Which Trinity? Whose Monotheism?

PHILOSOPHICAL AND SYSTEMATIC THEOLOGIANS ON THE METAPHYSICS OF TRINITARIAN THEOLOGY

Thomas H. McCall

WILLIAM B. EERDMANS PUBLISHING COMPANY
GRAND RAPIDS, MICHIGAN / CAMBRIDGE, U.K.

Published 2010 by
Wm. B. Eerdmans Publishing Co.
2140 Oak Industrial Drive N.E., Grand Rapids, Michigan 49505 /
P.O. Box 163, Cambridge CB3 9PU U.K.
www.eerdmans.com

Printed in the United States of America

16 15 14 13 12 11 10   7 6 5 4 3 2 1

Library of Congress Cataloging-in-Publication Data

McCall, Thomas H.
    Which Trinity? whose monotheism?: philosophical and systematic theologians
    on the metaphysics of Trinitarian theology / Thomas McCall.
        p.   cm.
    ISBN 978-0-8028-6270-9 (pbk.: alk. paper)
    1. Trinity.   2. Philosophical theology.
    3. Analysis (Philosophy)   I. Title.

BT111.3.M32   2010
231′.044 — dc22

                                                        2009043677

The editor and publisher gratefully acknowledge permission to include material from the
following sources:

    Part of chapter 7 appeared in the *Scottish Journal of Theology* as "Holy Love and Divine
    Aseity in the Theology of John Zizioulas," *SJT* 61 (2008): 191-205.

    Faith and Philosophy granted permission to use quoted material and to reproduce the chart
    appearing on page 48.

    Quotations and the chart that appears on page 30 are taken from *Philosophical Foundations
    for a Christian Worldview* by J. P. Moreland and William Lane Craig. Copyright © 2003 by
    J. P. Moreland and William Lane Craig. Used with permission of InterVarsity Press, PO Box
    1400, Downers Grove, IL 60515. ivpress.com.

To my Jenny —
    with faith,
        with hope,
            and with all my love.

CONTENTS

vii

There is a great gulf fixed between most contemporary systematic or dogmatic theology and much of the theological work done by contemporary philosophers of religion. The tradition of philosophy loosely referred to as "the analytic tradition" is sometimes thought to be utterly inhospitable to theistic belief in general and to Christian theology in particular. Some theologians are surprised to learn that theological issues are under consideration at all in the analytic community, while other theologians are skeptical — to say that they are dubious that any good could come out of Notre Dame is to put it mildly. Such theologians are sometimes highly suspicious of the intrusion of philosophers into their field, and sometimes it appears that they hold in contempt the efforts of the philosophers. On the other hand, it is not at all hard to find philosophers who look with disdain at the work of the systematic theologians. Yes, there is a great gulf fixed between those philosophers of religion who explore theological issues, on one hand, and systematic theologians on the other hand. But while this divide is in some ways very understandable, it is also lamentable.

I. The Renaissance of Philosophical Theology

Some theologians seem unaware of the amount and intensity of interest in theological issues among philosophers. Their awareness of "analytic philosophy" sometimes appears to lag several decades behind reality; they assume that analytic philosophy has not moved beyond the work of previous generations that indeed were largely hostile to Christian belief (and to theistic belief more generally). Thus one can peruse many contemporary works in systematic theology and find little or no reference to what is going on in, say, analytic epistemology or metaphysics, and any mention of analytic philosophy is in reference to logical positivism or "ordinary language philosophy." Theologians often regard the broad area of analytic philosophy as a vast — and very toxic — saline desert. They have heard of those who have ventured in and got lost, and they have posted signs that read "Warning: No (Theological) Food and Fuel for Next 900 Miles." In addition, they are suspicious of anything that comes out of this arid wasteland, and they worry that any creatures venturing out of the analytic desert must be dangerous.[1]

Some of these theologians might be surprised to learn of the changes that have taken place in the last few decades.[2] The labors of Alvin Plantinga, Nicholas Wolterstorff, Richard Swinburne, William P. Alston, Keith Yandell, and many others have brought us to a place where the well-known atheist Quentin Smith now says that following the publication of Plantinga's *God and Other Minds*[3] and *The Nature of Necessity*,[4] "it became apparent to the philosophical profession that realist theists were not outmatched by naturalists in terms of the most valued standards of analytic philosophy: conceptual precision, rigor of argumentation, technical erudition, and an in-depth defense of an original worldview. . . . In philosophy, it became, almost overnight, 'academically respectable' to argue for theism,

---

1. Dean Zimmerman's observation deserves attention: "analytic philosophy left some very negative impressions upon theologians who abandoned it several generations ago. I merely want to point out that the analytic philosophy they rejected was something of an aberration within the tradition: it was quite unlike analytic philosophy in its earliest days and the analytic philosophy of the past thirty or forty years. Most of the philosophical work that has been called 'analytic' throughout the last hundred years bears little resemblance to the narrow and stultifying doctrines that ruled when theologians set off for what seemed, then, to be friendlier waters." "Three Introductory Questions," in *Persons: Human and Divine*, ed. Peter van Inwagen and Dean Zimmerman (Oxford: Oxford University Press, 2007), p. 6.

2. For parts of this story, see Kelly James Clark, ed., *Philosophers Who Believe: The Spiritual Journeys of Eleven Leading Thinkers* (Downers Grove, Ill.: InterVarsity, 1993), and Thomas V. Morris, ed., *God and the Philosophers: The Reconciliation of Faith and Reason* (Oxford: Oxford University Press, 1994).

3. Alvin Plantinga, *God and Other Minds: A Study of the Rational Justification of Belief in God* (Ithaca, N.Y.: Cornell University Press, 1967).

4. Alvin Plantinga, *The Nature of Necessity* (Oxford: Oxford University Press, 1974).

making philosophy a favored field of entry for the most intelligent and talented theists entering academia today."[5] He concludes that "God is not 'dead' in academia; he returned to life in the late 1960's and is now alive and well in his last academic stronghold, philosophy departments."[6] Now a new generation of Christian philosophers has come onto the scene, and it is fair to say that work on philosophical issues of interest and importance to Christians is increasing in volume and sophistication. They are interested in the timeworn discussions of issues related to "philosophy of religion" (e.g., religious epistemology, theistic arguments, the nature of religious experience, problems of religious pluralism, etc.), but their interest often goes far beyond these issues. Many of them are keenly interested in topics once thought to be the province of theologians. Discussions of divine attributes such as omniscience, omnipotence, omnibenevolence, eternity, simplicity, immutability, impassibility, and others are found interesting. Beyond this, though, specifically Christian doctrines are addressed as well: perhaps most notable are the doctrines of original sin, incarnation, atonement, providence, resurrection, and even heaven and hell.

Important for our purposes is the conversation, one that is often direct and pointed, that has arisen among these philosophical theologians on the doctrine of the Trinity. Philosophers in the analytic tradition are now keenly interested in the classical doctrine of the Trinity, and their work shows evidence of commitment (and sometimes passion), as well as the clarity of expression and rigor of argumentation that are characteristic of the discipline. While there is nothing even approaching consensus on several important issues among them, it is evident that they take the doctrine very seriously.

II. Modern and Contemporary Systematic Theology

Modern and contemporary theologians often look beyond the analytic tradition for conversation partners. They often engage in dialogue with such disciplines as sociology, psychology, and anthropology, and sometimes with such disciplines as physics and neuroscience. When they do attend to their traditional "handmaiden," however, theologians almost al-

---

5. Quentin Smith, "The Metaphilosophy of Naturalism," *Philo* 4, no. 2 (2001): 2.
6. Smith, "The Metaphilosophy of Naturalism," p. 3.

ways engage with "continental" or "postmodern" philosophy.[7] The reasons for this are varied, and they have been explored elsewhere.[8] What is clear is that there is a dearth of engagement with the work being done by analytic philosophical theologians.

Nowhere is this more true than in discussions of the doctrine of the Trinity. Thomas R. Thompson notes that "the last couple of decades have seen a resurgence of interest in the Trinity and its relevance for the life and mission of the church."[9] Yet apart from a few notable exceptions, the "renaissance of trinitarian theology" has proceeded in almost complete isolation from what is taking place in analytic philosophical theology.[10] As Dean Zimmerman points out, "there has been very little dialogue between Christian philosophers in the analytic tradition and Christian theologians . . . when the groups do interact, terminological and methodological differences (and sometimes, sadly, prejudice and mistrust) hinder fruitful exchange."[11]

III. An Overview

This book proceeds out of a dissatisfaction with the current state of affairs, and from a conviction that both disciplines would benefit from interaction. I agree with Zimmerman that "unless philosophy always trumps theology, or vice versa, the only way to tackle the problems of philosophical theology is to keep both philosophical and theological considerations on the table, after the manner of Augustine or Edwards."[12] The theologians need — sometimes *desperately* need — the kind of assistance that might be found in the analytic toolkit. The theologian R. R. Reno sees this clearly,

7. E.g., Kevin J. Vanhoozer, ed., *The Cambridge Companion to Postmodern Theology* (Cambridge: Cambridge University Press, 2003).

8. An interesting set of essays relevant to this discussion can be found in William J. Wainwright, ed., *God, Philosophy, and Academic Culture* (Atlanta: Scholars, 1996).

9. Thomas R. Thompson, "Trinitarianism Today: Doctrinal Renaissance, Ethical Relevance, Social Redolence," *Calvin Theological Journal* 32 (1997): 11.

10. One of these notable exceptions is Bruce D. Marshall's *Trinity and Truth* (Cambridge: Cambridge University Press, 2000), although Marshall deals more with the relation of the Trinity to the debates over realism than to the doctrine itself.

11. Zimmerman, "Three Introductory Questions," pp. 3-4.

12. Zimmerman, "Three Introductory Questions," p. 12.

and he sounds a clarion call for theologians to employ the conceptual tools offered by the analytic tradition. As he sees things, analytic methodology bears a close resemblance to scholasticism, and he thinks that contemporary theology could use a good dose of it. He says that although the "overwhelming majority of theologians today sift through Heidegger and his philosophical children and grandchildren to try to find useable material," this impulse is fundamentally "misguided."[13] Reno concludes that analytic philosophy might be an important ally for theology, and this is "because analytic philosophy is unequivocally and fundamentally a force for the strengthening of truth, not its weakening."[14]

More particularly, this interaction needs to take place with regard to the doctrine of the Trinity. Theologian Fred Sanders recognizes this when he warns that future generations of theologians working on the doctrine of the Trinity could easily (and quickly) "develop into separate communities of discourse which are increasingly isolated from each other's literature and argumentation . . . if serious interdisciplinary work is not undertaken soon, the two traditions will harden into separate tracks and set the stage for great conflicts later." Sanders advocates another approach: "the kind of systematic theology that is heavily informed by biblical exegesis and the history of doctrine would benefit greatly from the conceptual clarity which could be provided by the kind of philosophical theology which concentrates on analytic tasks."[15]

On the other hand, the conversations on the doctrine of the Trinity taking place among analytic philosophers need to be informed by the insights and concerns of the theologians. As Zimmerman points out, while some of these analytic philosophical theologians have formal theological training and/or a long history of engaging theologians and theological issues, "most Christian philosophers in the analytic tradition have little, if any, training in biblical criticism or the history of doctrine, for instance." As this analytic metaphysician admits, when it comes to theological issues, "we have plenty to learn."[16] Sanders concurs. He notes that "what is generally omitted from these philosophical considerations is the host of concerns which generated the original propositions in the first place: the logic

13. R. R. Reno, "Theology's Continental Captivity," *First Things* 162 (April 2006): 29-30.

14. Reno, "Theology's Continental Captivity," p. 33.

15. Fred Sanders, "The State of the Doctrine of the Trinity in Evangelical Theology," *Southwestern Journal of Theology* 47 (2005): 170.

16. Zimmerman, "Three Introductory Questions," p. 12.

by which Jesus Christ was confessed to be divine, and the revision in the existing concept of God necessitated by that recognition, along with the careful Scriptural reasoning that made the process possible."[17] Sanders then concludes: "philosophical theology could benefit greatly from a closer encounter with the great themes of the Christian heritage, and a better understanding of the Biblical logic by which these themes merged into conceptual forms."[18]

So in this book I am working to build a bridge between the disciplines. In section 1 I bring some important and distinctly theological considerations to bear upon the current analytic debates. In chapter 1 I offer an overview of the current (and very lively) discussions of the "threeness-oneness problem" in analytic philosophical theology; here I describe the strategies known as "Social Trinitarianism," "Relative Trinitarianism," and "Latin Trinitarianism." I follow this in chapter 2 by raising some important theological issues (the nature of monotheism, the worship of Jesus in context, and important definitions of views deemed heretical) that I do not think are being adequately addressed within the current analytic discussions. In chapter 3 I draw together some of these conclusions, and I evaluate the various analytic proposals and Trinitarian "models" in light of the theological desiderata.

In section 2 I turn the tables; here I bring some of the conceptual tools of the analytic approach to the contemporary "renaissance of Trinitarian theology" in systematic theology. Here I choose several representative theologians. Using them as case studies of how analytic metaphysics can clarify, inform, and otherwise assist the work of the theologian, I focus on what I take to be crucial issues in the thought of several influential theologians. While my concerns and disagreements with these theologians will be evident, I trust that this will not obscure my respect for them. In each case I think they are raising important issues, and I share their driving concern that the doctrine of the Trinity really *matters*. In chapter 4 I look at Robert Jenson's account of the "identity" of the triune God, in chapter 5 I explore some issues related to Jürgen Moltmann's influential advocacy of perichoresis, in chapter 6 I examine recent discus-

17. Sanders, "Doctrine of the Trinity," p. 169.

18. Sanders, "Doctrine of the Trinity," p. 170. Sanders also notes that "philosophers sometimes seem to think of the ancient texts as cumbersome delivery systems containing ideas which it is their job to extract from the delivery systems and do something with" (p. 169).

sions among evangelical theologians about the subordination of the Son to the Father, and in chapter 7 I analyze two important theological themes in John Zizioulas's doctrine of the Trinity. Finally, in section 3 I offer some theses for scholastic disputation on the future of Trinitarian theology that is both faithful to its truly theological heritage and attentive to contemporary metaphysical issues.

Perhaps I should try to clarify what I am *not* trying to do. And the first thing to say is that I am *not* trying to be anything other than a theologian of the Word of God. Nicholas Wolterstorff offers a salutary challenge at this point:

> to my young grad students who aim to be theologians I say, with all the emphasis I can muster: *be theologians.* Do not be ersatz philosophers, do not be ersatz cultural theorists, do not be ersatz anything. Be genuine theologians. Be sure-footed in philosophy, sure-footed in cultural theory, and the like. And struggle to find a voice that can be heard, if not agreed with, not just by theologians but by others as well. But then: be theologians . . . what we need to hear from you is how things look when seen in light of the triune God — may his name be praised! — who creates and sustains us, who redeems us, and who will bring this frail and fallen, though yet glorious, humanity and cosmos to consummation.[19]

I take Wolterstorff's advice to heart. I want to foster a conversation between theologians and philosophers on the doctrine of the Trinity, and I do so with the conviction that theology stands to benefit from this interaction. But I do so as a theologian.

Nor am I trying to offer a comprehensive overview of the last few decades of Trinitarian theology (in either its philosophical or systematic forms). With respect to the analytic conversation, I focus on what I take to be the more influential and important works; when it comes to the systematic discussions, on the other hand, I concentrate on some important issues in the thought of several representative theologians. Nor yet am I trying to get the last word on any of the challenging issues related to the doctrine. Again, I want to foster and facilitate a conversation — not end it. I do not at this point try to justify the conversation at all (I take some steps in that direction elsewhere, where I work to defuse some of the more com-

---

19. Nicholas Wolterstorff, "To Theologians: From One Who Cares about Theology but Is Not One of You," *Theological Education* 40, no. 2 (2005): 91-92, emphasis in original.

mon objections from the side of the theologians);[20] rather than spend valuable resources displaying the documentation and permits for the building project, I simply get to the business of bridge building. By this I do not intend to leave the impression that such issues are irrelevant (or that I am unaware of them), but since I think the work of bridge building can actually begin, I do not bother to display the permits and polish the machinery on both sides of the divide.

I realize that what I do will at points be less than satisfying to partisans in both camps. As Zimmerman points out, "Naturally, each party to an interdisciplinary conversation of this sort runs the risk of saying things that will sound shockingly naive to the other."[21] I am sure that in places I will say things that are "shockingly naive" to the philosophers, while at other points I will disappoint my fellow theologians who think I have conceded far too much to the concerns of the philosophers. Be that as it may, I am convinced that a partnership between Trinitarian theologians who do constructive or systematic theology and those who are analytic philosophical theologians is both possible and potentially mutually beneficial, and I think it is time to begin. Thus I try to bring theological desiderata to bear upon the work of the philosophers, focus some metaphysical concerns upon the work of systematic theology, and suggest the next steps forward.

20. See my "Philosophers, Theologians, and the Doctrine of the Trinity," in *These Three Are One: Theological and Philosophical Essays on the Doctrine of the Trinity,* ed. Thomas McCall and Michael Rea (Oxford: Oxford University Press, 2009), pp. 336-49.

21. Zimmerman, "Three Introductory Questions," p. 12.

Which Trinity? Whose Monotheism?

CHAPTER ONE

Which Trinity? The Doctrine of the Trinity in Contemporary Philosophical Theology

The "threeness-oneness problem" of the Trinity is well known.[1] And it is, as Jeffrey E. Brower and Michael C. Rea point out, "a deep and difficult problem."[2] The problem is not simply that there is mystery here — if the doctrine of the Trinity is true, after all, we should hardly be surprised that it is mysterious. The problem is that the doctrine seems to be logically inconsistent and thus necessarily false.

Furthermore, the conundrum arises at the very heart of the Christian faith. Christians, along with other monotheists, believe that there is exactly one God. Christians also believe that the Father is God, the Son is God, and the Holy Spirit is God. They believe further that the Father is not the Son, nor is the Son or the Father the Holy Spirit. As the venerable Athanasian Creed puts it, "So the Father is God, the Son is God, and the Holy Spirit is God; and yet they are not three Gods, but one God." Belief in both the distinctness and divinity of the three persons, on one hand, and belief in the oneness or unity of God, on the other hand, are essential to orthodox Christian belief.

Systematic theology of recent vintage has done surprisingly little to address the dilemma. Given that many of these theologians criticize the traditional (especially Latin) formulations, it is both surprising and disap-

---

1. For a more formal statement of the problem, see, e.g., Thomas McCall and Michael C. Rea, introduction to *These Three Are One: Philosophical and Theological Essays on the Doctrine of the Trinity*, ed. Thomas McCall and Michael C. Rea (Oxford: Oxford University Press, 2009), pp. 1-15.

2. Jeffrey E. Brower and Michael C. Rea, "Understanding the Trinity," *Logos* 8 (2005): 145-57.

pointing that they have not set themselves to the task of addressing the problem. Fortunately, however, philosophers of religion working in the so-called analytic tradition do address this issue, and in what follows I shall offer a descriptive overview of this work. What follows is far from exhaustive, but influential figures and important trends, as well as the major criticisms of the various proposals, are surveyed.

I. Social Trinitarianism

The work of Cornelius Plantinga, Jr., and Richard Swinburne has been especially influential in the advocacy of "Social Trinitarianism" (ST).[3] It has also drawn serious and probing criticism, and this criticism has itself engendered further defenses of ST. We shall explore some of the more prominent of these in turn.

A. "Early ST": Plantinga and Swinburne[4]

Usually drawing inspiration from the Cappadocian theologians of the fourth century, ST proponents conceive of the Holy Trinity according to the analogy of a society or family of three human persons; they are often said to "start from" plurality and then struggle to provide an adequate account of divine oneness or unity. As Plantinga describes it, ST is any theory of the Trinity that satisfies these conditions: "the theory must have Father, Son, and Spirit as distinct centers of consciousness . . . (and) Father, Son, and Spirit must be tightly enough related to each other so as to render plausible" claims to monotheism.[5]

---

3. Other important proponents of ST (other than those discussed here) are Timothy Bartel, "Could There Be More Than One Almighty?" *Religious Studies* 29 (1993): 465-95; Bartel, "Could There Be More Than One Lord?" *Faith and Philosophy* 11 (1994): 357-78; David Brown, *The Divine Trinity* (La Salle, Ill.: Open Court, 1985); C. Stephen Layman, "Tritheism and the Trinity," *Faith and Philosophy* 5 (1988): 291-98; Thomas V. Morris, *The Logic of God Incarnate* (Ithaca, N.Y.: Cornell University Press, 1986); C. J. F. Williams, "Neither Confounding the Persons Nor Dividing the Substance," in *Reason and the Christian Religion: Essays in Honor of Richard Swinburne*, ed. Alan Padgett (Oxford: Oxford University Press, 1994), pp. 227-43.

4. By "early ST" I mean "early" in the *recent* discussions.

5. Cornelius Plantinga, Jr., "Social Trinity and Tritheism," in *Trinity, Incarnation, and Atonement: Philosophical and Theological Essays,* ed. Ronald J. Feenstra and Cornelius

Plantinga begins his argument for ST with materials drawn directly from the biblical sources. He argues that Paul and the other earliest Christians include Jesus in their prayers and even in the Shema (e.g., 1 Cor. 8:6). For Paul, Plantinga says, "Jesus Christ is claimed to be equal with God, to be a cosmic ruler and savior, a person in whom the fullness of the Godhead lodges. He is a person, indeed, to whom Paul and other Christians *pray*" (p. 24). Plantinga thinks that "through John's Gospel runs an even richer vein for the church's doctrine of the Trinity — a deep, wide, and subtle account of divine distinction within unity" (p. 25). For here in the Fourth Gospel we find the basis for what will later become known as a theory or doctrine of perichoresis (where each divine person is said to be "in" the other), and here we see that "the primal unity of Father, Son, and Paraclete is revealed, exemplified, and maybe partly constituted by common will, work, word, and knowledge among them, and by their reciprocal loving and glorifying" (p. 25).

Plantinga is convinced that reading the Fourth Gospel as a source of Trinitarian theology forces the theologian to rethink strong doctrines of divine simplicity. Rather than understanding the Athanasian Creed to be saying that the divine persons are each identical to the divine essence (but somehow not to one another), Plantinga suggests that a reading of the creed that maintains "some continuity with the Fourth Gospel presentation" will take the creed to be saying that the persons are "wholly divine" (p. 27). And since "simplicity theories are negotiable in ways that Pauline and Johannine statements are not," then we should be willing to adjust (or even abandon) simplicity doctrine for the sake of Trinitarian theology that is grounded in and arises from Scripture (p. 39). And since such a robust doctrine of the Trinity *is* what arises from a natural reading of Hebrews, Paul, and John, then we are left with ST.

Plantinga's ST proposal is then that

> the Holy Trinity is a divine, transcendent society or community of three fully personal and fully divine entities: the Father, the Son, and the Holy Spirit or Paraclete. These three are wonderfully united by their common divinity, that is, by the possession of each of the whole generic divine essence . . . the persons are also unified by their joint redemptive purpose,

Plantinga, Jr. (Notre Dame, Ind.: University of Notre Dame Press, 1989), p. 22. Plantinga also stipulates that any accompanying doctrine of divine simplicity must be modest enough to fit with these conditions. Page numbers in the text refer to "Social Trinity and Tritheism."

revelation, and work. Their knowledge and love are directed not only to their creatures, but also primordially and archetypally to each other. The Father loves the Son and the Son loves the Father . . . the Trinity is thus a zestful community of divine light, love, joy, mutuality, and verve. (pp. 27-28)

Plantinga makes it plain that each divine person is a distinct center of consciousness and will, but he also is at pains to insist that while each person is genuinely (numerically) distinct, the divine persons are not separate or autonomous: "in the divine life there is no isolation, no insulation, no secretiveness, no fear of being transparent to another." Thus he says that we should "resist every Congregational theory of trinity membership," for the divine persons share much more than a generic substance and a decision to get along together. For in addition to the generic divine essence, each divine person bears "a much closer relation to each other as well — a derivation or origin relation that amounts, let us say, to a personal essence" (p. 28). This "mysterious in-ness or oneness relation in the divine life is short of personal identity, but much closer than mere membership in a class" (pp. 28-29). So each divine person possesses the whole generic divine essence, and each person possesses a personal essence as well. The personal essences distinguish each person from the others, but both the generic essence and the personal essences unify the persons. "The generic essence assures that each person is fully and equally divine. The personal essences, meanwhile, relate each person to the other two in unbreakable love and loyalty" (p. 29).

It should be clear that Plantinga conceives that the divine persons are persons who are really distinct; they are agents who are (or have) distinct centers of consciousness and will. But they are also still one God, and Plantinga points to three ways that proponents of ST "may cling to respectability as monotheists": they may say that there is only one God in the sense that the New Testament often uses the term, that is, as the "peculiar designator of the Father . . . [there is] only one God in *that* sense of *God*" (p. 31). Or if we use the name *God* to refer to the generic divine essence, there is only one God in that sense of the term. Finally, "*God* is properly used as designator of the whole Trinity — three persons in their peculiar relations with each other." Each of these ways, Plantinga concludes, is "perfectly standard and familiar in the Christian tradition. And in each case, social trinitarianism emerges as safely monotheistic" (p. 31).

But Plantinga worries further about charges of tritheism. He offers three lines of defense against such charges. The first is this: "to say that the Father, Son, and Spirit are the names of distinct persons in the full sense of *person* scarcely makes one a tritheist" (p. 34). Here Plantinga appears to rely upon both the recognition that such terms as "person" and "tritheism" are understood in particular contexts (rather than in a historical or intellectual vacuum) and his efforts at demonstrating that "such a claim makes oneself an ally with the best-developed biblical presentation on the issue and with three-quarters of the subsequent theological tradition."

Plantinga next argues that the classical tritheist heresy is specifiable: it is Arianism. According to Arianism, the Son and Spirit are not *homoousios* with the Father; they do not share the divine essence (generic or otherwise). And since "what is heretical is belief in three *ontologically graded* distinct persons" rather than distinct persons *simpliciter,* ST can readily "affirm the standard trinitarian tradition" (p. 34).

But perhaps, a critic might aver, ST has only avoided one kind of tritheism to fall into another kind (albeit one less specifiable). Plantinga's third line of defense then addresses the concern that he has escaped Arian tritheism only to run aground on the shoals of another version. Here he relies upon his account of the personal relations (that amount to personal essences) of interdependence and loyal love: "just as it is part of the generic divine nature to be everlasting, omnipotent, faithful, loving, and the like, so also it is part of the personal nature of each trinitarian person to be bound to the other two in permanent love and loyalty. Loving respect for the others is a personal essential characteristic of each member of the Trinity," and although each divine person has generic aseity with respect to creation, "within the Trinity each essentially has interdependence, agapic regard for the other, bonded fellowship" (p. 36). So his third line of defense, he says, "comes, then, to this: If belief in three *autonomous* persons or three *independent* persons amounts to tritheism, the social analogy fails to qualify. For its trinitarian persons are essentially and reciprocally dependent" (p. 37).

In the original (1977) edition of *The Coherence of Theism,* Richard Swinburne mounted an argument that there could be only one divine individual. He later came to see that this argument was "unsound," and endorsed a robust version of ST.[6] Swinburne is well aware of the challenges

6. Richard Swinburne, *The Christian God* (Oxford: Oxford University Press, 1994), p. 2. Swinburne goes on to note that his distinction between ontological necessity and metaphys-

posed to the doctrine, and he works hard to defend its coherence. He is critical of attempts to apply the logic of relative identity to the doctrine of the Trinity, for he worries both that the philosophical objections to relative identity are compelling and that such a strategy takes us to the place where "we deny any clear content to the doctrine of the Trinity at all" (p. 188). So Swinburne pursues an ST account, but he wants one that is able to repel charges of tritheism. He does not think that the assertions of theologians such as Jürgen Moltmann amount to "an adequate account of what binds the members of the Trinity together" (p. 189 n. 26). He wants to present a Trinitarian theory that allows for both intelligibility and consistency with the creeds. These desiderata lead him to conclude that any charitable reading of traditional, creedal orthodoxy will *not* take the creeds to be saying something as obviously outrageous as they would be if they were claiming both that there are *three* divine individuals *and* that there is only *one* divine individual. Swinburne reads the *deus (theos)* of the creeds differently where it refers to the divine persons than he does where it "is said that there are not three *dei* but one *deus*. Unless we do this, it seems to me that the traditional formulas are self-contradictory. If we read all occurrences of *deus* as occurrences of the same referring expression, the Athanasian Creed then asserts that Father, Son, and Spirit are each of them the same individual thing, and also that they have different properties, for example, the Father begets but is not begotten" (p. 186). And since this obviously violates the Indiscernibility of Identicals, then such an interpretation cannot possibly be correct: "this is not possible; if things are the same, they must have all the same properties" (p. 186). No charitable reading of the creeds will conclude that they are claiming something so palpably incoherent and obviously false, so Trinity doctrine must give up on either the view that there are three individuals or the view that there is only one individual.

Swinburne opts for the latter; he insists that according to orthodox Christian theology there are three — rather than only one — divine individuals. He clearly conceives of the three divine persons as three individuals, three souls, three "persons" in the most robust sense. A person is "sim-

---

ical necessity is important in this respect, and he goes on to argue that "a divine individual is properly thought of as having metaphysical but not ontological necessity, and that there is reason to suppose that there are three such mutually dependent individuals; but that the three together form a whole (the Trinity) which is ontologically necessary." The page numbers in the discussion of Swinburne refer to *The Christian God*.

ply a rational individual" (p. 182). Swinburne's divine persons are, in the words of Marilyn McCord Adams, "three numerically distinct souls of the Divine essential kind, each instantiating the universal Divinity, each inevitably everlasting but individuated from one another by relations of origin."[7] Swinburne proposes (again as a possible reading of the major creedal statements) that the Godhead is made up of three individuals, each of whom is a distinct center of consciousness and will who is in full possession of the divine kind-essence. It is, says Swinburne, "exactly the instantiation of the same essence of divinity that makes the Father God, as makes the Son God, as makes the Spirit God. They would be the same individual but for the relational properties which are distinct from the divine essence and which distinguish them" (Swinburne, p. 189).

Swinburne offers this as a theory that is consistent with the tradition, and presumably he is convinced that it also accords well with Scripture. Interestingly, however, he also offers an a priori argument for the doctrine. Echoing a long line of medieval Trinitarian theorizing, he argues that perfection includes perfect love: "there is something profoundly imperfect and therefore inadequately divine in a solitary divine individual. If such an individual is love, he must share, and sharing with finite beings such as humans is not sharing all of one's nature and so is imperfect sharing. A divine individual's love has to be manifested in a sharing with another divine individual, and that (to keep the divine unity) means (in some sense) within the godhead, that is, in mutual dependence and support" (p. 190). This is so because "love involves sharing, giving to the other what of one's own is good for him and receiving from the other what of his is good for one; and love involves co-operating with another to benefit third parties" (p. 177). But then, an interlocutor might ask, why only three? Why not more divine persons? Swinburne admits that his "ethical intuitions are inevitably highly fallible here," but he suggests that, while there is a "qualitative difference between sharing and co-operating in sharing, and hence overriding reasons for both kinds, [there is] no similar qualitative difference between co-operating with one in sharing and co-operating with two" — thus there is no reason for the existence of more than three divine persons (p. 179). He thus offers the tentative conclusion that "necessarily if there is at least one divine individual, and if it is logically possible that there be more than

---

7. Marilyn McCord Adams, *Christ and Horrors: The Coherence of Christology* (Cambridge: Cambridge University Press, 2006), p. 116.

one divine individual, then there are three and only three divine individuals" (p. 179).

Swinburne is well aware that his view will prompt charges of tritheism. He responds by making a case that his view is consistent with the early creedal statements that were formulated with the express purpose of ruling out all forms of polytheism (with Arianism as exhibit A of polytheism). He insists that we cannot read the creeds as affirming that there are both only one divine person and also three divine persons, for "no person and no Council affirming something which they intend to be read with utter seriousness can be read as affirming an *evident* contradiction" (p. 180). So whatever is being ruled out in the creedal statements is *not* the view that there is more than one divine "individual." But just what *is* being ruled out in the denunciation of tritheism? Swinburne's understanding is that the denial of tritheism amounts to this: "they were denying that there are three *independent* divine beings, any of which could exist without the other; or which could act independently of each other" (p. 180).

And of course, Swinburne's theory avoids such tritheism, for on his account "the three divine individuals taken together would form a collective source of being of all other things; the members would be totally mutually dependent and necessarily jointly behind each other's act. This collective would be indivisible in its being for logical reasons . . . the claim that 'there is only one God' is to be read as the claim that the source of being of all other things has to it this kind of indivisible unity" (pp. 180-81). This mutual dependence is taken by Swinburne to be equivalent to perichoresis. He relates this to what have been termed the *opera ad extra* in the tradition, and he interprets the venerable slogan *omnia opera Trinitatis ad extra indivisa sunt* to mean that "in acting toward the outside world (i.e. in creating or sustaining other substances), although (unless there is a unique best action) one individual initiates any action, the initiating act (whether of active or permissive causation) is backed by the co-causation of the others" (p. 184). Furthermore, with respect to the *opera ad intra,* there is mutual dependence — even though Swinburne will admit some "asymmetry of dependence" in the Father's causation of the other persons, he also insists that the Father is "permitted to exist by the others" (p. 185). All the divine persons exist everlastingly; they are "metaphysically necessary" but not "ontologically necessary." But the three together "form a whole (the Trinity)," which is both everlasting and uncaused and therefore "ontologically necessary" (pp. 2-3). So each of the persons is "God" — that is, each is fully divine, each is in possession of such properties as omnipotence, omniscience, etc. And there is one God in the sense that there is one collective being (the three divine persons who are logically inseparable) that is the source of all else that has being.

B. Anti–Social Trinitarianism

ST is seen by many as an attractive option; Dale Tuggy even refers to a "rush to ST."[8] But ST has also drawn fire from various quarters. Critics of ST charge the view with running afoul of the creeds and confessions of historic orthodoxy; with wreaking havoc on traditional doctrines of divine omnipotence, omniscience, and goodness; and even with sliding into Arianism — and, of course, with doing violence to any intuitively acceptable notion of monotheism.

Some critics charge ST with "the naughtiness of novelty."[9] They question the tendency of ST's proponents to assert that the Cappadocian theologians were early advocates of ST; Sarah Coakley, for example, mounts a spirited argument that Gregory of Nyssa was *not* a Social Trinitarian.[10] Tuggy takes this a step further back; he argues that ST does not fit well with scriptural portrayals of God. He makes the rather surprising claim that ST is cut off from the belief that God is divine. His explanation goes like this: "whatever is divine in the primary sense is a person, a personal being. But according to ST, God is *not* a person, but only a group of persons. What is not a person is not divine, not a divinity. Thus, God is not divine. Sadly, for all its lovely virtues, this seems to be the death of ST."[11] Tuggy further worries that if ST is true then at least one of the divine persons is implicated in "what looks like wrongful deception," for the believers portrayed in the

---

8. Dale Tuggy, "Divine Deception, Identity, and Social Trinitarianism," *Religious Studies* 40 (2004): 269.

9. This term was used by Thomas P. Flint in another context; see *Divine Providence: The Molinist Account* (Ithaca, N.Y.: Cornell University Press, 1998), p. 112.

10. Sarah Coakley, "'Persons' in the 'Social' Doctrine of the Trinity: A Critique of the Current Analytic Discussion," in *The Trinity: An Interdisciplinary Symposium on the Trinity*, ed. Stephen T. Davis, Daniel Kendall, S.J., and Gerald O'Collins, S.J. (Oxford: Oxford University Press, 1999), pp. 123-44.

11. Dale Tuggy, "The Unfinished Business of Trinitarian Theorizing," *Religious Studies* 39 (2003): 168.

Old and New Testaments were convinced (by what most Christians accept as divine revelation) that there is only one divine person.[12] His conclusion leaves no room for doubt: "the kind of ST we are exploring is simply a dead end."[13] Finally, he argues that ST amounts to tritheism, and he responds to ST's appeals to perichoresis by complaining that "this kind of *perichoresis*-talk seems firmly stuck at the metaphorical level" and concluding that "such metaphors simply hide an unintelligible claim."[14]

Arguments come from other angles as well.[15] Recognizing that definitions of monotheism and polytheism are not quite as straightforward as one might initially think, Michael C. Rea compares ST to "Amun-Re theology" of Egypt's New Kingdom period. He argues that ST is "directly analogous" to Amun-Re theology, and he concludes that, since Amun-Re theology is clearly polytheistic, then so too is ST.[16]

The most sustained criticisms, however, have come from Brian Leftow. In his appropriately titled article "Anti Social Trinitarianism," Leftow poses two major problems for ST: the first is "to explain why its three Persons are 'not three Gods, but one God,' and to do so without transparently misreading the Creed."[17] The second "hard task for ST is providing an account of monotheism which is both intuitively acceptable and lets ST count as monotheist."[18] Leftow is convinced that ST cannot handle these tasks, and he mounts a spirited argument that "ST cannot be both orthodox and a version of monotheism."[19]

Although Leftow recognizes that the strategies sometimes "overlap," he considers three distinct routes of defense for ST: "Functional Monotheism," "Group Mind Monotheism," and "Trinity Monotheism." Leftow forcefully rejects Functional Monotheism. Here he targets Swinburne. Swinburne, he rightly notes, conceives of the divine being as a collective

---

12. Tuggy, "Divine Deception," p. 285.

13. Tuggy, "Divine Deception," p. 285.

14. Tuggy, "The Unfinished Business," pp. 170-71.

15. E.g., Kelly James Clark, "Trinity or Tritheism?" *Religious Studies* 32 (1996): 463-76; Edward Feser, "Swinburne's Tritheism," *International Journal for Philosophy of Religion* 42 (1997): 175-84.

16. Michael C. Rea, "Polytheism and Christian Belief," *Journal of Theological Studies*, n.s., 87 (2006): 145.

17. Brian Leftow, "Anti Social Trinitarianism," in *The Trinity: An Interdisciplinary Symposium on the Trinity*, p. 206.

18. Leftow, "Anti Social Trinitarianism," p. 207.

19. Leftow, "Anti Social Trinitarianism," p. 203.

that is indivisible for logical reasons.[20] But Leftow thinks this leaves a lot to be desired. "One who worships addresses someone. So worship makes sense only if directed to someone who can be aware of being addressed."[21] But "collections are not conscious, nor are mereological sums conscious as such. So one cannot really appropriately worship Swinburne's collective, save as a way to worship its members" (p. 228). He compares Swinburne's account of perichoretic Trinitarian action with pagan polytheism: "on the functional-monotheist account, the reason the Persons are one God and the Olympians are not is that the Persons are far more alike than Zeus and his brood, far more cooperative, and linked by procession" (p. 232). But it is "hardly plausible," avers Leftow, "that Greek paganism would have been a form of monotheism had Zeus & Co. been more alike, better behaved, and linked by the right causal relations" (p. 232). Leftow concludes that there is more to monotheism — indeed much more — than functional monotheism.

According to Group Mind Monotheism, the three divine minds somehow "emerge" or meld into one divine mind. Despite its initial promise (Leftow admits that "group minds seem at least possible," and he explores several possible analogies from cerebral commissurotomy), Leftow rejects this strategy as a failure (pp. 221-24). For, taken one way, it would imply that there is really only one divine "I," one center of self-awareness, consciousness, and will. But this would, as Leftow notes, "forfeit one major motivation for ST, the desire to find true, perfect love in God's inner life," and at any rate it would seem to "invert orthodoxy, giving us not three Persons in one substance but one Person in three substances" (p. 224). Taken differently, the Group Mind strategy becomes part of the strategy of Trinity Monotheism.

But what about Trinity Monotheism? Leftow is convinced that Trinity Monotheism cannot provide acceptable accounts of either omniscience or omnipotence. He argues that ST entails the compromise of an adequate doctrine of divine omniscience. For if the Trinity is a fourth mind — perhaps, as David Brown seems to say, one that combines the knowledge of the distinct persons to amount to full omniscience — then it seems that we have a fourth person. We would have a Quaternity rather than a Trinity, and unfortunately only one of these persons would really be omniscient.

---

20. Swinburne, *The Christian God*, p. 181.
21. Leftow, "Anti Social Trinitarianism," p. 228. Page numbers are placed in the text.

Or if the Trinity is only a collection of the three divine persons, then "it literally does not know anything. A fortiori it is not omniscient" (p. 211). Leftow does recognize that perhaps there is a sense in which the divine persons share what we might call noetic or cognitive perichoresis. On this model "each Person has on his own a stock of knowledge. But each supplements his own stock by drawing on the others' stocks. Thus, each has by belonging to the Trinity knowledge he got from another, and so knowledge which was in some sense a collective possession" (p. 212). Leftow recognizes that this model ties the deity of each person to the other persons, "for each helps the others qualify as divine: the Persons are 'one God' in that they are divine due to the way that they are one . . . while there are three tropes of deity in the Trinity, it is as if there was but one, for no Person can have his trope unless the others have theirs" (pp. 212-13).

Leftow seems to think that this is the most hopeful strategy for ST. But he argues that "this scenario faces problems," and he rejects this strategy on the grounds that it compromises divine perfection. For he cannot conceive of how it might be that the divine persons acquire such knowledge; the only way that he can think of it is that they receive it by testimony or by inference from facts about other persons. But he is convinced that "true deity seems to require some more perfect mode of knowledge," so he concludes that this is not a promising strategy for ST (p. 213).[22]

Leftow raises further concerns about ST; he worries that ST destroys an acceptable notion of divine omnipotence. He wonders what would happen if the Father were to eternally will that there be some universe while the Son eternally wills that there be none. Leftow points out that "on pain of contradiction, they cannot both bring about what they will. If their power is truly equal, it cannot be the case that one succeeds and the other fails" (p. 218). Thus, concludes Leftow, "if there are two or more discrete omnipotent beings, as in ST, one must either concede that omnipotence can be thwarted, deny that the Persons are omnipotent (precisely because one can thwart another), or hold that the situation just described is not in fact possible — for for no P can it be the case that one Person tries to bring about P and another effects it that the first one fails." He recognizes that

---

22. Leftow also raises what he thinks are "unanswerable questions" for ST: "We must ask just where the line falls in each Person's case between what he knows on his own and what he knows *via* the other Persons, and why he knows no more on his own. If the Person can know more on his own, then why doesn't he, and if he can't, how is this compatible with deity?" (p. 214).

the last option is "clearly the most attractive theologically," and he explores how this might be so.

Leftow interacts with Swinburne's suggestion that "no divine Person might thwart another Person, because the Persons necessarily are disposed to cooperate." In some kind of perichoresis, the "Persons are perfectly joined, intertwined, and sympathetic, and *this* perfection rules out all attempts to thwart one another" (p. 218). He recognizes that this move is attractive in some ways, but ultimately Leftow rejects it as providing an insufficient account of omnipotence: "If neither Father nor Son can fail, and each can that P or -P, each has power enough to restrict the other's agency. For each, by willing -P, can make it the case that if the other tried to bring about P, he would fail. . . . So if the Father wills that -P, he keeps the Son from trying to use his power to bring about P: given that the Father has willed -P, the Son is unable to try to effect P. This limits the Son's divine agency and freedom, and being unable to use one's power sits ill with being divine" (pp. 218-19). This means that there are some things that the Son cannot even try *because* he cannot fail: "oddly, omnipotence hamstrings him" (p. 219).

Leftow thinks Trinity Monotheism is impaled on the horns of a serious dilemma.

> Either the Trinity is a fourth case of the divine nature, or it is not. If it is, we have too many cases of deity for orthodoxy. If it is not, and yet is divine, there are two ways to be divine — by being a case of deity, and by being a Trinity of such cases. If there is more than one way to be divine, Trinity monotheism becomes Plantingean Arianism. But if there is in fact only one way to be divine, then there are two alternatives. One is that only the Trinity is God, and God is composed of non-divine Persons. The other is that the sum of all divine Persons is somehow not divine. To accept this last claim would be to give up orthodoxy altogether. (p. 221)

Leftow sees no way forward for the Trinity Monotheist, and he concludes that "Trinity monotheism is not a promising strategy for ST" (p. 221).

C. Defending Social Trinitarianism

As direct and forceful as these criticisms are, however, they do not deter the defenders of ST. Stephen T. Davis takes up the challenge by defending ST against Leftow's charges. He clearly endorses a robust version of ST. He makes it just as clear that he wants to avoid polytheism, and "to say baldly that God *is* a community either embraces or at least comes dangerously near tri-theism. Three Gods who are united in will and purpose is not orthodox Trinitarianism."[23]

Davis explains his understanding of ST in more detail. First, he says, "God is like a community. The three persons are three distinct centers of consciousness, will, and action. There are three instances or cases of divinity" (p. 42). The divine persons are *persons* in a very robust sense; they engage in "'mental' or 'conscious' acts like feeling, willing, believing, remembering, and knowing"; they "have desires, intentions, and aims"; and they "have the ability to act, to do and achieve things" (p. 42). Furthermore, "each of the divine persons equally possesses the divine essence"; there are no gradations of divinity, they are all fully divine. They are "all equally and essentially divine, metaphysically necessary, eternal (or everlasting), uncreated, omnipotent, omniscient, and perfectly good" (p. 43). Within the immanent Trinity, "the basis of all differentiation among Father, Son, and Holy Spirit is their relations to each other" (p. 43). Moreover, Davis endorses the ancient principle (which he attributes to Augustine) that *omnia opera Trinitatis ad extra indivisa sunt,* for "all three Persons are involved in all extra-Trinitarian acts" (p. 44). Finally, Davis says, "the Persons are related to each other by perichoresis."

This latter point is crucial to Davis's defense of ST against Leftow's charges. He characterizes it as "mutual indwelling, interpenetrating, merging," a concept that "reaches toward the truth that the core of God's inner being is the highest degree of self-giving love." The persons are "fully open to each other, their actions *ad extra* are actions in common, they 'see with each other's eyes,' the boundaries between them are transparent to each other, and each ontologically embraces the others" (p. 44). Beyond this initial characterization, Davis offers an analogy of perichoresis. He invites us to imagine three sets of circles. In the first set ("State A"), the "circles border on each other, i.e., the circumference of each circle touches the circumferences of the two others" but without any overlap. In the second set ("State B"), the circles overlap partially but not entirely. In the third set, however,

---

23. Stephen T. Davis, "Perichoretic Monotheism: A Defense of a Social Theory of the Trinity," in *The Trinity: East/West Dialogue,* ed. Melville Y. Stewart (Dordrecht: Kluwer Academic Publishers, 2003), p. 38. The page references to this essay have been placed in the text.

the "circles have wholly merged; they circumscribe the same area." Davis then asks us to imagine something else: "imagine something that is impossible with geometrical objects like circles and physical objects like human persons. Imagine that the three circles are simultaneously in State A and State C. Then you could legitimately say, of any property *p* possessed by all three, that Circle 1 is *p*, that Circle 2 is *p*, and Circle 3 is *p*. You could even speak of the one circle that exists in State C — call it Circle 123 — and say that it is *p*. But you cannot say that there are four things that are *p*; that would simply be false" (p. 45). Davis recognizes that in the case of geometric shapes (such as circles) this is logically impossible, but he insists that this analogy "is not an attempt to solve the logical problem of the Trinity, i.e., demonstrate the logical coherence of the dogma." For "at the moment," he says, "I am simply trying to explain *perichoresis*," and he insists that his "claim is that perichoretically related persons *can be* or indeed *are* simultaneously in something like" this situation (p. 46). He admits that "the Trinity is at bottom mysterious," and that all analogies and illustrations are insufficient to fully illustrate the doctrine, but he insists nonetheless that "what my story about the circles illustrates — God simultaneously being three-in-one — *is* logically possible (for perichoretically related Persons)." Indeed, he concludes, "Christians believe that it is actual" (p. 46).

Armed with this account of perichoresis, Davis rises to the challenge of Leftow's criticisms. Leftow's worries that ST amounts to polytheism are unfounded, says Davis, because the Greek gods to which Leftow compares ST were *not* perichoretically related. Davis agrees with Leftow that a better-behaved and better-organized Greek pantheon "would still constitute a plurality of gods rather than one God," but his ST "is monotheistic not only because of the Persons' shared divine essence and their necessary agreement and cooperation, but also because of their loving, interpermeating, boundaryless relations with each other" (p. 47). And just what do proponents of ST mean when they say that the Father is God, the Son is God, and the Holy Spirit is God? With respect to the Trinity, the Godhead, when we say that this "is God" we mean this in the sense of strict numerical identity. But when we say this with respect to the persons, "we are not talking about strict numerical identity; it would be false to say that 'the Father exhausts God.' Here the predicate '. . . is God' does not refer to an individual but is a property meaning something close to 'is divine'" (p. 47).

Edward Wierenga also understands the phrase "is God" to mean "is divine" with reference to the divine persons. Noting that "philosophers commonly distinguish between the 'is' of identity and the 'is' of predication," he asks, "Why not apply that distinction to these Divinity claims . . . why not interpret it instead as making a *predication?*"[24] Why not understand "is God" as "is divine"? On this reading of the traditional formula, "a person is divine just in case that person has the divine attributes," and the problems with the traditional statements of the doctrine are avoided. The "heart" of Wierenga's suggestion is this: the claims that the Father is God, the Son is God, and the Holy Spirit is God attribute divinity to the three Persons; thus "there is no contradiction between holding that there are several divine Persons but one God, provided that what that God is is a unity of these persons. And there is no error in counting here, either. The number of distinct divine persons is three; the number of Gods is one."[25]

Wierenga is aware of looming objections. He works to show that his reading works with the Latin text of the Athanasian Creed, and he worries further lest his view be charged once more with incoherence. With respect to the latter concern, he considers an argument from Richard Cartwright. Cartwright says his argument is "very simple: every Divine Person is a God; there are at least three Divine Persons; therefore, there are at least three Gods."[26] Before arguing that the other premises follow from the main tenets of the orthodox doctrine, Cartwright says the first premise needs no argument. For it "is a trivial truth."[27] Wierenga recognizes that if Cartwright is correct then his view is in trouble: "but Cartwright alleges that any Divine Person — any person who has the property of divinity, that is — is a God and that this furthermore, is a trivial truth. So if there are three divine Persons, there are three Gods, after all."[28] But Wierenga asks if it is really true that

(G) necessarily, any divine person is a God.

He responds that he does not see that this is true — much less does he see that it is trivially true. While he admits that "one might have uncritically been inclined to accept [(G)]," reflection on the doctrine of the Trinity

---

24. Edward Wierenga, "Trinity and Polytheism," *Faith and Philosophy* 21 (2004): 288.

25. Wierenga, "Trinity and Polytheism," p. 289.

26. Richard Cartwright, "On the Logical Problem of the Trinity," in Richard Cartwright, *Philosophical Essays* (Cambridge: MIT Press, 1987), p. 196.

27. Cartwright, "Logical Problem," p. 196.

28. Wierenga, "Trinity and Polytheism," p. 290.

serves "to call into question such uncritical acceptance." He suggests that what the doctrine of the Trinity should teach us is that "a thing is identical with God just in case it is a trinity of divine Persons."[29] And since there is only one such Trinity, there is only one God.

But Wierenga's strategy has attracted criticism. Dale Tuggy's forceful response actually came to press before Wierenga's essay. As something of a preemptive strike, his criticisms target several key areas. Tuggy first raises again the dilemma posed by Leftow: either God is a communal collection of divine individuals, or God is a composite individual. Taking the first horn is criticized sharply by Tuggy; he charges that on this reading "God will not have any personal characteristics at all, except in the derivative sense in which communities have them. He, or rather it, will not be conscious, omniscient, omnipotent, compassionate, and so on." Tuggy blasts this as nothing less than the defeat of theism, and he sees this as a "devastating problem for this kind of Social Trinitarianism."[30] For while Tuggy admits that this doctrine is "perfectly consistent and intelligible," he concludes that it cannot come close to doing justice to the biblical data. Similarly with the second horn of the dilemma, Tuggy argues that if God is a complex or composite being, then he cannot be identified as the New Testament identifies him — that is, with *the Father.*[31]

Tuggy further charges Wierenga with a disingenuous reading of the Athanasian Creed, and he locates an area of further concern for Wierenga. Tuggy notes that Wierenga "affirms that there are three divine persons, but denies that there are three gods."[32] This, exclaims Tuggy, "makes about as much sense as asserting that one has three male children, but denying that one has three sons."[33] Here he says Wierenga's claim "runs aground on the shores of unintelligibility."[34] Agreeing with Cartwright that

(G) Necessarily, any divine person is a God

expresses a "trivial truth," he complains that Wierenga's position is inchoate.

---

29. Wierenga, "Trinity and Polytheism," p. 291.

30. Dale Tuggy, "Tradition and Believability: Edward Wierenga's Social Trinitarianism," *Philosophia Christi* 5 (2003): 448.

31. Tuggy, "Tradition and Believability," pp. 449-50.

32. Tuggy, "Tradition and Believability," p. 450.

33. Tuggy, "Tradition and Believability," pp. 450-51.

34. Tuggy, "Tradition and Believability," p. 451.

Jeffrey E. Brower also criticizes Wierenga's defense of ST. Although he allows that Wierenga's position is "logically coherent," he points to several problems that beset Wierenga's account.[35] Brower doubts very much that Wierenga's reading of the Athanasian Creed is plausible. "If there really were a distinction to be drawn between *divinity* and *deity*," he asks, "and if the creed writers really intended to be predicating *divinity* rather than *deity* of the Persons, wouldn't we have expected them to use the Latin term '*divinus*' rather than '*deus*'?" (p. 297). Moreover, he is skeptical that there is any important distinction between the meaning of the Latin terms; "indeed, the terms '*divinus*' and '*deus*' seem to me to function in Latin much the way that 'human' and 'man' function in English" (p. 298).

But not only does Brower find Wierenga's distinction between *divinity* and *deity* to be both "historically and theologically dubious," he finds it philosophically unattractive as well (p. 300). He thinks it is unacceptably ad hoc, for it has no independent motivation. Brower admits that "if recognizing this distinction were the *only* way to make sense of the Trinity, then assuming that one has good reason to accept the doctrine itself, one might have good reason to recognize the distinction." But Brower does *not* think this is the only (or even the best) way to understand the doctrine of the Trinity, and he sees it as being "as artificial or unnatural as it would be to distinguish the property of *being human* from *being a man*" (p. 300). Thus he regards Wierenga's approach as an extreme solution to the conceptual problems posed by the doctrine of the Trinity.

Brower worries that "Wierenga's defense does nothing to remove the charge of polytheism *as polytheism is traditionally understood*" (p. 299). Even though it is logically coherent and avoids any charges of modalism, he nonetheless concludes that "it still must be regarded as theologically unacceptable" (p. 300).

Perhaps the most substantial and interesting defense of ST to date is that of J. P. Moreland and William Lane Craig.[36] After offering an overview of the biblical basis of the doctrine, Moreland and Craig briefly survey its historical development. They discuss both the major heresies (e.g.,

---

35. Jeffrey E. Brower, "The Problem with Social Trinitarianism: A Reply to Wierenga," *Faith and Philosophy* 21 (2004): 295. The page references to this essay have been placed in the text.

36. J. P. Moreland and William Lane Craig, *Philosophical Foundations for a Christian Worldview* (Downers Grove, Ill.: InterVarsity, 2003), pp. 575-95. The page references to this book have been placed in the text.

modalism and Arianism) and the responses of developing orthodoxy. They note the tendency to accentuate divine oneness and simplicity in the Latin tradition, and they are critical of Thomas Aquinas's anti–social Trinitarianism (pp. 585-87). But Moreland and Craig also highlight the ST elements in the Christian tradition. For instance, in their discussion of Tertullian's criticisms of modalism, they note Tertullian's arguments for a robust view of divine plurality; here they worry that Tertullian "at times seems to court tritheism" (p. 579), and they conclude that Tertullian "implicitly affirms that the persons of the Trinity are three distinct, self-conscious individuals" (p. 580). Similarly, they argue that the intention of the Cappadocians "was to affirm that there really are three persons in a rich psychological sense who are the one God" (p. 583), and they make a case that "Latin" theologians such as Hilary and even Augustine should not be interpreted as anti–social Trinitarians (pp. 585, 591).

Moreland and Craig clearly endorse ST, and they say that its "central commitment" is the conviction that "in God there are three distinct centers of self-consciousness, each with its proper intellect and will" (p. 583).[37] But they do not rest content with the standard defenses of ST, and indeed they are quite critical of the strategies of Gregory of Nyssa and Richard Swinburne (pp. 583-84, 587-88). They admit that "the most pressing task of contemporary social trinitarians is to find some more convincing answer as to why, on their view, there are not three Gods" (p. 584). They then set themselves to this task by addressing directly the challenge of Leftow.

Moreland and Craig apparently think that Leftow's criticisms of "Functional Monotheism" are appropriate, for they agree that "there is no salient difference between functional monotheism and polytheism" (p. 588). They also find the "Group Mind" strategy implausible, so they defend ST by opting for "Trinity Monotheism." They quote Leftow's challenge:

> Either the Trinity is a fourth case of the divine nature, in addition to the divine persons, or it is not. If it is, then we have too many cases of deity for orthodoxy. If it is not, and yet is divine, there are two ways to be divine — by being a case of deity, and by being a Trinity of such cases. If there is more than one way to be divine, Trinity monotheism becomes

---

37. They contrast this with "the central commitment of anti social trinitarianism": this is the conviction "that there is only one God, whose unicity of intellect and will is not compromised by the diversity of the persons."

Plantingean Arianism. But if there is in fact only one way to be divine, then there are two alternatives. One is that only the Trinity is God, and God is composed of non-divine persons. The other is that the sum of all divine persons is somehow not divine. To accept this last claim would be to give up Trinity monotheism altogether. (p. 589)[38]

Moreland and Craig represent Leftow's challenge as

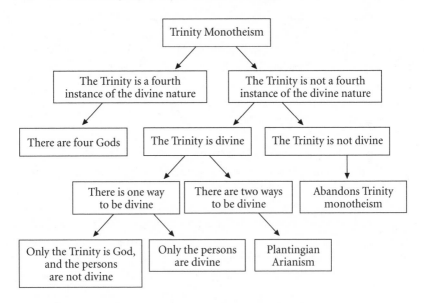

Responding to Leftow's challenge, Moreland and Craig deny that the Trinity is a fourth instance of the divine nature. They agree that the Trinity *is* divine, "since that is entailed by Trinity monotheism" (p. 590). Leftow thinks this means that there is more than one way to be divine, and this is what Leftow has labeled "Plantingean Arianism." Moreland and Craig are unsatisfied with Leftow's explanation of just what "Plantingean Arianism" *is* — simply to say (as Leftow does) that it is "the positing of more than one way to be divine" is "uninformative," and they want to know just why this would be objectionable. They put their finger on the "alleged problem": "if only the Trinity exemplifies the divine nature, then the way in which the persons are divine is less than fully divine."

38. Quoting Leftow, "Anti Social Trinitarianism," p. 221.

But Moreland and Craig protest that the "inference would follow, however, only if there was one way to be divine (namely, by instantiating the divine nature); but the position asserts that there is more than one way to be divine." They deny that the only way to be divine is to instantiate the divine nature.

> The persons of the Trinity are not divine in virtue of instantiating the divine nature. For presumably *being triune* is a property of the divine nature (God does not just happen to be triune); yet the persons of the Trinity do not have that property. It now becomes clear that the reason that the Trinity is not a fourth instance of the divine nature is that there are no other instances of the divine nature. The Father, Son, and Holy Spirit are not instances of the divine nature, and that is why there are not three Gods. The Trinity is the sole instance of the divine nature, and therefore there is but one God. (p. 590)

Moreland and Craig handle the familiar problems associated with identity statements as follows: "So while the statement 'The Trinity is God' is an identity statement, statements about the persons like 'The Father is God' are not identity statements." So what are they? They are statements that "perform other functions, such as ascribing a title or an office to a person (like 'Belshazzar is king,' which is not incompatible with there being coregents) or ascribing a property to a person (a way of saying, 'The Father is divine' as one might say 'Belshazzar is regal')" (pp. 590-91).

But if the persons are not instantiations of the divine nature, then just what are they? What makes them divine? Moreland and Craig invite us to consider an analogy with a cat. They point out that one way (perhaps the most obvious way) of "being feline is to instantiate the nature of a cat" (p. 591). But Moreland and Craig point out that there are also other ways to be feline: "A cat's DNA or skeleton is feline, even if neither is a cat. Nor is this a sort of downgraded or attenuated felinity: A cat's skeleton is fully and unambiguously feline. Indeed, a cat just is a feline animal, as a cat's skeleton is a feline skeleton." They then ask the obvious question: "Now if a cat is feline in virtue of being an instance of the cat nature, in virtue of what is a cat's DNA or skeleton feline?" One plausible answer, they say, "is that they are parts of a cat," and they then suggest that "we could think of the persons of the Trinity as divine because they are parts of the Trinity, that is, parts of God." Although they are quick to allow for significant disanalogies, they conclude that "given that the Father, for example, is not the whole Godhead, it seems clear that there is some sort of part-whole relation obtaining between the persons of the Trinity and the entire Godhead."

Moreland and Craig do not think this diminishes the divinity of the persons in any way. To the contrary, they find this account helpful in understanding the divine attributes. "For parts can possess properties which the whole does not, and the whole can have a property because some part has it. Thus, when we ascribe omniscience or omnipotence to God, we are not making the Trinity a fourth person or agent; rather, God has these properties because the persons do. Divine attributes." But as for such attributes as necessity, aseity, and eternity, on the other hand, "the persons have these properties because God as a whole has them" (p. 591).

Moreland and Craig recognize that their proposal is unusual, and they admit that this view conflicts with several post-Nicene statements (both of individual theologians and of creeds such as the Athanasian Creed and those of the Eleventh Council of Toledo and the Fourth Lateran Council). But they insist that since Protestants judge all doctrinal statements ("especially creeds of nonecumenical councils") by Scripture, since "nothing in Scripture warrants us in thinking that God is simple and that each person of the Trinity is identical to the whole Trinity," and since "nothing in Scripture prohibits us from maintaining that the three persons of the Godhead stand in some sort of part-whole relation to the Trinity," then their version of mereological ST cannot be condemned as heterodox and "seems to be thus far vindicated" (pp. 592-93).

But they are still sensitive to the charges of polytheism that haunt all versions of ST. "All of this still leaves us wondering," they readily admit, "how three persons can be parts of the same being, rather than three separate beings. What is the salient difference between three divine persons who are each a being and three divine persons who are together one being?" (p. 593). Moreland and Craig respond by again offering an analogy. They remind us of Cerberus, the three-headed dog who guarded Hades. They ask us to suppose that this animal has three brains, three centers of consciousness. We could even, they suggest, give "proper names to each of them: Rover, Bowser, and Spike." Moreland and Craig think there is exactly one dog guarding the gates of Hades; "despite the diversity of his mental states, Cerberus is clearly one dog. He is a single biological organism having a canine nature" (p. 593). So Rover, Bowser, and Spike may be said to be canine even though they are distinct and even though they are not three dogs but one dog. So too, the Father, Son, and Holy Spirit are all fully divine even though they are distinct and even though they are not three Gods but one God.

Moreland and Craig draw together the meaning of this for the doctrine of the Trinity: "suppose then, that God is a soul which is endowed with three complete sets of rational cognitive faculties, each sufficient for personhood. Then God, though one soul, would not be one person but three, for God would have three centers of self-consciousness, intentionality and volition, as social trinitarians maintain" (p. 594). God would not, on this view, "be three discrete souls because the cognitive faculties in question are all faculties belonging to one soul, one immaterial substance. God would therefore be one being who supports three persons, just as our own individual beings each support one person." Moreland and Craig conclude that this "model of Trinity monotheism seems to give a clear sense to the classical formula 'three persons in one substance'" (p. 594).

But not everyone is convinced of the viability of such a model. Daniel Howard-Snyder says the Trinity Monotheism of Moreland and Craig is both unstable on the periphery and rotten at the core, and he concludes that this model is not a version of monotheism at all. He raises several worries about the analogies; he wonders if there could be such a thing as Cerberus at all, and even if there could be he insists that it would be "an unnatural composite whose proper parts are three dogs, Rover, Bowser, and Spike; as such, Cerberus — Rover, Bowser, and Spike 'as a whole,' you might say — is not a dog at all."[39] Howard-Snyder pushes further and says that if the Cerberus analogy works at all, it works only to provide an analogy for Swinburne's Functional Monotheism, and Howard-Snyder calls this "avowedly tritheistic" (p. 396). Moreover, he argues that since "brains individuate mammals," then a single dog could not have "three distinct, complete, independently functioning brains" (p. 397). He believes that considering the possibility of surgical separation makes this obvious, and he thinks the most plausible option here is that they are distinct dogs "both prior to and after surgery." And at any rate, says Howard-Snyder, "even if Moreland and Craig were right about Cerberus, we have not the

39. Daniel Howard-Snyder, "Trinity Monotheism," *Philosophia Christi* 5 (2003): 396. The page references to this essay have been placed in the text.

foggiest idea what they are saying" (p. 397). He is not at all impressed with the analogies; he thinks it is obvious that "with the slightest bit of pressure, both the Cerberus analogy and the individual human analogy buckle" (p. 398).

But Howard-Snyder does more than merely point out the shortcomings of the analogies; he also raises several further metaphysical and theological concerns. He is concerned that Moreland and Craig do not offer adequate explanations of composition and support. He complains that the Moreland-Craig proposal leaves vague the mode of being of the divine persons: Are they individual substances or are they not (pp. 393-95)? He worries further that Moreland and Craig somehow diminish the divinity of the persons. He asks us to consider what someone utterly alien to the doctrine of the Trinity might think if he or she encountered this model, and he concludes that the alien "should concede that something's *being a proper part of the Trinity 'as a whole' that possesses powers of rationality, volition, and so forth, that are logically sufficient for full divinity* is, indeed, logically sufficient for its being fully divine" (p. 392). Despite this, however, Howard-Snyder insists that our alien should be unsatisfied with such an answer, because it leaves unexplained "how it could be" that the persons are fully divine without being instantiations of the divine nature (p. 392).

Howard-Snyder also raises concerns about the divinity of the Trinity as a whole. On the Moreland-Craig view, it seems that the one soul that is the triune God is not identical with any person. Howard-Snyder draws out some unwelcome consequences: "God is not 'equipped' with rational faculties of intellect and volition which enable it to be a self-reflective agent capable of self-determination," and although this does not mean that God "does not have proper parts that are thus equipped," it does mean that "God itself lacks the equipment" (p. 399). Thus God cannot perform intentional actions such as creation, and we are left with the result that the "first sentence in the Bible expresses a necessary falsehood" (p. 399). In addition, he charges that "Judeo-Christian anthropology will have to be remade," for if God is not a personal agent, then he cannot create personal agents in his image. Finally, Howard-Snyder says that because the Trinity "as a whole" both exemplifies the divine nature and yet is not a person, we are left with "an abysmally low view" of the divine nature (p. 400). This causes him to exclaim: "God is not a person or an agent, yet God is omnipotent, omniscient, and the like. What! If God is not a person or an agent, then God does not know anything, cannot act, cannot choose, cannot be morally good, cannot be worthy of worship. This is the God of Moreland's and Craig's Trinity Monotheism" (p. 401).

Perhaps Howard-Snyder's harshest criticisms come in his discussion of monotheism. He states that "monotheism is a thesis about Gods and the thesis is this: there is one and only one of them" (p. 401). He appeals to history here; he asserts that "there are no monotheists unless traditional Jews are monotheists, and when *they* assert that there exists exactly one God, they affirm that there exists a certain number of Gods and the number is one. Moreover, traditional Christians agree with traditional Jews on this score" (pp. 401-2). The "upshot" of all this is "that academic Trinitarians cannot mean whatever they like when they insist that they are monotheists" (p. 402). Howard-Snyder is clear about the real meaning of monotheism: "monotheists insist that the divine nature does not include the property of being triune and they insist that the divine nature does include the property of being worthy of worship, which implies being a person in a minimal sense. . . . [A]ccording to Monotheism, something can be a God without exemplifying the property of being triune and nothing can be a God without exemplifying a nature that includes the property of being a person. Either way, Moreland and Craig offer us a version of Trinity Monotheism that is *not* a version of Monotheism" (pp. 402-3).

In his response to the criticisms of Howard-Snyder, Craig offers a summative restatement of the model: "God is an immaterial substance or soul endowed with three sets of cognitive faculties each of which is sufficient for personhood, so that God has three centers of self-consciousness, intentionality, and will." He then points out that Howard-Snyder "fusses terribly over the analogies and suggestions that we offer as a springboard for arriving at this model while having comparatively little to say about the coherence or acceptability of the model itself."[40] Craig makes it clear that his primary concern is with the model itself rather than the analogies, but he defends the analogies nonetheless. For instance, to Howard-Snyder's claim that a three-headed dog would really be three partially overlapping dogs, Craig retorts that he finds this claim "astonishing," and he says that photographs show that multiheaded animals exist in the real world (as well as in mythology) (p. 102). Craig also responds to Howard-Snyder's

---

40. William Lane Craig, "Trinity Monotheism Once More: A Response to Daniel Howard-Snyder," *Philosophia Christi* 8 (2006): 101. The page references to this essay have been placed in the text.

claim that "brains individuate mammals" by calling this a "mere assertion!" (p. 102).

More important is Craig's interaction with Howard-Snyder's more substantive criticisms. Craig thinks Leftow begs the question by presupposing that there is only one way to be divine, and he is convinced as well that Howard-Snyder has repeated this mistake: Howard-Snyder's "reprise of Leftow's objection is as question-begging as the original, (for) it assumes that the only way to be divine is to exemplify the divine nature" (p. 110).

In response to Howard-Snyder, Craig says that whether or not the divine persons are actually parts of God is a "very difficult question"; surprisingly, however, he says "our final model leaves this an open question" (p. 110). If the divine persons are parts of the triune God, then Craig offers two options: the Trinity might be an individual composed of individuals or a collection (or group) composed of individuals. Either way, he thinks the model is unobjectionable, for the three persons are "indisputably divine" and as such are omnipotent, omniscient, worship-worthy, and so forth (p. 111).

But are the persons individual substances? Craig thinks this is a tougher question, but he does not commit himself either way. The answer to this question, he says, "will depend on whether we think that inseparable parts of a substance are themselves substances" (p. 113). He suspects that parts that were never separate, such as hands, don't have the "stand alone quality that something must have in order to be a substance." But even if they are not substances in their own right, they do have "enough integrity to have natures. A hand, for example, seems to have certain essential properties, such as having digits and having an opposable thumb. The persons of the Trinity could likewise share a certain nature, just as my hands do, without being substances in their own right." And since this nature includes all the properties of divinity, we would have three persons of one substance. Or if we do conclude that inseparable parts are substances, then we would be faced with the conclusion that the persons are individual substances. But not to worry, says Craig, for "as inseparable parts they are still three persons in one substance. They are no more instances of the nature of that unique substance than my hands are instances of the human nature." So either way, there is nothing for the Trinity Monotheist to fear, for both the full divinity of the persons and the unity of the triune God are preserved. "The crucial fact is that these individuals compose one unique, indivisible individual which is a substance" (p. 113).

Craig is willing to let the mereologists have their disputes about some of these issues, and he is reticent to commit himself on several of these points. But on another crucial theological issue he is exercised to defend his model against Howard-Snyder's criticisms. Recall Howard-Snyder's charge that Trinity Monotheism is not really a version of monotheism at all: monotheism insists both that the divine nature does not include the property of being triune and that God is *a* person. Craig admits that Howard-Snyder is correct in his assessment that according to Trinity Monotheism God is not *a* person, but Craig objects to the way Howard-Snyder "cashes this out" so "tendentiously" (p. 104). From the statement that "God is not *a* person," Howard-Snyder draws the conclusion that God lacks whatever it takes to be a rational agent. Craig retorts that this "is very misleading, as though God were not on our view a personal being. But in fact on our view God has the cognitive equipment sufficient for personhood three times over and so is tri-personal" (p. 105). He insists that Trinitarians — *all* Trinitarians, even those opposed to ST — affirm that God is personal but deny that God is *a* person. This, he says, is simply "part and parcel of Trinitarian orthodoxy," and in turn he charges Howard-Snyder with evincing "a dangerous proclivity toward unitarianism" (p. 105). The "real sticking point," he says, is Howard-Snyder's claim that "all monotheists concur that God is a person" (p. 106). Craig is convinced that this is nothing but the rank confusion of unitarianism with monotheism, and he concludes that the real heart of monotheism is that there is one God who is personal. And since Trinity Monotheism satisfies this criteria, Trinity Monotheism really is monotheism.

But Michael C. Rea raises additional concerns. He says the part-whole model offered by Moreland and Craig comes with "two problems, both apparently devastating." The first problem, he says, is that the part-whole Trinitarian cannot affirm the opening line of the Nicene Creed. Why not? Because the opening line says "We believe in one God, the Father Almighty" — but Moreland and Craig's model renders God "a fundamentally different thing from the Father." Worse yet, the part-whole theorist cannot affirm *homoousios,* for according to the part-whole account the Son is neither numerically the same essence as the Father nor of the same nature as the Father.[41]

---

41. Michael C. Rea, "The Trinity," in *The Oxford Handbook of Philosophical Theology*, ed. Thomas P. Flint and Michael C. Rea (Oxford: Oxford University Press, 2008), p. 709.

Keith Yandell offers another proposal.[42] Because God is triune, he argues, God is a complex being. Perhaps surprisingly, however, God is not composed of parts. In his specified sense of complexity, "X is complex if and only if there is a Y and a Z such that Y is not numerically identical to Z, it is logically impossible that Y exist and Z not exist, and Y and Z *together* are numerically identical to X in the sense of their together composing X."[43]

So God is complex, and God is complex in virtue of being three fully divine persons, each of whom is a conscious, rational agent. But according to Yandell's understanding of complexity and parthood, this complex God has no parts. This calls for some explanation. On Yandell's account of parts ("proper parts"), "if Y is a part of X, then Y can exist whether X exists or not. Further, if Y and Z are parts of X, then Y can exist without Z existing and Z can exist without Y existing."[44] Stated differently, "X is a *part* of Y if and only if X exists, Y exists, X plus something else is all of Y, X is not all of Y, and it is logically possible that X exist and Y not exist or Y exist and X not exist (or both)."[45]

Importantly, Yandell denies that the divine persons are parts of God. They are not, properly speaking, "parts" of God. For it is logically impossible that any of the divine persons exist without the others. Thus the God who is complex in virtue of triunity is also simple. For something is what he calls "simple(i)" if and only if it has no parts. He contrasts this account of simplicity with what he calls "simplicity(ii)" — which is what he says an entity would be just in case it were not complex. Thus God is both simple — in the sense of simplicity(i) — and complex in virtue of being triune. Indeed, God is necessarily simple(i) and necessarily not simple(ii).

All of this means that the God who is triune is not composed of parts or pieces. The divine persons are "necessarily strongly internally related," thus God is "necessarily particularly strongly internally complex."[46] The

---

42. Keith Yandell, "An Essay in Particularist Philosophy of Religion: A Metaphysical Structure for the Doctrine of the Trinity," in *These Three Are One: Philosophical and Theological Essays on the Doctrine of the Trinity,* ed. Thomas McCall and Michael C. Rea (Oxford: Oxford University Press, 2009). Although Yandell refrains from labeling his view ST, it bears many of the features that friends and foes alike ascribe to ST. At any rate, surely it is ST-friendly.

43. Yandell, "An Essay," p. 5.
44. Yandell, "An Essay," p. 6.
45. Yandell, "An Essay," p. 8.
46. Yandell, "An Essay," p. 21.

triune God is necessarily complex if and only if the triune God exists, is complex, and is complex (in the sense of complexity specified), and necessarily, were the triune God not complex then God would not exist. The triune God is particularly complex if and only if the triune God exists, is complex, and necessarily could not be complex in any other manner than that in which he is complex. And the triune God is internally complex if and only if the triune God exists, is complex, and it is logically impossible that that in virtue of which God is complex exists without everything else in virtue of which God is complex existing.[47]

What this yields, Yandell is convinced, is an account of the Trinity according to which God is both simple and triune. It rejects outright any notion that "there are three distinct omnicompetent beings," thus it is defensible against charges of tritheism.[48] What we are left with is a doctrine of one God who exists necessarily as triune.

II. Relative Trinitarianism

So ST wants to say that, while the divine persons are both distinct and discrete, there is but one God. Whether or not they can do so with consistency continues to be debated, and some Trinitarian theorists have looked elsewhere for help. The logic of relative identity is one such place to which they look.

A. The Logic of Relative Identity

As formulated by Peter Geach, the Relative Identity thesis holds that absolute identity is inexpressible; even though a language may have predicates expressing indistinguishability by the predicates it contains, a language cannot express indistinguishability *simpliciter*.[49] For the relative identity theorist, classical (or "absolute") identity, which holds that identity is reflexive, transitive, and symmetric, is mistaken. Leibniz's Law of the Indiscernibility of Identicals,[50]

---

47. Yandell, "An Essay," pp. 6-8.
48. Yandell, "An Essay," p. 21.
49. Peter Geach, *Logic Matters* (Berkeley: University of California Press, 1980), pp. 238-49.
50. This is not to be confused with the Identity of Indiscernibles (which is sometimes

(InId) For any objects x and y, if x and y are identical, then for any
property P, x has P if and only if y has P,[51]

is ill formed. All equivalence and identity relations are relative equivalence
and identity relations.

Consider such questions as these: "Is x the same as y?" or "Is x better
than y?" To the proponent of relative identity, trying to answer such questions — when asked as such — is a futile endeavor. We need to know if x is
a better *what* than y. And just how do we classify this "what"? The relative
identity theorist explains that these are *sortals;* they are general nouns that
denote objects of one particular kind.

So according to the theory of relative identity, objects may be identical
under one sortal concept but distinct under another.[52] Things can be said
to be the *same relative to* one kind of thing, but *distinct relative to* another
kind of thing. Purported examples of this include such statements as "the
couch and the chair are the same color — but different pieces of furniture,"
"'I' and 'I' are the same letter-type — but different letter-tokens," "the ship
Theseus sailed in as a youth and the ship his grandchildren gave to the
Athenian naval museum are the same ship — but different collections of
planks," "the soft clay statue of Pegasus and the (previously formed) soft
clay statue of Mercury are the same hunk of stuff — but different statues,"
"the man I spoke to last week and the man to whom I am currently speaking are the same official — but different men," or "the mayor and the high
seneschal are the same man — but different officials."[53] As Michael C. Rea
summarizes it, the theory of relative identity holds that

(R1) statements of the form 'x = y' are incomplete and therefore ill-
formed. A proper identity statement has the form 'x is the same
F as y.'

---

also called "Leibniz's Law"): "if any objects x and y share all of the same properties, then x
and y are identical."

51. In symbols: $(\forall x) (\forall y) [x = y (\forall F) (F(x) F(y))]$.

52. See Harold Noonan, "Relative Identity," in *A Companion to the Philosophy of Language,* ed. Bob Hale and Crispin Wright (Oxford: Blackwell, 1997), pp. 634-52.

53. This list is drawn from Christopher Hughes (who in turn credits Perry and
Wiggins), *A Complex Theory of a Simple God: An Investigation in Aquinas' Philosophical Theology* (Ithaca, N.Y.: Cornell University Press, 1989), p. 159. See further John Perry, "The Same
F," *Philosophical Review* 78 (1970): 181-201; David Wiggins, *Sameness and Substance* (Cambridge: Harvard University Press, 1980).

and (R2) states of affairs of the following sort are possible: x is an F, y is an
F, x is a G, y is a G, x is the same F as y, but x is not the same G
as y.[54]

Some entity may be the same as another relative to some sortal, but truly
be distinct relative to another sortal.

B. Relative Identity and the Doctrine of the Trinity

If the Relative Identity thesis is correct, then things can be said to be the
same relative to one sortal but *distinct relative to* another sortal. Relative
Trinitarianism (RT) employs this with respect to the doctrine of the Trinity, and with obvious payoff: the Father, Son, and Holy Spirit are *distinct
persons,* but they are the *same God.* So far, however, this leaves a lot unsaid,
and it could be taken in any of several different directions.

Drawing analogies with some of these purported examples might lead
away from an interpretation of Trinitarian theology that is compatible
with Christian orthodoxy. Such examples as ships and constituent collections of planks or of the same human person who occupies various roles
and wears various "hats" would, without careful qualification, offer analogies to modalism. For instance, John Macnamara, Marie La Palme Reyes,
and Gonzalo E. Reyes offer the analogies of a single person who travels on
several flights and thus is several passengers, a single person who is major-
ing both in the department of philosophy and in the department of mathematics, and a single person who is both the patient of a urologist and a
heart specialist. In the first instance we are faced with one person but several passengers, in the second instance we meet one person who is counted
as a major in multiple departments, and in the third instance we encounter
one person who is counted both as a patient and as an employee at the
hospital.[55] Such examples are "particularly relevant," they say, "because the

---

54. Michael C. Rea, "Relative Identity and the Doctrine of the Trinity," *Philosophia
Christi* 5 (2003): 434. I say "the" theory of relative identity; what this means is "the operative
theory of relative identity" (Rea surveys other theories as well).

55. John Macnamara, Marie La Palme Reyes, and Gonzalo E. Reyes, "Logic and the Trinity," *Faith and Philosophy* 11 (1994): 7-8. Interestingly, however, they deny the logic of relative
identity. John S. Feinberg also employs such analogies, but he distances himself from
modalism. *No One Like Him: The Doctrine of God* (Wheaton, Ill.: Crossway, 2001), pp. 496-98.

Divine Persons, being eternal, are simultaneously a single God."[56] As Edward Feser argues, however, such examples are misleading at best. We might admit that there is a *sense* in which the philosophy student is distinct from the mathematics student, but this is decidedly *not* the sense in which the divine persons are distinct from one another: "the same thing, however, can only be said in the case of the Divine Persons and God on pain of Sabellianism."[57]

The most impressive and sophisticated of the applications of the logic of relative identity to the doctrine of the Trinity shows no hints of tendencies toward modalism, however. In his elegant essay entitled "And Yet They Are Not Three Gods but One God," Peter van Inwagen applies the logic of relative identity to Trinitarian theology while maintaining that modalism is "a far more dangerous heresy to fall into in our time," and thus deciding to "risk" tritheism.[58] Van Inwagen makes plain his conviction that the term "person" in Trinitarian theology means the same as it does in everyday usage, and he spells this out further by saying that "persons are those things to which personal pronouns are applicable: a person can use the word 'I' and be addressed as 'thou' . . . [and] it is evident that the Persons of the Trinity *are* in this sense 'persons,' *are* someones: if the Father loves us, then someone loves us, and if the Son was incarnate by the Holy Ghost of the Virgin Mary, then someone was incarnate by the Holy Ghost of the Virgin Mary."[59]

Van Inwagen tells us that his version of RT does not attempt to penetrate or dispel the mystery of the doctrine, nor does he attempt to explain just how it is that God is three and that God is one. In fact, he does not actually endorse his proposal — he remains neutral on whether or not there are any actual cases of relative identity.[60] Instead, he offers the RT strategy as one way of meeting the charge that the traditional doctrine is incoherent.

---

56. Macnamara, Reyes, and Reyes, "Logic and the Trinity," p. 8.

57. Edward Feser, "Has Trinitarianism Been Shown to Be Coherent?" *Faith and Philosophy* 14 (1997): 91.

58. Peter van Inwagen, *God, Knowledge, and Mystery: Essays in Philosophical Theology* (Ithaca, N.Y.: Cornell University Press, 1995), p. 230.

59. Van Inwagen, *God, Knowledge, and Mystery,* pp. 264-65.

60. Van Inwagen, *God, Knowledge, and Mystery,* p. 227. Interestingly, van Inwagen explicitly rejects all of A. P. Martinich's "supposed examples of nontheological 'cases of relative identity'" (p. 228 n. 7). Van Inwagen states elsewhere that the logic of identity he proposes "turns on the idea that there is not one relation of identity but many." "Three Persons in One Being: On Attempts to Show That the Doctrine of the Trinity Is Self-Contradictory," in *The Trinity: East/West Dialogue,* p. 92.

After outlining a formal system of the logic of relative identity, van Inwagen applies this to the central theses of Trinitarian theology. He concludes that this gives us the result that

(1) Something is a divine person if it is a divine being

is formally consistent with

(2) there are three divine persons

and

(3) there is one divine being.

His philosophical explanation is that "without classical identity, there is no absolute counting: there is only counting by Ns."[61] So if we are counting "divine Beings by beings, there is one; counting divine Persons by beings, there is one; counting divine Beings by persons, there are three; counting divine Persons by persons, there are three."[62] Thus even though we may not be able to explain just *how* God is three distinct persons yet only one being, van Inwagen concludes that when seen through the lens of the logic of relative identity, "'is the same being as' does not dominate 'is the same person as.'"[63] Thus "all the constituent propositions of the doctrine of the Trinity can be expressed in the language of relative identity, and they can be shown to be mutually consistent, given that the correct logic of identity is the logic of relative identity."[64] There is but one God — in the strong numerical (rather than generic) sense of *one* — and there are three divine persons. Is this not what Trinitarian orthodoxy requires?

C. Objections to Relative Trinitarianism

Despite the elegance and rigor of van Inwagen's formulations, however, not all philosophical theologians find RT persuasive. Some critics cast doubts upon the very notion of relative identity; they find the logic of rela-

---

61. Van Inwagen, *God, Knowledge, and Mystery,* p. 250.
62. Van Inwagen, *God, Knowledge, and Mystery,* p. 250.
63. Van Inwagen, *God, Knowledge, and Mystery,* p. 259.
64. Van Inwagen, "Three Persons," p. 97.

tive identity itself to be problematic. They worry that it works only so long as it trades in ambiguity, and once the sortals in question are made explicit we see that the "relative identity" is only apparent and instead there is at the end of the day only absolute identity. Moreland and Craig point out that even van Inwagen, who is without doubt RT's most illustrious contemporary defender, "has no answer to the questions of how x and y can be the same N without being the same P," and they conclude that "the ability to state coherently the trinitarian claims under discussion using the device of relative identity is a hollow victory."[65] Swinburne and Christopher Hughes echo and endorse the criticisms of the logic of relative identity made by David Wiggins and John Perry.[66] They worry that RT violates (InId), and they think this is much too high a price to pay. As Hughes puts it, if x and y are discernible, then they cannot be the very same N — because if they are discernible, they cannot be the very same anything.[67]

Other critics are unconvinced that the logic of relative identity helps with the doctrine of the Trinity (whatever its merits — or demerits — elsewhere). Again following Wiggins, James Cain points out that some of the problems associated with the logic of relative identity become *more* complicated when we bring in the Trinity.[68] In the most penetrating of the engagements of RT to date, Rea distinguishes between what he calls "pure" and "impure" forms of RT. He raises objections to both versions.

The "pure" version of RT endorses both

(RTa) some doctrine of relative identity is true;

and (RTb) the words "is God" and "is distinct from" in Trinitarian formulations express relativized identity and distinctness relations rather than absolute identity and distinctness relations.[69]

The problems with the "pure" version, as Rea sees things, are "catastrophic." At best it leads to modalism; what is much worse is the conclusion that "the doctrine of relative identity seems to presuppose an

---

65. Moreland and Craig, *Philosophical Foundations*, p. 592.

66. E.g., Swinburne, *The Christian God*, pp. 14-16, 187-88. Cf. Wiggins, *Sameness and Substance*, and Perry, "The Same F."

67. Hughes, *A Complex Theory*, p. 157.

68. James Cain, "The Doctrine of the Trinity and the Logic of Relative Identity," *Religious Studies* 25 (1989): 145.

69. Rea, "Relative Identity," p. 437. The page references to this essay have been placed in the text.

antirealist metaphysic" (p. 442). Accepting this as a solution would be nothing short of "disastrous," says Rea, for surely orthodoxy would license us to say neither that "the very existence of Father, Son, and Holy Spirit is a *theory-dependent* matter" nor that "the distinctness of the divine Persons is somehow relative to our ways of thinking and theorizing" (p. 443).

Nor does the "impure" version look all that much better to Rea. The "impure" strategy endorses (RTb) while remaining neutral on (RTa). In other words, it withholds opinion on the possibility of absolute identity while using the logic of relative identity for help in theological matters. Rea asks whether, if we grant his use of the logic of relative identity, van Inwagen has shown that the doctrine of the Trinity is coherent. Surprisingly, he says, "the answer is no" (p. 440). For in remaining neutral on relative identity, van Inwagen "leaves open the possibility that Father, Son, and Holy Spirit are absolutely distinct, and if they are absolutely distinct, it is hard to see what it could possibly mean to say that they are the same *being*" (p. 441). So the "impure" RT theorist, on Rea's account, must either commit to the truth of relative identity, thus converting to "pure RT" (and thus be prepared to grapple with the problems that come with the adoption of the "pure" strategy), or tell a "supplemental story to explain the metaphysics of the RI [Relative Identity] relations" (p. 442).

D. Constitution and the Trinity

Telling such a story is what Rea and Brower do in their appropriation of an account of material constitution. They begin by drawing attention to another well-known problem in metaphysics: the problem of material constitution. As they explain it, "this problem arises whenever it appears that an object a and an object b share all of the same parts and yet have different modal properties."[70] They ask us to consider a bronze statue and the lump of bronze that constitutes the statue. On one hand, it seems obvious that we have two entities at hand, for the statue (which presumably cannot survive being melted down) and the lump of bronze (which could be melted down and recast) have different modal properties. But on the other hand, "our ordinary counting practices lead us to recognize only *one* mate-

---

70. Jeffrey E. Brower and Michael C. Rea, "Material Constitution and the Trinity," *Faith and Philosophy* 22 (2005): 57. The page references to this essay have been placed in the text.

rial object in the region" (p. 57). They admit that the analogy is far from perfect, but they think that one way of dealing with the problem of material constitution can be applied to the doctrine of the Trinity. The "guiding intuition," they say, "is the Aristotelian idea that it is possible for an object a and an object b to be 'one in number' — that is, numerically the same — without being strictly identical" (p. 58).

Brower and Rea work to show how a proposed solution to the problem of material constitution may be applied to Trinitarian theology, and they make it clear just what doctrine of the Trinity they seek to defend. They spell out five desiderata that they take to be basic to any acceptable doctrine of the Trinity:

> (D1) An acceptable doctrine of the Trinity is clearly consistent with the view that Father, Son, and Holy Spirit are divine individuals, and that there is exactly one divine individual.
>
> (D2) It does not conflict with a natural reading of either the Bible or the ecumenical creeds.
>
> (D3) It is consistent with the view that God is an individual rather than a society, and that the Persons are not parts of God.
>
> (D4) It is consistent with the view that classical identity exists and is not to be analyzed in terms of more fundamental sortal-relativized sameness relations like *being the same person as*.
>
> (D5) It carries no anti-realist commitments in metaphysics. (p. 59)

We are able to see that they want the most robust version of divine unity or oneness; they insist on nothing less than numerical oneness. They also, however, hold to a robust notion of the distinctness of the persons.[71] They worry that extant defenses of ST violate D1-D3, while they also think that existing versions of RT (such as van Inwagen's) violate D1, D4, or D5. Thus they seek to bolster RT by employing the notion of numerical sameness without identity.

How is this strategy to work? Taking Aristotle's notion of "accidental sameness" as their "point of departure," Brower and Rea argue that the Philosopher's account of hylomorphic compounds accords well with common

---

71. They don't deny that the divine persons compose a society; what they reject instead are the views that (a) the name "God" refers to this society and (b) the divine persons should be thought of as parts of God; see Brower and Rea, "Material Constitution," p. 75 n. 7.

sense and helps solve some notorious metaphysical puzzles. Common sense, they suggest, leads us to believe in things that are "very plausibly characterized as hylomorphic compounds whose matter is *a familiar material object* and whose form is an accidental property. For example, we believe in fists and hands, bronze statues and lumps of bronze, cats and heaps of cat tissue, and so on" (p. 61). They argue that their view is a common-sense way of looking at things: "if you sell a piano, you won't charge for the piano *and* for the lump of wood, ivory, and metal that constitutes it. As a fan of common sense, you will probably believe that there are pianos and lumps, and that the persistence conditions of pianos differs from the persistence conditions of lumps" (p. 62). Again, reflection on the modal conditions of pianos and lumps pushes us to admit that while there is one material object for sale, the lump and the piano are nonetheless really distinct. This does not mean that we can no longer count by identity; it means only that "it simply requires us to acknowledge a distinction between sortals that permit counting by identity and sortals that do not" (p. 63).

Brower and Rea are careful to point out the significant disanalogies between material constitution and the doctrine of the Trinity. Of course, the Trinity is not an example of *material* constitution; the role of matter in material constitution is played by nonmatter. Furthermore, the form in hylomorphic compounds is commonly instantiated only contingently by the matter in question, but the constitution of the Trinity is necessary. Additionally, while the constitution relation is typically between a substance and a hylomorphic structure that is built out of the substance and an accidental property, the Trinitarian account is different. "The Persons, however, are not like this. Thus, it is at best misleading to say that the relation between them is one of *accidental sameness*. Better instead to go with the other label we have used . . . the persons stand in the relation of numerical sameness without identity" (p. 69).

Brower and Rea are *not* merely taking an existing metaphysical notion and then somehow forcing Trinitarian doctrine to fit into that paradigm. This can be seen in their diagram on page 48 of the different senses of the copula "is" (p. 71).[72] Brower and Rea clearly reject the "is" of predication; they are convinced that this tilts toward an unacceptable account of ST. Instead they endorse the "is" of numerical sameness, but they do not opt for

---

72. The chart appears in *Faith and Philosophy* 22, no. 1 (2005): 71, and is used here with permission.

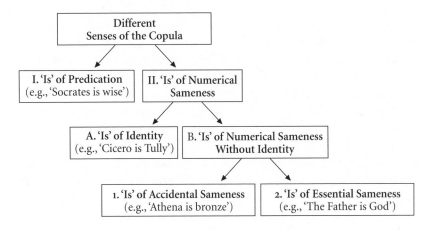

the "is" of identity. Here they show their colors; they endorse a version of "impure" RT (p. 76 n. 23).[73] But it is at this juncture that they break with Aristotle, and, by my lights, they do so on theological grounds. They take the route of numerical sameness without identity, but they do not hold that statements such as "the Son is God" are statements of *accidental* sameness. Instead, we have a new category, and one apparently occasioned by theology: the "is" in "the Son is God" is the "is" of essential sameness rather than accidental sameness.

Brower and Rea spell out the conclusions for Trinitarian theology:

[T]he Persons of the Trinity can also be conceived of in terms of hylomorphic compounds. Thus, we can think of the divine essence as playing the role of matter, and we can regard the properties *being a Father, being a Son,* and *being a Spirit* as distinct forms instantiated by the divine essence, each giving rise to a distinct Person. As with matter, we regard the divine essence not as an individual thing in its own right but rather as that which, together with the requisite "form," constitutes a Person. Each Person will then be a compound structure whose matter is the divine essence and whose form is one of the three distinctive Trinitarian properties. On this way of thinking, the Persons of the Trinity are directly analogous to particulars that stand in the familiar relation of material constitution. (p. 68)

73. I take them to deny the commitments of "pure" versions of relative identity; they do not commit to the view that Leibniz's Law is ill-formed or that sortal-relative identity statements are more fundamental than absolute identity statements.

They obviously think the analogy of material constitution has the resources to make the standard charges of incoherence dissipate:

> It seems not at all inappropriate to think of the divine Persons on analogy with hylomorphic compounds; and once they are thought of this way, the problem of the Trinity disappears. According to the Aristotelian solution to the problem of material constitution, a statue and its lump are *two* distinct hylomorphic compounds; yet they are numerically one material object. Likewise, then, the Persons of the Trinity are *three* distinct Persons but numerically one God . . . there will be three distinct Persons, each Person will be God (and will be the same God as the other Persons); and there will be exactly one God. (p. 69)

Brower and Rea think that a major advantage of their version of RT is that it allows for the satisfaction of their desiderata. Like ST, their view posits three divine persons who are really distinct. Unlike ST, however, their position also insists that there is *one* divine individual, thus allowing for the full satisfaction of D1. Although they do not deal with issues at any length, presumably they think their view coheres well with Scripture and the ecumenical creeds, thus not running aground of D2. It also denies that God is composed of parts, thus satisfying D3. Like RT, it holds to both numerical sameness and real distinction between the divine persons. But unlike RT, it is consistent with the view that classical identity exists and is not to be analyzed in terms of more fundamental sortal-relativized sameness relations like *being the same person as,* nor does it carry any antirealist commitments. Thus it satisfies D4 and D5 as well (p. 70). "For all of these reasons," they conclude, "our Aristotelian solution to the problem of the Trinity seems to us to be the most philosophically promising and theologically satisfying solution on offer" (p. 70).

III. "Latin" Trinitarianism

There is, however, another possibility — perhaps the view flying under the flag of Latin Trinitarianism (LT) offers a better way forward.[74] In what

74. This label has been affixed by Brian Leftow; see, e.g., "A Latin Trinity," *Faith and Philosophy* 21 (2004): 304-33. Peter Forrest offers a similar proposal in "The Trinity and Personal Identity," in *The Trinity: East/West Dialogue,* pp. 75-82.

Leftow calls "Latin Trinitarianism," there is just one divine substance, and the three "Persons are somehow God three times over."[75] He draws a sharp contrast between LT and ST. For ST, the persons are both distinct and discrete. But for LT, the persons are distinct but not discrete. For ST, there are three tropes of divinity, three individualized cases of deity. Why object to that? Because, says Leftow, "whatever has a deity-trope is an instance of this kind. An instance of the kind *deity* is a God. So: three tropes of deity, three Gods."[76] For LT, on the other hand, there is only one individualized case of an attribute: "while both Father and Son instance the divine nature (deity), they have but one trope of deity between them, which is God's."[77] "Abel and Cain," Leftow explains, "were both human. Yet they had the same nature, humanity. Yet each also had his own nature, and Cain's humanity was not identical with Abel's. Abel's perished with Abel's, while Cain's went marching on." This is because "bearers individuate tropes: Cain's humanity is distinct from Abel's just because it is Cain's, not Abel's."

Leftow employs this conceptual framework to make clear what he means by LT: "while both Father and Son instance the divine nature (deity), they have but one trope of deity between them, which is God's. While Cain's humanity ≠ Abel's humanity, the Father's deity = the Son's deity = God's deity. But bearers individuate tropes. If the Father's deity is God's, this is because the Father just *is* God" (p. 305).

Leftow is well aware that his claim that the persons are distinct but not discrete is puzzling. He wants to show how the divine persons might be distinct but not discrete. To this end, he employs a fascinating time-travel analogy:

> You are at Radio City Music Hall, watching the Rockettes kick in unison. You notice that they look quite a bit alike. But (you think) they just must be made up to look that way. After all, they came on-stage at once, each from a different point backstage, they put their arms over each others' shoulders for support, smile and nod to each other, and when the number is over, they scatter offstage each in her own direction. So they certainly seem to be many different women. But appearances deceive. Here

---

75. Leftow, "A Latin Trinity," p. 304.

76. Leftow, "Modes without Modalism," in *Persons, Human and Divine*, ed. Peter van Inwagen and Dean Zimmerman (Oxford: Oxford University Press, 2007), p. 358.

77. Leftow, "A Latin Trinity," p. 305. The page references to this essay have been placed in the text.

is the true story. All the Rockettes but one, Jane, called in sick that morning. So Jane came to work with a time machine . . . ran on-stage to her position at the left of the chorus line, kicked her way through the number, then ran off. She changed her makeup, donned a wig, then stepped into her nephew's Wells-o-matic, to emerge from a point to the right of her first entry, stepped into line second from the chorus line's left, smiled and whispered a quip to the woman on the right, kicked her way through the number, then ran off. She then changed her makeup again. . . . (p. 307)

Leftow asks the crucial question: "Can one person thus be wholly in many places at once?" His "short answer" is this: "she is in many places at the same point in *our* lives, but not the same point in *hers*" (p. 307).[78]

In the Rockettes, as in LT, there is but one trope. Leftow recognizes that the cases differ in some important ways, and that there is a significant disanalogy here as well. But he thinks the analogy succeeds in showing that as there is but one Jane who is nonetheless present several times over in the chorus line, so also God lives his life in three discrete strands at once. In "one strand God lives the Father's life, in one the Son's, and in one the Spirit's. The events of each strand add up to the life of a Person. The lives of the Persons add up to the life God lives *as* the three Persons." He concludes that "there is one God, but He is many in the events of His life, as Jane was in the chorus line: being the Son is a bit like being the leftmost Rockette" (p. 312).

So what does it mean to be a "person" in LT? Leftow's initial response to this question is that "they are whatever sort God is — the Persons just *are* God . . . the Persons have the same trope of deity" (p. 314). In what ways are they really distinct? Well, "just as Jane does not think her leftmost thoughts at the point in her life at which she is rightmost, God does not think his Father-thoughts at the points in His life at which He is Son" (pp. 314-15). And "just as Jane can token the truth 'I am the leftmost Rockette' and 'I am the rightmost,' God can token with truth 'I am the Father' and 'I am the Son.'" But as Leftow sees things, it is also true that "just as Jane cannot token both claims with truth at the same points in her life, God cannot token with truth 'I am the Son' at the points in His life at which He is Father"; furthermore, "just as Jane at the leftmost chorus line has no internal

---

78. Of course, there is much more to Leftow's theory than his "short answer" might indicate.

access to and is not thinking the thoughts she thinks at the rightmost spot, God as Father has no internal access to and is not thinking the thoughts of God as Son." The upshot of all this is that "the Son is distinct from the Father as leftmost Jane is from rightmost, and the Son's mind is distinct from the Father's as leftmost is from rightmost" (p. 315).

Leftow introduces a technical phrase: "phased sortal." "'Infant' and 'man' are phased sortals: they pick out a substance under a description which essentially involves a particular case of its life" (p. 324). So in the case of the Rockettes, the "'leftmost Rockette' and the 'rightmost Rockette' act as mutually exclusive phased sortals picking out Jane. . . . So too, on the account of the Trinity I've been suggesting, 'Father' and 'Son' are mutually exclusive phased sortals picking out God" (p. 324). The Father and Son are — or at least are much like — temporally located identities. But they are not themselves temporary; they are eternal. Indeed, they are timelessly eternal. The "basic point of the Rockette analogy" that Leftow draws out "is that one should approach the Trinity by asking in what ways God's life is free from ordinary temporal relations," and then find the answer that "it is free enough from ordinary temporal ordering that we can say that God lives His life in three streams at once, (and then) index Trinitarian truths to appropriate sets of events" (p. 326).

The distinctness of the divine persons is then "event-based" (p. 315). The divine persons "simply are God as in certain acts — certain events — in His inner life" (p. 316). But it is vitally important to remember that these events "have no temporal sequence. None succeeds the other, for none are in time. As they are not in time, they have no temporal parts. God just eternally *does* the acts which constitute His life; these acts render Him triune" (p. 316). Leftow turns to a rather surprising source (at least for LT) to flesh out the relevant notion of person: John Locke. Leftow thinks that what he calls "Locke-persons" are genuine persons; a Locke-person has "the full repertoire of person abilities: it is conscious, acts, loves."[79] But the existence-conditions make a Locke-person unique: "persons are identical over time just as far as a single 'consciousness' extends."[80] Locke-persons begin to exist when a single consciousness begins, and Locke-persons cease to exist when this single consciousness ends.

Leftow is well aware of the questions that nag and the problems that

---

79. Leftow, "Modes without Modalism," p. 367.
80. Leftow, "Modes without Modalism," p. 367.

plague Locke's proposal (is it really the case that "Tom sleeping" is not the same person as "Tom awake"?). But he is not committed to the entire Lockean picture, and he is surely not committed to the view that *we* are Locke-persons. The divine persons are omniscient; there is never a break in the consciousness of any of them. The obvious problems that dog Locke's theory need not worry the application of his view to the doctrine of the Trinity.

The moral Leftow draws from the story is this: even if we are not Locke-persons, there *could be* Locke-persons. Relevantly, the divine persons could be Locke-persons. Leftow summarizes his use of Locke's theory: "My Lockean 'mode'-based suggestion about the Trinity, then, is this. Perhaps the triune Persons are event-based persons founded on a generating substance, God . . . these streams are mental events, and each such stream is the life of a Locke-person. God never exists save *in* the Persons . . . there is just one God who generates and lives as the three Persons, by generating and living in three distinct mental streams."[81]

Is this enough to avoid modalism? Leftow is aware that this is the threat to his proposal. He recognizes that if, as his LT has it,

(1) the Father = God

and (2) the Son = God,

then transitivity would seem to push us to

(3) the Father = the Son.

And Leftow knows as well that if this is so, then "the Father suffered on the cross, and so LT falls into the heresy of Patripassianism."[82] The challenge looms large, and Leftow works to "skirt the Scylla of tri-theism and the Charybdis of modalism."[83]

And he thinks this can be done; Leftow denies that his view is a version of modalism. He says that "it is no easy thing to say just what Modalism *was,* or exactly why it was rejected."[84] He goes on to offer some snippets of descriptions drawn from theological reference works: modalism is the

---

81. Leftow, "Modes without Modalism," p. 374.
82. Leftow, "Modes without Modalism," p. 359.
83. Leftow, "A Latin Trinity," p. 326.
84. Leftow, "A Latin Trinity," p. 326.

view "that the persons are impermanent and transitory," that they are "a mere succession of modes or operations," that God is triune only in the *opera ad extra,* or that there is only a "Trinity of manifestation."[85] Leftow then points out that "nothing in my account of the Trinity precludes saying that the Persons' distinction is an eternal, necessary, non-successive and intrinsic feature of God's life, one which would be there even if there were no creatures." He denies that his view entails that the Father was crucified; although it *is* true that the same God who is the Father is crucified, it is not the case that the God who is the Father is crucified at the same Father-point in his life. Furthermore, he insists, his view can account for the important "anti-Modalist" biblical texts: "the Son cannot token truly 'I am the Father,' though He can token truly 'I am the God who is (at another point in his life) the Father.' "[86] None of the divine persons can say "I am at one point in my life the Father and at another point the Son," for it is not true either that God is the Son at any point in the life of the Father or that he is the Father at any point in the life of the Son.

Leftow thinks there is an important sense in which there is an "I-Thou" relationship within the life of the triune God. When the Son, for example, says "I," we are to understand this as meaning that he is — now at the point of being the Son — the one God who is Father at another point of his life. This means (among other things) that there is no simple divine "I," for if any "I" were what Leftow calls "purely referential" (a term whose contribution to a sentence is simply an individual to whom God refers), then "a purely referential 'I' would always contribute simply God to a sentence's content. No Person could speak as 'I' and refer to Himself as Person; the Son could not say with truth, 'I am not the Father,' for His 'I' would refer to God, and God *is* the Father."[87] Thus first-person divine reference always includes a "mode of presentation, a sense under which the speaker conceives and refers to Himself." This leads Leftow to the conclusion that the Son always speaks as Son, as an "I," as a distinct entity with his own mind and will, and this in turn assures him that "this is enough to make adequate sense of the texts" and to guarantee the "real distinctness of Father and Son."[88]

---

85. Leftow, "A Latin Trinity," p. 327.
86. Leftow, "A Latin Trinity," p. 327.
87. Leftow, "A Latin Trinity," p. 328.
88. Leftow, "A Latin Trinity," p. 328.

So God has three parts of his life, and these occur simultaneously. "God eternally has three parts of His life going on at once, without succession between them. One part is the Father's life, one the Son's, one the Spirit's."[89] God has these parts necessarily and eternally: "these three streams of consciousness and the Persons they generate are eternal, necessary, and intrinsic features of the divine inner life."[90] God has three parts, and these parts are streams of self-conscious life for God. Thus the triune God is three persons. But the triune God who has these parts has them eternally — simultaneously and everlastingly — and the triune God who has these parts exemplifies exactly one trope of divinity. Thus the triune God is exactly one God.

IV. Conclusion

In this chapter I have provided an overview of some important recent work on the doctrine of the Trinity done by analytic philosophical theologians. Without attempting to be exhaustive, I have offered a survey of some of the most interesting and influential statements. Several things should be clear: there is a lively and spirited conversation taking place among analytic philosophers of religion, these philosophers share a deep conviction that these issues matter greatly, and in general they desire to understand and defend an orthodox account. But beyond this there is very little consensus. For ST the charge of tritheism remains on the table. Worries about the coherence of RT have not yet been put entirely to rest, while LT, on the other hand, will surely face criticisms that it does not avoid modalism (in addition to the criticisms of the analogy itself).

All parties desire a statement or model that is both coherent and orthodox. They want to avoid both modalism and tritheism. Consideration of such issues is irreducibly *theological* — these discussions are not, and cannot be, reduced to metaphysics alone. How might more intensely theological concerns inform the current analytic debate? To this question we now turn.

89. Leftow, "Modes without Modalism," p. 374.
90. Leftow, "Modes without Modalism," p. 374.

CHAPTER TWO

Whose Monotheism? Jesus and His Abba

Just what violates the standards of monotheism? What really counts as an acceptable version of Trinitarian monotheism; what allows Trinitarians to "cling to respectability as monotheists"?[1] And what does it mean to charge someone with polytheism or Arianism? How does one make such charges really "stick"? These are vexed questions, and the process of coming to a satisfactory answer is complicated by the unfortunate fact that agreement about what really counts as monotheism (and, for that matter, what really counts as polytheism) is remarkably hard to come by. Of course, most everyone agrees that to be a monotheist is to believe that number is applicable to deity and that the number of Gods is one (and that polytheism is the view that the number of Gods is more than one). But beyond that we are hard pressed to find anything approaching consensus. Does commitment to monotheism flatly rule out belief in there being more than one divine agent? Is the monotheist committed to the belief that there is at most one trope of divinity?[2] Or is belief in a divine society — a divine society rightly ordered — acceptable as a form of monotheism? Is polytheism the belief that there are multiple divine entities who are in conflict with one another, or is it simply the belief that there is more than one trope of divinity?

1. Cornelius Plantinga, Jr., "Social Trinity and Tritheism," in *Trinity, Incarnation, and Atonement: Philosophical and Theological Essays*, ed. Ronald J. Feenstra and Cornelius Plantinga, Jr. (Notre Dame, Ind.: University of Notre Dame Press, 1989), p. 31.

2. As Brian Leftow seems to do; "Anti Social Trinitarianism," in *The Trinity: An Interdisciplinary Symposium on the Trinity*, ed. Stephen T. Davis, Daniel Kendall, S.J., and Gerald O'Collins, S.J. (Oxford: Oxford University Press, 1999), p. 204.

The situation is further complicated by the fact that arguments (pro and con) often hinge on intuitions; intuitions that apparently run deep but, alas, intuitions that are questioned by those who disagree. It is not all that hard to begin with, say, the view that multiple tropes of deity would individuate distinct gods and then show that, since Social Trinitarianism posits multiple tropes of deity, then Social Trinitarianism is obviously a version of polytheism. Nor is it all that difficult to identify "pagan polytheism" as the view that the gods are "in continual conflict" and then contrast this with Social Trinitarianism's claim that "the unity of the three persons consists, at least in part, in that very harmony of will" that they enjoy, concluding, of course, that Social Trinitarianism is not a version of polytheism but is indeed a kind of monotheism.[3]

What is much harder is finding a relevant account of monotheism that offers a plausible standard.[4] While there are other accounts that might be informative and helpful, I suggest that we take the monotheism of Second Temple Judaism as it was received and drawn upon by John, Paul, and the other authors of the New Testament. In what follows I offer a brief summary of this monotheism. I shall make a case that the worship of Jesus by the earliest Christians shows us that they understood him to be included in the identity of the one God, that they understood him to be what we might call a distinct speech-agent, and that they did so without seeing this worship as a compromise of their monotheism.[5] I then offer a brief overview of Arianism (the prototypical Christian version of tritheism), and I seek to unpack the understandings of modalism and polytheism that are to be found in some important statements. While I make no claim to either originality or comprehensiveness, this survey will allow us to gain a broader theological perspective.

---

3. Thomas V. Morris, *The Logic of God Incarnate* (Ithaca, N.Y.: Cornell University Press, 1986), p. 214. For a similar account of polytheism, see Keith Yandell, "The Most Brutal and Inexcusable Error in Counting? Trinity and Consistency," *Religious Studies* 30 (1994): 216.

4. An interesting and important step in this direction has been taken by Michael C. Rea, "Polytheism and Christian Belief," *Journal of Theological Studies,* n.s., 87 (2006): 133-48.

5. I leave aside here discussion of "centers of consciousness," although I must confess I have no idea how someone might be a distinct speech-agent (of the kind presented in the Gospels — wherein one who is not incarnate says to one who is incarnate, "you are my beloved son") and not be a center of consciousness.

I. Monotheism and Christology in the New Testament

Questions surrounding discussions of "monotheism" are hotly disputed by biblical scholars. Some scholars claim that monotheism as a category itself owes much to Enlightenment and post-Enlightenment forms of religious analysis; these scholars claim that discussions of monotheism are potentially more misleading than helpful.[6] Other scholars continue to work with the concept but deny that the religion of the Hebrew people was in any way recognizably monotheistic.[7]

Despite the lack of consensus, however, I think it safe to say that biblical scholarship offers strong support for the view that, at least by the period known as "Second Temple Judaism," we can see a strict monotheism.[8] Accordingly, in this section I shall offer a summary of this monotheism as it was received by Paul, John, and other authors of the New Testament, noting that worship is central to understanding monotheism. I will make a case that Jesus indeed was worshiped and thus included in the identity of the one God, and that the Jesus who was worshiped is portrayed as a divine

---

6. For this assessment, see Nathan MacDonald's insightful *Deuteronomy and the Meaning of "Monotheism"* (Tübingen: Mohr Siebeck, 2003).

7. The literature on this topic (a good deal of which was spawned by the discovery of several eighth-century Jewish texts that spoke positively of a consort — an *asherah* — of Yahweh) is enormous; representative of these studies is the work of Mark S. Smith. Smith sees the development of Israelite monotheism as very late; he calls it "evolutionary" while also admitting that it is "revolutionary"; see, e.g., *The Early History of God: Yahweh and the Other Deities in Ancient Israel* (Grand Rapids: Eerdmans, 1990), pp. 198-99; see also his *The Origins of Biblical Monotheism: Israel's Polytheistic Background and the Ugaritic Texts* (Oxford: Oxford University Press, 2001). It seems important to keep in mind an important distinction between the canonical *prescriptives*, on one hand, and on the other hand the *descriptions* of ancient Israelite religious practice found in various inscriptions. The insights that Israel was *not* exclusively devoted and did *not* practice monolatry to Yahweh are to be found in the prophets themselves; arguments to this conclusion from historical-critical studies are hardly shocking to those familiar with the canonical narrative.

8. I say "at least" because it is possible to mount good arguments that such monotheism precedes the era known as "Second Temple Judaism." Minimally, a good case can be made that the Old Testament is what James A. Sanders calls "monotheizing literature"; *Canon and Community: A Guide to Canonical Criticism* (Philadelphia: Fortress, 1984), p. 52. Similarly, Bernard Lang contends that the redactors of the canon were "committed monotheists." *Monotheism and the Prophetic Minority* (Sheffield: Almond Press, 1983), p. 53. But since these arguments are beyond the scope of this essay, I shall leave such complicated and important issues unaddressed.

agent who is distinct and discrete from his Father. Of course, I shall be able to offer only the briefest summary, but even such a summary should be enough to inform the current analytic discussion.

A. The "Strict" Monotheism of Second Temple Judaism: The Centrality of Worship

James D. G. Dunn puts it bluntly: "Monotheism was absolutely fundamental for the Jew of Jesus' day."[9] Richard Bauckham agrees that "the monotheism of Second Temple Judaism was indeed 'strict.'" He makes a case that "most Jews in this period were highly self-consciously monotheistic and had certain very familiar and well-defined ideas as to how the uniqueness of the one God should be understood. In other words, they drew the line of distinction between the one God and all other reality very clearly, and were in the habit of distinguishing God from all other reality by means of clearly articulated criteria."[10]

And what *are* these criteria? Well, for early Jewish monotheism, YHWH alone is the Creator and Ruler of all things. As the sole Creator and sole Ruler, YHWH is utterly unique. Bauckham notes that this theme, which is expressed so powerfully in Deutero-Isaiah, resounds throughout the literature of Second Temple Judaism: "the Lord is God, and there is no god besides him."[11] And because YHWH is utterly unique as Creator and Lord, worship is to be devoted exclusively to him. Thus worship is abso-

---

9. James D. G. Dunn, *The Partings of the Ways between Christianity and Judaism and Their Significance for the Character of Christianity* (Philadelphia: Trinity, 1991), p. 19. See also E. P. Sanders, *Judaism: Belief and Practice, 63 BCE–66 CE* (Philadelphia: Trinity, 1992), p. 242. Nancy Calvert-Koyzis argues that the importance of monotheism for Second Temple Judaism can be seen in the ways that Philo and Josephus (as well as others) portray Abraham as a monotheist. *Paul, Monotheism, and the People of God: The Significance of Abraham Traditions for Early Judaism and Christianity,* Journal for the Study of the New Testament Supplemental Series (London: T. & T. Clark, 2004).

10. Richard Bauckham, *God Crucified: Monotheism and Christology in the New Testament* (Grand Rapids: Eerdmans, 1998), p. 3.

11. Bauckham points out that this monotheistic formula appears frequently in this literature: e.g., Deut. 4:35, 39; 32:39; 1 Sam. 2:2; 2 Sam. 7:22; Isa. 43:11; 44:6; 45:5, 6, 14, 18, 21, 22; 46:9; Hos. 13:4; Joel 2:27; Wis. 13:3; Jth. 8:20; 9:14; Bel and Dragon 41; Sir. 24:24; 36:5; 4Q504 5:9; 1Q35 1:6; Bar. 3:35; *2 En. 33.8; 36.1; 47.3; Sib. Or.* 3.629, 760; 8.377; *T. Ab.* A8.7; Orphica 16; Philo, *Legum allegoriae* 3.4, 82; Bauckham, *God Crucified,* p. 11.

lutely central to early Jewish monotheism. As Bauckham puts it, "In the exclusive monotheism of the Jewish religious tradition . . . it was worship which was the real test of monotheistic faith in religious practice. . . . God must be worshiped; no creature may be worshiped. For Jewish monotheism, this insistence on the one God's exclusive right to religious worship was far more important than metaphysical notions of the unity of the divine nature."[12]

So worship is central to early Jewish monotheism. Monolatry is entailed by monotheism: "the exclusive worship of the God of Israel is precisely *a recognition of and response to* his unique identity."[13] And this monotheism is captured by the Shema: "Hear, O Israel, the Lord our God, the Lord is One," which — recited twice daily by Jews of the era and commonly echoed in the literature — is "central to the Jewish faith of the period."[14]

In summary, we can see that the religious faith of Second Temple Judaism indeed *was* reliably monotheistic, and that this monotheism is evidenced in their insistence on monolatry and articulated forcefully in the Shema. While we may not have a definition as tight as we might hope for, we should be in a position to see the central point: there is only one God, and this God is *the* Creator and Ruler. But it is important to see that this account of monotheism is not centered on numerical oneness, nor does it obviously dictate that there is at most one divine person. At least one prominent modern Jewish theologian agrees. As the contemporary Jewish theologian Pinchas Lapide notes, this account of monotheism is not primarily concerned with integers or with questions of how many tropes of divinity there are; it *is* centered on exclusive allegiance to the only Creator and Ruler. "The Oneness of God, which could be called Israel's only 'dogma,' is neither a mathematical nor a quantitative oneness . . . the difference between gods and the One God is indeed not some kind of differ-

---

12. Richard Bauckham, *The Climax of Prophecy: Studies on the Book of Revelation* (Edinburgh: T. & T. Clark, 1993) p. 118; see also Bauckham, *The Theology of the Book of Revelation* (Cambridge: Cambridge University Press, 1993), pp. 58-59; Dunn, *Partings of the Ways*, pp. 19-21; Paul Rainbow, "Jewish Monotheism as the Matrix for New Testament Christology: A Review Article," *Novum Testamentum* 33 (1991): 78-91.

13. Bauckham, *God Crucified*, p. 14, emphasis in original.

14. Richard Bauckham, "Biblical Theology and the Problems of Monotheism," in *Out of Egypt: Biblical Theology and Biblical Interpretation,* ed. Craig Bartholomew et al. (Grand Rapids: Zondervan, 2004), p. 218; see also N. T. Wright, *The Climax of the Covenant: Christ and the Law in Pauline Theology* (Minneapolis: Fortress, 1991), p. 129.

ence in number — a more miserable understanding there could hardly be — but rather a difference in essence. It concerns a definition not of reckoning but of inner content; we are concerned not with arithmetic but rather with the heart of religion, for 'one' is not so much a quantitative concept as a qualitative one."[15]

So while there is no precedent in Second Temple monotheism for the inclusion of more than one "personal" agent in the worship that rightly belongs only to YHWH, neither is there anything that prohibits it.[16] As Bauckham puts it, "Jewish monotheism clearly distinguished the one God and all other reality, but the ways in which it distinguished the one God from all else did not prevent the early Christians including Jesus in this unique divine identity. While this was a radically novel development . . . the character of Jewish monotheism was such that this development did not require repudiation of the ways in which Jewish monotheism understood the uniqueness of God."[17]

B. The Inclusion of Jesus in the Worship of YHWH

So worship is central to understanding Second Temple monotheism: YHWH alone is truly God, and therefore YHWH alone is to be worshiped. And Jesus *is* worshiped by the earliest Christians. Although arguments can be made for this in several ways, for our purposes we need look no further than the way the New Testament includes Jesus in the classic statements of monotheism.[18]

The first of these statements can be found in Philippians 2:5-11.[19] Here

15. Lapide then informs us of the central objections to Trinity doctrine: it violates a doctrine of divine simplicity, and it violates the dictum that "two or more cannot be absolute. Two or more also cannot be timeless or eternal. If there are two or more, there can be no concept of omnipotence. Two or more must lead to a division of labor and to conflict." *Jewish Monotheism and Christian Trinitarian Doctrine: A Dialogue by Pinchas Lapide and Jürgen Moltmann* (Philadelphia: Fortress, 1981), pp. 29-31.

16. For discussion of the claims that angels and other intermediary creatures are worshiped, see Loren T. Stuckenbruck, *Angel Veneration and Christology: A Study in Early Judaism and in the Apocalypse of John* (Tübingen: J. C. B. Mohr, 1995).

17. Bauckham, *God Crucified*, p. 4.

18. For a detailed and impressive tour of these arguments, see Larry W. Hurtado, *Lord Jesus Christ: Devotion to Jesus in Earliest Christianity* (Grand Rapids: Eerdmans, 2003).

19. What I say here assumes the majority reading (both traditional and contemporary)

Jesus is included in what C. F. D. Moule refers to as a "great monotheistic passage" of the Old Testament (Isa. 45:23): "that at the name of Jesus every knee should bow, in heaven and on earth and under the earth, and every tongue confess that Jesus Christ is Lord, to the glory of God the Father."[20] Here language reserved strictly for God is used directly of Jesus. But Jesus is nonetheless seen to be distinct from his "Father": while "in very nature God," only the Son "made himself nothing, taking the very nature of a servant . . . humbled himself and became obedient to death — even death on a cross!" (vv. 6-8). In other words, Jesus is included in the identity of YHWH, even though he is still portrayed as someone whose actions are distinct from those of "God the Father." Commenting on this passage, N. T. Wright says that "it should be clear that Paul remained a monotheist, and never sold out this position to any sort of hellenistic ditheism or polytheism. It is also clear from dozens of passages that he regarded Jesus Christ as still Jesus Christ, not simply absorbed into God the Father. . . . But if Jesus is not one-for-one identical with the Father, and if Paul is still a monotheist, then the assertions of 2.9-11 must mean that Jesus — or, more accurately, the one who *became* Jesus — must have been from all eternity 'equal with God' in the sense of being himself fully divine."[21] Paul is convinced that Jesus is fully divine, but he understands him to be distinct from the Father even as preincarnate.

The second of these is the inclusion of Jesus in the Shema in 1 Corinthians 8:1-6.[22] Here Paul reformulates the Shema to explicitly include Jesus within it: "but for us there is one God, the Father, from whom are all things and for whom we live, and there is but one Lord, Jesus Christ, through whom all things came and for whom we live." Bauckham points out that if Paul were adding "one Lord" to the one God of the Shema, then he would

---

that this passage refers to a preexistent Christ. For recent arguments to this conclusion, see L. D. Hurst, "Re-Enter the Pre-existent Christ in Philippians 2:5-11," *New Testament Studies* 32 (1986): 449-57; Ralph P. Martin, *A Hymn of Christ: Philippians 2:5-11 in Recent Interpretation and in the Setting of Early Christian Worship* (Downers Grove, Ill.: InterVarsity, 1997); C. A. Wanamaker, "Philippians 2.6-11: Son of God or Adam Christology," *New Testament Studies* 33 (1987): 179-93; Wright, *Climax of the Covenant*, pp. 56-98.

20. C. F. D. Moule, *The Origin of Christology* (Cambridge: Cambridge University Press, 1977), p. 41.

21. Wright, *Climax of the Covenant*, p. 94.

22. Of course, other examples — such as the Fourth Gospel's portrayal of Jesus as alluding to the Shema with reference to himself (e.g., John 10:1-18; 17:1-23) — could easily be used. For a brief discussion of these see Bauckham, "Biblical Theology," pp. 227-29.

be guilty of contradicting or radically subverting the Shema and thus rejecting Judaism. But he insists that this is *not* what Paul is doing; Paul is including Jesus within the unique identity of the one God: "but this is in any case clear from the fact that the term 'Lord,' applied to Jesus as the 'one Lord,' is taken from the Shema itself. Paul is not adding to the one God of the Shema a 'Lord' the Shema does not mention. He is identifying Jesus as the 'Lord' whom the Shema affirms to be one. In this unprecedented reformulation of the Shema, the unique identity of the one God *consists of* one God, the Father, *and* the one Lord, his Messiah (who is implicitly regarded as the Son of the Father)."[23] N. T. Wright concurs: "there can be no mistake . . . Paul has placed Jesus *within* an explicit statement, drawn from the Old Testament's quarry of monotheistic texts, of the doctrine that Israel's God is the one and only God, the Creator of the world." Thus Paul has redefined the Shema, "producing what we can only call a sort of christological monotheism."[24]

But does this not violate the original meaning of the Shema; does it not radically subvert the original meaning of "Hear, O Israel, the Lord our God, the Lord is one"? Surprisingly, the answer is negative — there is no good reason to think of this as a violation of the Shema. For the original formulation of the Shema (Deut. 6:4) is not about the number of tropes of divinity any more than is Paul's reformulation; its primary purpose is to call the children of the covenant to exclusive devotion to the only God there is. After surveying the textual and interpretive problems associated with this text (as well as canvassing the major exegetical options), Daniel I. Block concludes that what this passage declares is that "Israel's love for Yahweh is to be absolute, total, internal, communal, public, and transmitted from generation to generation."[25] Moreover, the very use of *'echad* for

---

23. Bauckham, "Biblical Theology," p. 224. Bauckham also points out the way that Paul includes Christ in the work of creation in this passage; he states that in Second Temple Judaism there is "no more unequivocal way of including Jesus in the unique divine identity . . . conceivable."

24. Wright, *Climax of the Covenant*, p. 129; see also Donald A. Hagner, "Paul's Christology and Jewish Monotheism," in *Perspectives on Christology: Essays in Honor of Paul K. Jewett*, ed. Marguerite Shuster and Richard Muller (Grand Rapids: Zondervan, 1991), pp. 19-38, and David B. Capes, *Old Testament Yahweh Texts in Paul's Christology* (Tübingen: J. C. B. Mohr, 1992), pp. 181-83.

25. Daniel I. Block, "How Many Is God? An Investigation into the Meaning of Deuteronomy 6:4-5," *Journal of the Evangelical Theological Society* 47 (2004): 212. See also R. W. L.

"one" is suggestive here; the word used here is a word that actually allows for interpersonal relationship — it is the very word used of a man and woman becoming "*one* flesh." The original Shema *is* a statement of monotheism, but it is much more concerned with exclusive devotion than with informing us about the acceptable maximum number of divine tropes.[26]

C. Jesus and His Abba: Distinction and Relationship

With this as background, the New Testament's portrayal of the relation of Jesus to his Father is striking.[27] For the New Testament authors do not hesitate to describe them as distinct in speech and action. Only the Son becomes incarnate, suffers under Pontius Pilate, is crucified, dead, and buried, and raised again on the third day (to use the creedal summary of the New Testament's picture). Only the Son is baptized at the river Jordan, and only the Father says to the Son: "You are my Son, whom I love; with you I am well pleased" (Luke 3:22b). The actions of the (incarnate) Son are distinct from those of the Father,[28] and we see that the Father and Son use first-person and second-person indexicals: "I know you" (John 17:25).

Moberly, "Toward an Interpretation of the Shema," in *Theological Exegesis: Essays in Honor of Brevard A. Childs*, ed. Christopher Seitz and Kathleen Greene-McCreight (Grand Rapids: Eerdmans, 1999), especially pp. 132-41.

26. I don't mean to suggest that concern about the maximum number of divine tropes is illegitimate; I mean only to make clear that it is not the point of the Shema.

27. My purpose here is *not* to offer anything approaching a full statement of a scriptural basis for a doctrine of the Trinity. This has been done often enough in the Christian tradition, and at any rate is beyond the scope of the current project. What I am working for here is much more modest: I only wish to see how it is that Jesus is portrayed as distinct from yet related to his Father. As to the relationship between Scripture and creedal orthodoxy, I am in fundamental agreement with C. Kavin Rowe when he argues that there is an "exegetical necessity" to Trinitarian doctrine. He recognizes that "there is an organic connection between the biblical testimony and the early creeds, and the creeds can function as hermeneutical guides to reading the bible because it is in fact the biblical text itself that necessitated the creedal formulations." "Luke and the Trinity: An Essay in Ecclesial Biblical Theology," *Scottish Journal of Theology* 56 (2003): 4.

28. I think this need not conflict with the traditional Christian affirmation that the *Opera Trinitatis ad extra sunt indivisa*. Although only the Son becomes incarnate, he does so in concert with the will of the Father and in the power of the Spirit; thus the Trinity is operative in the incarnation even though only the Son is born of a virgin, suffers under Pontius Pilate, etc. Richard Swinburne quotes Maximus the Confessor to illustrate this: "the Father

For instance, consider the prayer of Jesus in John 17.[29] It is important to note what is *not* in this passage. Contrary to what is sometimes claimed, the social analogy as it is commonly conceived is not here. There is no hint that the oneness of Father and Son is nothing more than a generic oneness. There is no hint that the disciples are like the Trinity simply by virtue of being human or sharing the kind-essence humanity. As Royce Gordon Gruenler points out, "not all the world belongs to the new society of God but only those who are kept and guarded by the Family of God."[30] In fact, Jesus does not say that the disciples *are* "one" as the Father and Son are one in the loving communion of the Holy Trinity — instead he prays that they "*may* be one" as the Father and Son are one (17:21). He implores his Father to protect the disciples "*so that* they may be one as we are one" (17:11). Leon Morris thinks there is a sense in which the unity or "oneness" referred to here is complete; he interprets the present subjunctive to have the force of a completed reality: "The unity prayed for is a unity already given: Jesus does not pray that they may 'become' one, but that they may 'continually be' one." But Morris also recognizes that the prayer of Jesus in 17:23 petitions the Father for a greater or superior unity: "It looks for the disciples to be 'brought to complete unity.' They already had unity of a sort. But this unity is not regarded as being sufficient. There is to be a closer unity, a 'perfected' unity."[31] Similarly, D. A. Carson holds that "some measure of unity is assumed, but Jesus prays that they may *be brought to complete unity,* sharing richly in both the unity of purpose and the wealth of love that tie the Father and the Son together."[32]

---

and Spirit 'themselves did not become incarnate, but the Father approved and the Spirit co-operated when the Son himself effected his Incarnation.'" *On the Lord's Prayer* (Patrologia Graeca 90:876), Swinburne, *The Christian God* (Oxford: Oxford University Press, 1994), p. 181 n. 7. The *Opera ad intra,* on the other hand, may be entirely the work of one or another of the divine persons, e.g., only the Father generates the Son.

29. D. A. Carson sees "a summary of the entire Fourth Gospel to this point" in this prayer of Jesus. This includes especially the "unity of the disciples modeled on the unity of the Father and the Son." *The Gospel according to John* (Grand Rapids: Eerdmans, 1991), p. 551.

30. Royce Gordon Gruenler, *The Trinity in the Gospel of John: A Thematic Commentary on the Fourth Gospel* (Grand Rapids: Baker, 1986), p. 126.

31. Leon Morris, *The Gospel according to John,* rev. ed. (Grand Rapids: Eerdmans, 1995), pp. 644, 650-51.

32. Carson, *John,* p. 569. See also Barnabas Lindars, *New Century Bible: The Gospel of John* (London: Oliphants, 1972), p. 531; Herman Ridderbos, *The Gospel of John: A Theological Commentary* (Grand Rapids: Eerdmans, 1997), p. 561; and C. K. Barrett, *The Gospel according*

But there is *something* of a social analogy used here, and it is not simply a device used to illustrate the distinctness of the divine persons (while relying upon other analogies to illustrate the unity or oneness). The analogy is not employed here to illustrate how the divine persons are three; instead it is used with reference to divine unity. Pheme Perkins comments, "the unity of the community is founded in and testifies to the truth of this basic Christological insight: Jesus and the Father are one."[33]

The "oneness" of human persons that is shared commonly is *not* the pattern or model for the divine life. The direction is reversed: the unity of the divine persons in the Trinity is the pattern for the "oneness" of those who come to know the triune God and who are sanctified by this relationship. As Gruenler puts it, "The plurality and unity of the persons of the divine Community becomes the pattern for a new community of believers. Jesus prays fervently for the vindication of the social model in the new society, just as it is a reality in the Triune family. The reality of the distinct personalities within essential unity is attested in the formula 'we . . . one,' and is to be replicated in the circle of the redeemed 'they . . . one.'"[34]

Jesus' prayer is that the disciples *will be* "one" as is the Trinity; he prays that this oneness will become a reality as the disciples experience and come to know the loving relations that the divine persons share among themselves in the loving communion of the triune life. Gruenler comments that "the way of the higher Family is to share what is received, so that there is perfect oneness in love. As (kathos) the persons of the divine family are one, so, Jesus prays, may the believing family become perfectly one."[35] C. K. Barrett states that the unity of the church both "is modeled upon, and springs from, the unity of the Father and the Son."[36] Gruenler con-

---

to John: An Introduction with Commentary and Notes on the Greek Text (Philadelphia: Westminster, 1978), p. 502.

33. Pheme Perkins, *The Gospel according to John: A Theological Commentary* (Chicago: Franciscan Herald Press, 1978), p. 204. This does not mean, of course, that the personal distinctions are ever blurred in this passage; see also T. E. Pollard, *Johannine Christology and the Early Church* (Cambridge: Cambridge University Press, 1970), p. 18, and Mark L. Appold, *The Oneness Motif in the Fourth Gospel* (Tübingen: J. C. B. Mohr, 1976).

34. Gruenler, *The Trinity*, p. 125.

35. Gruenler, *The Trinity*, p. 128. Ridderbos understands *kathos* in a causative sense; see, e.g., *The Gospel of John*, pp. 463, 519, 561-62. Carson takes it as purposive, *John*, p. 554, while Raymond Brown sees it as both "comparative and causative." Brown, *The Gospel according to John*, Anchor Bible 29A (New York: Doubleday, 1970), p. 769.

36. Barrett, *John*, p. 508.

cludes that "Jesus' prayer reveals that the goal of the divine family is to bring the separated and fallen into a redeemed and unified family that reflects the relationship of the divine persons in their ultimate oneness."[37]

Thus it seems as though there is in this prayer at minimum the potential for a social analogy in the human relations of the disciples. As his disciples and future believers are sanctified (17:17-19) and "indwell" the Trinity (17:23), Jesus is convinced that the human persons who come into the communion of the triune God will come to the "complete unity" shared by the divine persons. Raymond Brown concludes that this means that "some type of vital, organic unity seems to be demanded by the relationship of the Father and Son that is held up as the model of unity. The Father-Son relationship involves more than mere moral union; the two are related because the Father gives life to the Son (6:57). Similarly the Christians are one with one another and with the Father and Son because they have received of this life."[38]

So there is *something of* a social analogy here, even though it is not the garden variety version.[39] It is not the unity of three human persons who share a generic essence, nor is it the unity of three human persons who get along well. It is much more than that. Nonetheless, the analogy is here. The Son prays that the human persons who know God will come to be "one" just as the Father and Son are one. As Barrett puts it, the "unity of the church is strictly analogous to the unity of the Father and the Son."[40] There is no sense in which the distinctness of the persons is ever blurred, either between the Father and the Son, between the divine persons and the disciples, or between the disciples themselves. But this distinction in no way compromises the "complete unity" spoken of by the Son. Some sort of social analogy is at work here.

John 17 also presents the divine persons as distinct agents. We can see this both in the distinct actions of the Father that are depicted here and in the distinct actions of the Son. The Father gives authority "over all people" to the Son (17:2). The Father gives those who will be saved to the Son (17:2, 6). The Father gives "work" to the Son (17:4). The Father gives "words" to the Son (17:8); the Father is also said to give his "name" (17:11). The Father

---

37. Gruenler, *The Trinity*, p. 129.

38. Raymond Brown, *John*, p. 776.

39. Whether or not this gets us all the way to "Social Trinitarianism" is an issue to be explored in subsequent chapters.

40. Barrett, *John*, p. 512. See also Leon Morris, *John*, p. 649.

sends the Son into the world (17:18, 21, 25). The Father gives glory to the Son (17:22), and the Father loves the Son (17:26).

We also see the distinct actions of the Son. Of course, these are closely related to the Father; they are always done in dependence on the Father and in accord with the will of the Father. As Ridderbos points out, "this is the case in the mutuality based upon his unity with the Father: 'all yours are mine.'"[41] But these are ascribed to the Son in distinction from the Father. Here the Son prays *for* his disciples and all future believers; here he prays *to* the Father (17:1). Jesus gives eternal life to those whom the Father has given to him (17:2). He brings glory to the Father (17:4); he does this by completing the work that the Father has sent him to do (17:4). He asks the Father to "glorify me in your presence with the glory I had with you before the world began" (17:5; cf. 1:1). He states that he has revealed the Father "to those whom you gave me out of the world" (17:6). The Son informs the Father that he has given the disciples the "words" (17:8) and the "word" (17:14) that the Father had entrusted to the Son.[42]

Jesus testifies that he has "protected" his disciples; he has "kept them safe" by the "name" that the Father had given to him (17:12). He speaks so that the disciples may have the "full measure" of his joy (17:13). The Son says that "I sanctify myself" so that the disciples may be "truly sanctified" as well (17:19). Carson thinks this speaks of "Jesus' determination to co-operate with the Father's sanctification of him. Jesus is as determined to set himself apart for his Father's exclusive service as the Father is to set him apart."[43] Jesus states that he has given to the disciples the glory that the Father has given to him, and he clearly insists that the purpose of this is that the disciples "may be one as we are one" (17:22).

Here we see that the actions of the Father and Son are distinct; they interact as personal agents. As Leon Morris puts it, the Father and Son are so "closely connected" that "to glorify the Son is to glorify the Father."[44] Yet the distinction is never removed or blurred. As Gruenler summarizes this

41. Ridderbos, *The Gospel of John*, p. 552.

42. According to Carson, "a good case can be made that when in the Fourth Gospel Jesus refers to his *words* (plural) he is talking about the precepts he lays down, almost equivalent to his commands . . . but when he refers to his *word* (singular) he is talking about his message as a whole, almost equivalent to 'gospel.'" Carson, *John*, p. 559. Raymond Brown, on the other hand, thinks that such distinctions are "tenuous." Brown, *John*, p. 743.

43. Carson, *John*, p. 567.

44. Leon Morris, *John*, p. 636.

point, "the Father glorifies the Son and makes himself available to him, the Son glorifies the Father and defers to him."[45] The Father and the Son are united in what they are working to achieve, but they operate in distinct ways to bring their work to fulfillment or completion. Carson's comments on 17:21 capture this well: "The Father is actually in the Son, so much so that we can be told that it is the Father who is performing the Son's works (14:10); yet the Son is in the Father. . . . The Father and Son are distinguishable (the pre-incarnate Word is 'with' God, 1:1, the Son prays to his Father; the Father commissions and sends, while the Son obeys), yet they are one. Similarly, the believers, while distinct, are still to be one in purpose, in love, in action undertaken with and for one another, in joint submission."[46]

The mutual love of the Father for the Son and the Son for the Father is evident in John 17 as well. In fact, it is almost taken for granted here — the point of the requests of Jesus is for the disciples and future believers (and indeed the world) to see, experience, "know," and share that love! Gruenler points out that the "Father and Son are utterly at the disposal of one another in selfless and dynamic love, and manifest this generosity to the new society, which in turn is empowered to pass it on to others."[47] F. F. Bruce comments that "the Father and Son know each other in a mutuality of love, and by the knowledge of God men and women are admitted to the mystery of this divine love, being loved by God and loving him — and one another — in return."[48] Jesus thus prays that the disciples and believers will be brought to "complete unity" in order "to let the world know" that the Father sent Jesus and has "loved them even as you have loved me." Again, Jesus prays, "Father, I want those you have given me to be with me where I am, and to see my glory" (17:24). This glory is the glory that the Father gave to the Son (17:24). Barrett thinks this glory "is the essential inward love of the Godhead, the love with which the Father eternally loves the Son (the love which God *is,* 1 John 4:8, 16)."[49] And the reason for this gift of glory is clear: it is "because you loved me before the creation of the world" (17:24). Thus Jesus concludes his "high priestly prayer" with these words: "I have made you known to them, and will continue to make you

45. Gruenler, *The Trinity,* p. 122.

46. Carson, *John,* p. 568.

47. Gruenler, *The Trinity,* p. 127.

48. F. F. Bruce, *The Gospel of John: Introduction, Exposition, and Notes* (Grand Rapids: Eerdmans, 1983), p. 329.

49. Barrett, *John,* p. 515.

known in order that the love you have for me may be in them and that I myself may be in them" (17:26).

The reason for the revealing work of the Son is obvious enough. The Son reveals the Father (and the Father-Son relationship) "in order that" *(hina)* the mutual love of the Father and the Son may be shared with the disciples and the world. As Beasley-Murray summarizes it, "the statement of this goal has a variety of significations: (i) it implies an ever increasing understanding of the love of the Father for the Son; (ii) an ever fuller grasp of the wonder that that love is extended to believers also; and (iii) an ever more responsive love on their part toward the Father."[50] Gruenler's conclusion makes clear the love of the Father for the Son and the Son for the Father in this passage: "In the final refrain of his prayer Jesus acclaims once more the likeness of the Father's love for believers and his love for the Son, the equality of Father and Son, and the inexhaustible and dynamic love of the divine Community for the redeemed community as divine knowledge and love are to be poured out in mutual indwelling and interpersonal communion."[51]

That the Father and Son are (or have) distinct centers of consciousness and will is also clear from this passage. First, there is here — as elsewhere — the explicit statement of Jesus Christ to the Father that makes use of first-person and second-person indexicals: "I know you" (17:25). O'Day notes that this passage reveals the intimacy of Jesus' relationship with the Father; there is a "tone of intimacy, for the whole prayer is built around an I/you axis of communication."[52] Much more pervasive, however (and likely much more important), are the implications drawn from the other explicit statements in this prayer. Gruenler states that "Jesus can think of himself in personal terms because he consciously and voluntarily merges his will with the Father's and because he chooses to be at the disposal of the faithful."[53] In 17:1-2 Jesus shows awareness of sharing in the glory of the Father in a preincarnate state, and in 17:4 he testifies that he "has glorified you on earth, having accomplished the work" the Father had given him to do. In 17:5 Jesus

---

50. G. R. Beasley-Murray, *John*, Word Biblical Commentary 36 (Waco: Word, 1987), p. 305.

51. Gruenler, *The Trinity*, p. 130.

52. Gail R. O'Day, "The Gospel of John," in *The New Interpreters Bible: General Articles and Introduction, Commentary and Reflections for Each Book of the Bible Including the Apocryphal/Deuterocanonical Books in Twelve Volumes*, vol. 9 (Nashville: Abingdon, 1995), p. 798.

53. Gruenler, *The Trinity*, pp. 122-33.

prays that the Father will again glorify him with the glory they shared prior to creation. Gruenler comments that "Jesus displays again his consciousness of preexistence and correlativity with the Father (cf. 8:58) and prays for the restoration of his glorious status in the divine ascent that follows the divine descent and shapes the U of divine disposability (cf. Phil. 2:5-11)."[54] Or as Carson puts it, "the petition asks the Father to reverse the self-emptying entailed in his incarnation and to restore him to the splendour that he shared with the Father before the world began."[55]

The allusion to Philippians 2 is instructive here. For there, as here in John 17, the decision made by the person of the Son is made *prior to* his incarnation. It will not do, then, simply to attribute the distinctness of the Son's will and consciousness to his *humanity*. It is the preincarnate Son who willingly humbles himself and empties himself. It is not the case that the Son is distinct with respect to consciousness and will *because* he is incarnate; rather he is incarnate because he is a distinct person prior to his incarnation.

To summarize, in John 17 we find that the Father gives authority (17:2), work (17:4), words (17:8), his name (17:11), and glory to the Son (17:22), and that the Father loves the Son (17:23, 24, 26). The Son prays *to* the Father (17:1), gives eternal life to those whom the Father has given to him (17:2), and brings glory to the Father (17:4). It seems reasonable, then, to conclude that in John 17 there is some sort of "social analogy" being employed, that we see the Father and Son portrayed as distinct agents, that we see their love for one another, and that indeed they are presented as distinct centers of will and consciousness. James D. G. Dunn is convinced that modern notions of personhood should not be read into the early church, but he nonetheless admits that John's Gospel "does seem to present Jesus as a 'being self-consciously distinct' from his Father."[56] Gruenler's summary of the depiction of the Trinity in John 17 is helpful:

> Jesus' high-priestly prayer to the Father discloses the social nature of the divine Family. It underscores Jesus' teaching throughout his ministry that God is social and that creation, insofar as it images God, is also social in nature. Individuality is real, as are Father, Son, and Holy Spirit; however, true individuality is not separateness or egocentricity but faithful interrelatedness in oneness. As with believers in the new community, so

---

54. Gruenler, *The Trinity,* p. 124.
55. Carson, *John,* p. 554.
56. James G. D. Dunn, *Christology in the Making* (London: SCM, 1980), p. 264.

with the divine Community in the highest and most original sense: reality lies in generous love and being at one another's disposal. As he faces his final act of disposability, Jesus proclaims in intercessory prayer that this is the highest and final glory for God as well as believers.[57]

It is worth pointing out that even the strongest statements of unity or oneness made by the Johannine Jesus use the language of personal indexicals in this way. Consider such statements as "I and the Father are one" (10:30) and "I am in the Father and the Father is in me" (10:38). Both were considered blasphemous, but the charges of blasphemy seem to arise because a *human* makes such claims; these charges do not come from the threat of there being some interpersonal relationship within the divine identity. Bauckham notes that saying that "Jesus and the Father are one is [saying] that the unique divine identity comprises the relationship in which the Father is who he is only in relation to the Son, and vice versa. It is in the portrayal of this intra-divine relationship that John's Christology steps outside the categories of Jewish monotheistic definition of the unique identity of the one God."[58] But, as Bauckham goes on to point out, since the Shema "asserts the uniqueness of God, not his lack of internal self-differentiation," the result is that "this does not at all deny or contradict any of these [categories], but from Jesus' relationship of sonship to God it redefines the divine identity as one in which the Father and Son are inseparably united in differentiation from each other."[59]

Even from this brief summary, we should be in a position to see several things with clarity. First, while there is no precedent for such an understanding of multiple divine speech-agents in the monotheism of Second Temple Judaism, neither, on the other hand, does Second Temple monotheism rule it out. As Bauckham puts it, "nothing in the Second Temple Jewish understanding of divine identity contradicts the possibility of interpersonal relationship within the divine identity."[60] Second, Jesus Christ clearly *is* worshiped as divine — Paul, John, and the other authors of the New Testament are convinced that Jesus belongs on the divine side of the hard line that separates the one God from all else that exists, and that he deserves the worship appropriate to that position. And third, the

---

57. Gruenler, *The Trinity*, p. 131.
58. Bauckham, "Biblical Theology," p. 228.
59. Bauckham, "Biblical Theology," p. 228.
60. Bauckham, *God Crucified*, p. 75.

Jesus who is worshiped is portrayed in the New Testament as someone who is distinct from his Father — distinct in speech and act.

II. Polytheism and Modalism in the Christian Tradition

We may also benefit from seeing how polytheism and modalism have been defined in the Christian tradition. Although this brief survey is far from comprehensive or exhaustive, in what follows I shall highlight some important points drawn from several important controversies and key conciliar statements.

A. Arianism: Archetypal Polytheism

As we have seen, Brian Leftow charges Social Trinitarianism with "Plantinga's sort of Arianism."[61] But what does that mean? And is Leftow right? It is undeniable that Arianism is the archetypal Christian version of polytheism. But just what is it? In this section I draw upon some relevant historical scholarship on the Arian controversies of the fourth century. Focusing on early Arianism (the Arianism associated with Arius himself rather than "Homoian Arianism" or "neo-Arianism"), I shall summarize its major characteristics. My goal here is simply to summarize the main tenets of Arianism. I am not trying to add anything to what Christopher Haas has called "the stream of scholarly studies on the Arian controversy [that] has risen to a veritable floodtide."[62] I am not, for instance, attempting to break new ground in the discovery of the antecedents of Arius. My goal is not to write nor even to sketch a history of the events and developments of the fourth-century theological scene. For instance, I am not arguing nor even conjecturing about the possible influence of Athenagoras, Clement, Origen, Dionysius, Lucian, or others on Arius,[63] nor am I taking sides in the discussions of possible Platonic, Plotinian, or Aristotelian in-

---

61. Leftow, "Anti Social Trinitarianism," p. 208.

62. Christopher Haas, "The Arians of Alexandria," *Vigiliae Christianae* 47 (1993): 234.

63. E.g., L. W. Barnard, "The Antecedents of Arius," *Vigiliae Christianae* 24 (1970): 172-88; Christopher Stead, "Arius in Modern Research," *Journal of Theological Studies* 45 (1994): 30-36; R. P. C. Hanson, *The Search for the Christian Doctrine of God: The Arian Controversy, 318-381* (Edinburgh: T. & T. Clark, 1988), pp. 60-84.

fluences on Arius.[64] I am not trying to ascertain "Alexandrian" or "Antiochene" provenance of Arian thought.[65] Nor am I worrying about such issues as the role of the West at Nicea,[66] the disputed authorship of various works,[67] the sociopolitical aspects of these controversies,[68] the relations of the "Arians" and various sympathizers to Arius,[69] or the role and behavior of Athanasius.[70] Further, I am not trying to sort out the various debates on whether Arianism was primarily a cosmological scheme or a soteriological system,[71] or whether Arius and the early Arians were pri-

---

64. E.g., T. E. Pollard, "The Origins of Arianism," *Journal of Theological Studies* 9 (1958): 104-5; Christopher Stead, "The Concept of Divine Substance," *Vigiliae Christianae* 29 (1975): 1-14; Hanson, *Christian Doctrine of God*, pp. 84-94.

65. E.g., Rebecca Lyman, "Arians and Manichees on Christ," *Journal of Theological Studies* 40 (1989): 495-98. Rowan Williams concludes that it is "perfectly valid" to locate Arianism "well within the Origenian mainstream of Alexandrian exegesis." *Arius: Heresy and Tradition* (London: Darton, Longman, and Todd, 1987), p. 17.

66. Jorg Ulrich, "Nicea and the West," *Vigiliae Christianae* 51 (1997): 10-24; Daniel H. Williams, "Another Exception to Later Fourth-Century 'Arian' Typologies: The Case of Germinius of Sirmium," *Journal of Early Christian Studies* 4 (1996): 335-57.

67. E.g., R. P. C. Hanson, "The Source and Significance of the Fourth *Oratio Contra Arianos* Attributed to Athanasius," *Vigiliae Christianae* 42 (1988): 257-66; Charles Kannengiesser, *Holy Scripture and Hellenistic Hermeneutics in Alexandrian Christology: The Arian Crisis* (Berkeley: Center for Hermeneutical Studies, 1982), pp. 54-57.

68. E.g., Haas, "The Arians of Alexandria," pp. 234-45; Charles Kannengiesser, *Arius and Athanasius: Two Alexandrian Theologians* (Brookfield, Vt.: Variorum, 1991), pp. 460-65.

69. E.g., Christopher Stead, "Eusebius and the Council of Nicaea," *Journal of Theological Studies* 24 (1973): 85-100; R. D. Williams, "Arius and the Meletian Schism," *Journal of Theological Studies* 37 (1986): 35-52; Maurice Wiles, "Attitudes to Arius in the Arian Controversy," in *Arianism after Arius: Essays on the Development of the Fourth Century Trinitarian Conflicts*, ed. Michel R. Barnes and Daniel H. Williams (Edinburgh: T. & T. Clark, 1993), pp. 31-44; Dennis E. Groh, "New Directions in Arian Research," *Anglican Theological Review* 68 (1986): 350-51. Hanson lists Eusebius of Nicomedia (whom Arius had called a "co-Lucianist"), Asterius, Athanasius of Anarzarbas, Theognis, George of Laodicea, and Eusebius of Caesarea as prominent contemporary supporters of Arius. *Christian Doctrine of God*, pp. 19-59.

70. E.g., Hanson, *Christian Doctrine of God*, pp. 239-73; Timothy D. Barnes, *Athanasius and Constantius: Theology and Politics in the Constantinian Empire* (Cambridge: Harvard University Press, 1993).

71. Robert C. Gregg and Dennis E. Groh argue that Arianism (at least in its early versions) was primarily a view of salvation, albeit one that entailed some broader theological and cosmological ramifications that were not lost on the Arians themselves. *Early Arianism: A View of Salvation* (Philadelphia: Fortress, 1981). Much of the older scholarship either argued for or simply assumed the view that Arianism was at base a cosmological system, e.g.,

marily philosophical or biblical theologians.[72] I do not mean to deny the importance of such studies, but I see them as peripheral to the goal before us. So I shall happily leave such interesting issues, and the questions and debates spawned by them, to the historical theologians who explore them. Instead I shall outline some important identifying characteristics of Arianism.

R. P. C. Hanson offers a convenient summary of the core tenets of Arianism.[73] He highlights the following points:

(A1) God was not always Father; he was once in a situation where he was simply God and not Father.

Arianism places stress on the incomparability and solitude of God. Kelly insists that the "fundamental premise" of Arius's system "is the affirmation of the absolute uniqueness and transcendence of God, the unoriginate source *(agennetos arche)* of all reality."[74] Grillmeier maintains that the Arians hold that "only the first hypostasis, the Monad, is God in the real and unqualified sense . . . the Son does not arise from eternity *in* God, as Origen and Gregory Thaumaturgus have it, but *outside*."[75] As Hanson puts

---

H. M. Gwatkin, *The Arian Controversy* (London: Longmans, Green, and Co., 1903); G. L. Prestige, *God in Patristic Thought* (London: SPCK, 1952), pp. 155-56; J. N. D. Kelly, *Early Christian Doctrines* (New York: Harper and Row, 1960), p. 225. The thesis of Gregg and Groh has not gone unchallenged; see, e.g., Rowan D. Williams, "The Logic of Arianism," *Journal of Theological Studies* 34 (1983): 57, 80; Kannengiesser, *Arius and Athanasius*, pp. 471-73; Aloys Grillmeier, *Christ in Christian Tradition*, vol. 1 (Philadelphia: John Knox, 1975), p. 231. Hanson argues that Gregg and Groh were (a) right to bring soteriology into the discussion, for it indeed is an essential element of the theory; (b) wrong to conjecture (at least with such confidence) the influence of Stoicism; (c) perhaps wrong about "moral progress" and the perfection of Christ in Arius's thought; and (d) wrong to insist that the Son is, for Arius, an example of human achievement. *Christian Doctrine of God*, pp. 96-98.

72. Here I am inclined to accept the verdict of Rowan D. Williams that "Arius' aim was to develop a biblically-based and rationally consistent" position. *Arius,* p. 111. See also Rowan Williams, "The Logic of Arianism," p. 56; Colin E. Gunton, "And in One Lord Jesus Christ . . . Begotten Not Made," *Pro Ecclesia* 10 (2001): 261; Christopher Stead, "The *Thalia* of Arius and the Testimony of Athanasius," *Journal of Theological Studies* 29 (1978): 38; R. P. C. Hanson, "The Doctrine of the Trinity Achieved in 381," *Scottish Journal of Theology* 36 (1983): 53.

73. For the sake of brevity I here summarize it a bit further.

74. Kelly, *Early Christian Doctrines*, p. 227.

75. Grillmeier, *Christ in Christian Tradition*, p. 227.

it, God "was once in a situation where he was simply God and not Father . . . the majestic solitariness of God was a central point of this theology." Gregg and Groh show that "in Arian usage, the term 'Father' signifies a relationship which God has to the Son, not an attribute which he has in himself. This is attested to in the care with which Arius distinguishes between God and Father. God only receives the name Father, he argues, upon the creation of the Son."[76] Therefore "Fatherhood and Sonship are neither absolute nor essentialist words in Arian vocabulary."[77] The Father-Son relationship is relational *rather than* ontological, and it is characterized by dependence and subordination rather than equality. As Williams puts it, "to be Father is, *as it happens,* an identifying and thus inalienable characteristic of God, but it is not part of the 'essential' definition of God, since God as such, being self-subsistent, cannot be defined as to *what* he is by reference to anything else. So 'Father' and 'Son' are not, *in divinis,* mutually definitory."[78]

(A2) The Logos/Son is a creature. God made him out of nothing.[79]

Kelly explains that because "begat" and "create" were synonymous for the Arians, "the Word must be a creature, *(ktisma* or *poiema),* Whom the Father has formed out of nothing by mere fiat."[80] As a creature the Word must have a time of beginning; it must be true "that there was when he was not."[81] Hanson states that for the Arians, the Son "cannot be related by nature or substance *(ousia)* to God who is the Unoriginated, the Eternal."[82] Gregg and Groh explain that

> The Jesus of history and the preexistent "Son" for the Arians were not only twin aspects of the same christological reality; they were two harmonious ways to safeguard their cardinal principle — that all creatures, the redeemer notwithstanding, were ultimately and radically dependent on a Creator whose sole method of relating to his creation was by his

---

76. Gregg and Groh, *Early Arianism,* p. 83.
77. Gregg and Groh, *Early Arianism,* p. 84.
78. Rowan Williams, "The Logic of Arianism," p. 61.
79. Hanson, *Christian Doctrine of God,* p. 20.
80. Kelly, *Early Christian Doctrines,* p. 227.
81. Kelly, *Early Christian Doctrines,* p. 228.
82. Hanson, *Christian Doctrine of God,* p. 20.

will and pleasure, there is no better-attested Arian principle. . . . This meant to Arius, as to his cohorts, that the mediator was not an extension of the divine nature but a creation of the divine will.[83]

The Son exists by the creative will of the Father — *not* of his substance. In his discussion of the "rationale of Arianism," Hanson points out that the Logos/Son is thus a reduced deity; the Son is "God" but is not fully God (in the same sense that the Father is God). This entails for the Arians the imperfection and inferiority of the Logos qua Logos; the divine Word (not just the human body or human nature) is imperfect and thus inferior to the high God.[84]

Arius insisted that the Son is not a creature *like one of the (other) creatures.* Williams states that "the Arian Son stands at the absolute summit of creaturehood, and because he praises and worships God as his Father, he shows that what is glorious and honorable in creation has its roots beyond creation."[85] Nonetheless, the Arians still held that the Son was a creature who was created ex nihilo. Thus to call the Son "God" or even "the Son of God" is to bestow what Kelly refers to as "courtesy titles."[86] For, as Arius himself spelled it out, "He is not God truly, but by participation in grace. . . . He too is called God in name only."[87] This brings us to

(A3) The Logos is alien from the divine being; he is not true God because he has come into existence.[88]

Hanson's explanation goes like this:

Arius does not fight shy (as the later Neo-Arians tended to) of speaking of the Father begetting the Son. But for him begetting and creating were identical, and both always meant dependence. His school of thought believed that their opponents taught a physical begetting of the Son, and they insisted on the other side that the Son was given existence from the Father's will. He and his followers insist again and again that the Son

---

83. Gregg and Groh, *Early Arianism,* p. 5.
84. Hanson, *Christian Doctrine of God,* pp. 106-8.
85. Rowan Williams, "The Logic of Arianism," p. 80.
86. Kelly, *Early Christian Doctrines,* p. 229.
87. Quoted in Kelly, *Early Christian Doctrines,* p. 229.
88. Hanson, *Christian Doctrine of God,* p. 21.

was produced before times and ages, yet they hold onto the conviction that there was a time when the Son did not exist, and again there was another time when he was in existence.[89]

Again, there is no common divine nature or substance.[90] Williams is convinced that, for the early Arians, "Father" and "Son" are titles that "name two individuals whose essential properties are different."[91] In the words of Gregg and Groh, the Father and the Son are thus "foreign in essence, related by will."[92]

(A4) A Trinity of dissimilar hypostases exists.[93]

Gregg and Groh are convinced that the "preserved utterances of Arius about the Trinity" illustrate this well: "[T]here is a Triad not in equal glories; their subsistences *(hypostases)* are unmixed with each other, one infinitely more inestimable in glories than the other. The essences *(ousai)* of the Father and the Son and the Holy Spirit are separate in nature *(phusei)*, and are estranged, unconnected, alien, and without participation in each other. . . . They are utterly dissimilar from each other with respect to both essences and glories to infinity."[94]

Hanson's summary is clear indeed: "A Trinity of dissimilar hypostases exists: the three existing realities are unlike in their substances *(ousia)*. The union which makes them a Trinity is a purely moral one, a unity of will and disposition."[95] Gregg and Groh remark that "the Arians appear to have described the unity of the Son with the Father as an agreement with God, an agreement in the sense of harmony rather than identity."[96] Kelly captures well this Arian conclusion: "the Three he envisages are entirely different beings, not sharing in any way in the same nature or essence."[97]

89. Hanson, *Christian Doctrine of God*, p. 22.
90. Hanson, *Christian Doctrine of God*, p. 104.
91. Rowan Williams, "The Logic of Arianism," p. 61.
92. Gregg and Groh, *Early Arianism*, p. 91.
93. Hanson, *Christian Doctrine of God*, p. 23.
94. Gregg and Groh, *Early Arianism*, p. 98.
95. Hanson, *Christian Doctrine of God*, p. 23.
96. Gregg and Groh, *Early Arianism*, p. 26.
97. Kelly, *Early Christian Doctrines*, p. 229.

B. Condemnations of Tritheism

But what about forms of tritheism beyond Arianism? Surely Arianism is not the *only* form or version of polytheism rejected in the Christian tradition. Just what was ruled out when various views were rejected as tritheistic?

The Fourth Lateran Council's rejection of Joachim of Fiore's Trinitarian theology — perhaps the prototypical instance of tritheism rejected in Latin Christianity — is instructive here. Fiona Robb notes that this controversy "has never received the attention from intellectual historians which it deserves."[98] She notes that "the full meaning of Joachim's attack on Peter Lombard has perplexed and eluded scholars."[99] Despite this cautionary note, however, much is reasonably clear about this debate.

Joachim was worried that Lombard's view of the divine essence as a *quaedam summa res* resulted in a Quaternity. As Robb explains it, Joachim "understood the *summa res* as a thing in addition to the three divine Persons and thus accused Lombard of putting forward a doctrine of Quaternity in place of the Trinity."[100] Joachim thinks this is not only the denial of the orthodox faith; it is also madness *(vesania)*.[101] As he sees things, the *quaedam summa res* is another divine object, and cannot be countenanced:

> O how perversely in every way did he correct both these errors, who said that one divine substance is one supreme reality [*quaedam summa res*]

---

98. Fiona Robb, "The Fourth Lateran Council's Definition of Trinitarian Orthodoxy," *Journal of Ecclesiastical History* 48 (1997): 23. For this reason, as well as the fact that "explanations predicated upon purely social and political factors are inadequate," Robb insists that "reconsideration of the decree in meticulous detail is necessary."

99. Robb, "Fourth Lateran Council's Definition," p. 30. Referring to this as "Joachim's attack on Peter Lombard" should not obscure the fact that Joachim was not alone in raising worries about encroaching forms of Sabellianism in the twelfth century. Robb notes several important predecessors who launched similar attacks on "the same trend in twelfth-century thought": Bernard of Clairvaux attacks Gilbert of Poitiers for Quaternism, Walter of St. Victor accuses Peter Lombard of this, and the (unknown) author of the *Liber de vera philosophia* (ca. 1179) raises similar concerns; see pp. 31-34.

100. Robb, "Fourth Lateran Council's Definition," p. 25. She notes that Joachim is the theological conservative at this point; his hostility to Lombard's view "was entirely consistent with his wider methodological objection to the introduction of new concepts and terms with no scriptural or patristic basis."

101. Robb, "Fourth Lateran Council's Definition," p. 26.

common to three Persons, and that each individual person is that same substance. For it is as if for the substance, the number one hundred was substituted, but for the Persons, three tens [*denarii*]. Or, if he did not mean to say that the substance is greater than each of the Persons, it is as if three ten pieces [*tres denarii*] were substituted for the Persons, and a fourth ten piece [*quartus denarius*] for the substance, as though God were not Trinity but Quaternity. Yet they endeavor to conceal this mad doctrine [*vesania*] in this way, and thus they say that each one of the Persons is the substance, as if they had said that three ten pieces [*tres denarii*] are one ten piece [*unus denarius*] is three. But both are bad. For one ten piece [*unus denarius*] pertains to the Father, one to the Son, and one to the Holy Spirit, all three ten pieces [*trice denarius*] together to the Trinity . . . the value of the ten pieces [*denarius*] is meant to designate the perfection of the Person, and not to signify quantity. Similarly, a thirty piece [*ternarius*] is used to designate trinity, not to signify quantity. . . . Therefore, three ten pieces [*tres denarii*] designate the three Persons, of whom each one is perfect God. A thirty piece [*unus tricenarius*], which is the collection of the *denarii*, designates the Trinity of one substance, because perfect God is the Trinity and perfect God is each individual Person.[102]

Joachim's primary concerns seem to be these: first, if the *summa res* really is the supreme reality, then we seem to have a Quaternity rather than a Trinity. We have three personal realities combined with one supreme reality, and what is that if not a Quaternity? Moreover, if this *res* really is *the* supreme reality, then it is greater than the persons. So not only do we have a fourth thing, this fourth thing is superior to the other three, and we end up downgrading the divinity of the persons. Whether taken separately or collectively, the persons are still inferior to the divine essence. Nor is Joachim at all impressed with the claim that the divine persons just *are* the divine essence: attempting to conceal this *vesania* with claims that each of the divine persons *is* the divine substance only brings further incoherence. As Robb puts it, "the number 100 (essence) is not equal to 3 × 10 (Persons), nor does 3 × 10 (Persons) equal 10 (essence)."[103] Joachim is convinced that to call the divine essence a *summa res* is to either make it equal to the per-

102. Quoted in Robb, "Fourth Lateran Council's Definition," p. 27. For the full Latin text, see p. 27 n. 23.
103. Robb, "Fourth Lateran Council's Definition," p. 28.

sons, so that it "becomes a fourth Person," or give it such a status that it "dwarfs the Persons altogether."[104] Neither option is attractive to Joachim.

In its place he offers a different account of divine unity. He proposes what Robb calls a "collective" account of divine unity: "three ten pieces [*tres denarii*] designate the three Persons, of whom each is perfect God. A thirty piece [*unus tricenarius*], which is the collection of denarii, designates the Trinity of one substance, because perfect God is the Trinity and perfect God is each individual Person."[105] As Robb notes, this "passage *could* be interpreted as putting forward a doctrine of unity of collection."[106]

At any rate, this was how the Lateran Council took it. It criticized Joachim for his overreliance on analogy, and it took him to task for the content of his theology as well. With respect to the former, Robb points out that the attitude of the council to Joachim "was as much the result of twelfth-century disquiet about extensive analogies as it was of Joachim's own particular use of them."[107] But with respect to the material content, the council saw Joachim's doctrine resulting in what Robb describes as "the dilution of the type of unity appropriate to the Trinity from a unity of essence to a mere collection, no more binding than the spiritual unity among the faithful as expounded in many passages in the Bible."[108] In response to Joachim's charge of Quaternism, the council mounts its own "counter-charge that Joachim's own doctrine of divine unity was one of collectivity and resemblance, rather than a true and proper unity of essence."[109] The council thus concludes that

> in this way he does not confess a true and proper unity, but one of collectivity and resemblance, in the way that many men are called one people, and many believers one Church, according to: "the multitude of believers had but one heart and one soul" [Acts iv.32], and: "He who is joined to the Lord is one spirit with him" [1 Cor vi.17]; also "He that

104. Robb, "Fourth Lateran Council's Definition," p. 28.

105. Robb, "Fourth Lateran Council's Definition," p. 27.

106. Robb, "Fourth Lateran Council's Definition," p. 28. She notes further that this interpretation would be consistent with Joachim's "predilection for collective analogies found throughout his works."

107. Robb, "Fourth Lateran Council's Definition," p. 34.

108. Robb, "Fourth Lateran Council's Definition," p. 22.

109. Robb, "Fourth Lateran Council's Definition," p. 29.

planteth and he that watereth are one" [1 Cor iii.8], and all of us "are one body in Christ" [Rom xii.5]; again in the Book of Kings: "My people and your people are one" [1 Kings xxii.4]. But above all to prove this opinion, he refers to what Christ says in the Gospel concerning the faithful: I wish, Father, "that they may be one" in us, "as we also are one" [John xvii.22] "that they may be made perfect in one" [John xvii.13]. For, as he says, the Christian faithful are not one, that is a single reality which is common to them all, but they are one in this way, that is one Church on account of the unity of the catholic faith and finally one kingdom on account of the dissoluable union of charity.[110]

Thus Joachim is criticized, and his doctrine of the Trinity decisively rejected, on two fronts: first, his use of analogy is too direct; second, his account of divine unity is insufficient to secure monotheism and avoid tritheism.

C. Condemnations of Modalism

But what about, on the other hand, the condemnations of modalism? Surely the use of the term "mode" itself does not qualify as modalism (at least not a version of modalism deemed heretical), for even the Cappadocians referred to the Father, Son, and Holy Spirit as *tropoi hyparxeos*.[111] Brian Leftow points out that exact definitions of modalism are surprisingly hard to come by.[112] Despite this, however, it is possible to make some progress on understanding it. At the most basic level, it is the denial that there is more than one divine person. As Harold O. J. Brown puts it, "modalism upholds the deity of Christ, but does not see him as a distinct person vis-a-vis the Father. It holds that God reveals himself under different aspects or modes in different ages — as the Father in Creation and in the giving of the Law, as the Son in Jesus Christ, and as the Holy Spirit after Christ's ascension."[113]

Kelly notes that as early as Justin's time "we read of objections to his

---

110. Translation by Robb, "Fourth Lateran Council's Definition," pp. 36-37.

111. See the discussion in Kelly, *Early Christian Doctrines*, p. 266.

112. Brian Leftow, "A Latin Trinity," *Faith and Philosophy* 21 (2004): 326.

113. Harold O. J. Brown, *Heresies: Heresy and Orthodoxy in the History of the Church* (Peabody, Mass.: Hendrickson, 1984), p. 99.

teaching that the Logos was 'something numerically other' than the Father," but he says the first theologian to formally embrace modalism was Noetus of Smyrna.[114] These early modalists denied that the terms "father" and "son" stood for real distinctions; they thought these were "mere names applicable at different times."[115] Similarly, the shadowy Praxeas apparently believed they "were one identical Person *(duos unum volunt esse, ut idem pater et filius habeatur),* having no independent existence."[116]

Central to a proper understanding of what the rejection of modalism amounts to is the rejection of patripassianism. And here we come to the crux of an important argument against modalism. As Brown summarizes it, the problem is this: "when modalism teaches the incarnation of God in Christ, it logically implies patripassianism and even the death of God; if it attempts to say that God did not suffer, and thus to preserve the classical conviction of philosophical theology that God is impassible, then it must make a distinction between God in Christ and the man Jesus and in effect revert to kind of adoptionism."[117]

This is an important point, because it adds something important to our understanding of modalism. Consider two analogies. In the first, Damon is first a cornerback for the Ohio State Buckeyes, then a safety for the Philadelphia Eagles, then finally a kickoff specialist for the Chicago Bears. In the second, Damon is a football player, a husband, and a Sunday school teacher. The first scenario illustrates the type of modalism that incorporates sequence: Damon first plays for the Buckeyes, then for the Eagles, and finally for the Bears. He plays only one position at a time, and he plays for only one team at a time. He is one person who can be identified by the various "modes" (or indeed uniforms) that proceed sequentially. But the second analogy shows us that sequence is not a necessary condition for modalism. Damon is (or at least can be) *simultaneously* a football player, a husband, and a Bible study leader. But this is modalism nonetheless; if Damon the football player is injured, then Damon the husband and Damon the Bible study leader suffer too. In fact, the "too" is redundant, and quite obviously so. Likewise with modalism; to hold that there is only one divine person appearing in three modes is to hold as well that if that

---

114. Kelly, *Early Christian Doctrines,* pp. 119-20.
115. Kelly, *Early Christian Doctrines,* p. 120.
116. Kelly, *Early Christian Doctrines,* p. 121.
117. Brown, *Heresies,* p. 101.

one divine person suffers in any of its modes, then it is the one divine *person* who suffers. So if Jesus Christ just is the one divine person incarnate, and if Jesus Christ suffers and dies on the cross, then it simply is true that the divine person suffered and died on the cross.

III. Summary

However brief, this survey of some important theological controversies and issues puts us in a position to better evaluate the various options in contemporary philosophical theology. From our overview of monotheism and Christology in the New Testament, we can see that commitment to monotheism is simply not negotiable for orthodox Trinitarianism. The exact process (and the exact time) by which the Hebrew people came to embrace monotheism may not be as clear as we would hope, but what is clear enough is this: by the Second Temple era and the writing of the documents that came to be known as the "New Testament" there is an unwavering commitment to monotheism. We can also see that worship is vitally important. Because there is only one God, only he is to be worshiped.

Interestingly, however, this commitment to monolatry and monotheism did not rule out the possibility that a second divine agent could be understood to be included in the "identity" of God. As Bauckham puts it, "Jewish monotheism clearly distinguished the one God and all other reality, but the ways in which it distinguished the one God from all else did not prevent the early Christians including Jesus in this unique divine identity. While this was a radically novel development . . . the character of Jewish monotheism was such that this development did not require repudiation of the ways in which Jewish monotheism understood the uniqueness of God."[118]

We also see that Jesus indeed *is* worshiped as divine by the earliest Christians. Such passages as Philippians 2:5-11 and 1 Corinthians 8:6 clearly include Jesus in quotations of the highest statements of monotheism drawn from the Old Testament. This leads N. T. Wright to conclude that "there can be no mistake . . . Paul has placed Jesus *within* an explicit statement, drawn from the Old Testament's quarry of monotheistic texts, of the doctrine that Israel's God is the one and only God, the Creator of the

---

118. Bauckham, *God Crucified*, p. 4.

world." Thus Paul has redefined the Shema, "producing what we can only call a sort of christological monotheism."[119]

Furthermore, we see that the Jesus who is worshiped as divine is portrayed throughout the New Testament as being distinct from his Abba (and from their Spirit as well). He is distinct enough to love the Father and be loved by his Father. He is a distinct agent; only the Son becomes incarnate, suffers under Pontius Pilate, is crucified, dead, and buried, and only the Son is raised again on the third day. Given this, and considering the ways that the Son submits to the will of the Father, it is reasonable to conclude that the Father and Son are (or have) distinct centers of will and consciousness. Indeed, even the strongest statements of oneness in the Fourth Gospel employ personal indexicals in a manner consistent with this conclusion.

Similarly, from our overview of Arianism we see that any model of the Trinity that entails ontological subordination of the Son to the Father is to be rejected out of hand. Any view that maintains that God was not always Father and Son, or that the Father-Son relation is somehow accidental to God, cannot be acceptable. Any model that posits that the Son is a creature is heterodox. And any theory of the Trinity according to which the Son is less than fully divine — according to which he belongs to a lower kind of deity — is beyond the pale of orthodoxy. As Kelly summarizes it, the central conviction of Arianism that "the Three are entirely different beings, not sharing in any way in the same nature or essence," will be unacceptable to anyone committed to an orthodox doctrine of the Trinity.[120]

Moreover, models of the Trinity should work hard to keep a safe distance from other forms of polytheism as well. If commitment to the Latin tradition is deemed important, then such models will try to come into line with what is arguably the "high-water mark" of the Latin tradition and avoid posting any concepts of divine oneness that amount to no more than generic, perichoretic, or collective accounts while showing proper caution regarding the use of analogies.

In addition, an acceptable doctrine of the Trinity will avoid any view that embraces or entails modalism. It will not embrace any model that makes the divine persons to be sequentially related, nor will it lose the distinct and real personal relationships between the Father, the Son, and the Holy Spirit.

119. Wright, *Climax of the Covenant*, p. 129.
120. Kelly, *Early Christian Doctrines*, p. 229.

This brings us to the following theological desiderata. First, any acceptable doctrine of the Trinity must be a version of monotheism. Second, it will be wary of claims either that monotheism (or "real" monotheism) excludes real distinctions between the divine persons or that the divine "persons" must not be at all like "persons" in the more normal use of the term. To the contrary, a doctrine of the Trinity that arises from, and is consistent with, the biblical witness will maintain that the divine persons are persons in a robust sense of the term, and the proponents of such a view will insist that this is consistent with the account of monotheism that should matter most to Christians — it is consistent with the (Second Temple) monotheism of Paul, John, and the other authors of the New Testament. Third, such a doctrine will likewise insist that the Father, Son, and Holy Spirit are *homoousios*. Thus it will avoid all views that entail ontological subordination, and it will hold to the full divinity of the Son and Spirit as well as the Father. Finally, it will look for the strongest possible account of divine oneness or unity, and it will understand the "possible" in this instance to be constrained by the foregoing commitments (e.g., to the full divinity and real distinction of the Son and Spirit). And depending upon the degree of commitment to the authority of the Latin tradition (and especially such statements as that of the Fourth Lateran Council), it will be wary of accounts of divine oneness that rely strictly on generic, functional, or collective unity.

CHAPTER THREE

Doctrine and Analysis

S o how are we to evaluate the various proposals with such theological desiderata in mind? In this chapter I shall take a close look at this question, and I point out the strengths and weaknesses of the various proposals vis-à-vis the primary theological concerns.

I. Social Trinitarianism Again

We begin with Social Trinitarianism. After first canvassing its strengths, I seek to evaluate it in light of some of the major criticisms of the model. I then turn to a discussion of some of the remaining questions and potential liabilities.

A. Theological Strengths of Social Trinitarianism

A great strength of ST is its quite obvious fidelity to the way the New Testament depicts the real distinction of the divine persons in their relations. Recall Cornelius Plantinga's initial characterization of ST as any theory of the Trinity that satisfies these conditions: "the theory must have Father, Son, and Spirit as distinct centers of knowledge, will, love, and action . . . as distinct centers of consciousness . . . (and) Father, Son, and Spirit must be tightly enough related to each other so as to render plausible" claims to monotheism.[1]

---

1. Cornelius Plantinga, Jr., "Social Trinity and Tritheism," in *Trinity, Incarnation, and*

ST's position on the distinctness of the divine persons surely seems to be warranted by the witness of the New Testament. Indeed, it seems to be demanded by this witness. After all, it is only the Son who is baptized at the Jordan River, and it is the voice of the Father that is heard in the words "this is my beloved Son, whom I love, and with whom I am well pleased." Only the Spirit descends upon Jesus at his baptism and on the 120 followers who are gathered in the Upper Room as recorded in Acts 2. Only the Father sends, and only the Son descends and humbles himself by taking on the form of a servant. Only the Spirit is said to come as "another Comforter" (John 15:26). To borrow the creedal summary of the New Testament teaching, only the Son is conceived of the Holy Spirit, only the Son is born of the Virgin Mary, only the Son suffers under Pontius Pilate, only the Son is crucified, only the Son is buried, only the Son is raised again on the third day, and only the Son ascends to his Father. Only the Son becomes incarnate and is thus *homoousios* with us while also being *homoousios* with the Father and their Spirit. Similarly with the Holy Spirit. As Plantinga points out, "the Spirit searches, for example, and intercedes. The Spirit apportions gifts and can be grieved. These are personal acts and capacities."[2] The actions of the incarnate Son are distinct from those of the Father, and the Son and the Father freely use personal indexicals: "I know you" (John 17:25).

This is no idle consideration. Consider the statements of such important twentieth-century theologians as Karl Rahner and Karl Barth that resolutely deny that there are three centers of consciousness and will within the triune God. Rahner says there is only one "self-utterance" in God.[3] He denies that the Father and Son love one another, for there is "properly no mutual love between the Father and Son, for this would presuppose two acts."[4] Rather, there is in God "one consciousness that exists in a threefold way."[5] Similarly, and perhaps even more forcefully, Barth exclaims that there is "only one Willer and Doer that the Bible calls God."[6] We are not,

---

Atonement: Philosophical and Theological Essays, ed. Ronald J. Feenstra and Cornelius Plantinga, Jr. (Notre Dame, Ind.: University of Notre Dame Press, 1989), p. 22.

2. Plantinga, "Social Trinity and Tritheism," p. 24.

3. Karl Rahner, *The Trinity,* translated by Joseph Donceel with an introduction, index, and glossary by Catherine Mowry LaCugna (New York: Crossroad, 1997), p. 106.

4. Rahner, *The Trinity,* p. 106.

5. Rahner, *The Trinity,* p. 107.

6. Karl Barth, *Church Dogmatics* I/1 (Edinburgh: T. & T. Clark, 1975), p. 348.

he insists, "speaking of three divine 'I's' but thrice of the one divine 'I.'"[7] What "we call the 'personality' of God," says Barth, "belongs to the one unique divine essence of God."[8] There is only one divine Subject, "one speaking and acting divine Ego"; if there were three of these then "we should obviously have to do with three gods."[9] Three divine speakers and agents would be the "worst and most extreme expression of tritheism," and of course Christian orthodoxy will not allow for that![10]

Despite their stature as important theologians, however, it is hard to see how Rahner and Barth might be right on this point. The Son very clearly is presented in the New Testament as an "I" in relation to another divine "Thou." Only the Father sends, only the Son becomes incarnate, and only the Spirit comes at Pentecost. Only the Son is baptized, only the Father says, "this is my beloved Son," and only the Spirit descends in the form of a dove. Only the Son prays "not my will but yours be done," and he prays it to his Father. For orthodoxy, it is undeniable that "one of the Trinity suffered in the flesh." As the early controversies with modalism made clear, to deny this is to make a charade of the narrative drama of Scripture, and especially of the paschal mystery of Christ and his Abba.

Nor will it do to offer as a rejoinder the observation that these statements come from (or refer to) the *incarnate* Son — in other words, it is the humanity of Jesus that is the referent of the "I" when Jesus refers to himself in relation to a "Thou." This will not do for several reasons: it does not take into account the way the Holy Spirit is portrayed as personally distinct (though obviously not incarnate), and it does not provide us with a satisfactory explanation of the biblical witness that the Son became incarnate *because* he humbled himself and took on human nature (Phil. 2:5-11).

Is this an outright violation of monotheism? Is it really the "worst and most extreme expression of tritheism"? The advocates of ST can readily argue that it is not. They can claim that their view is consistent with the monotheism inherited and adapted by John, Paul, and the other authors of the New Testament. Recall the summary of Richard Bauckham: Second Temple "Jewish monotheism clearly distinguished the one God from all other reality, but the ways in which it distinguished the one God from all else did not

---

7. Barth, *Church Dogmatics* I/1, p. 351.
8. Barth, *Church Dogmatics* I/1, p. 350.
9. Karl Barth, *Church Dogmatics* IV/1 (Edinburgh: T. & T. Clark, 1956), p. 205.
10. Barth, *Church Dogmatics* I/1, p. 351.

prevent the early Christians including Jesus in this unique divine identity. While this [inclusion of Jesus in the worship of the unique divine identity] was a radically new development . . . the character of Jewish monotheism was such that this development did not require any repudiation of the ways in which Jewish monotheism understood the uniqueness of God."[11]

Proponents of ST can make a good case that their view fits well with this understanding of monotheism. They can claim that they are following Paul in promoting what N. T. Wright and Gordon Fee (among others) call "christological monotheism,"[12] and they can say that when combined with the New Testament portrayal of the Holy Spirit, what they hold to is a form of Trinitarian monotheism — it is a form of monotheism consistent with and indeed demanded by the New Testament. It may not be a strict enough form of monotheism to satisfy, say, the theologians of later Judaism.[13] Of course, it will not satisfy Islamic philosophers and theologians, and it might not satisfy the conditions of monotheism laid down by scholars of Egyptian religion.[14] But the advocates of ST can retort that while such accounts of monotheism are surely interesting, they are not the *relevant* or *decisive* accounts of monotheism for Christians. For Christians, ST theorists can say, the relevant account of monotheism is the one to which the authors of the New Testament were committed. And while we might hope

11. Richard Bauckham, *God Crucified: Monotheism and Christology in the New Testament* (Grand Rapids: Eerdmans, 1998), p. 4.

12. E.g., N. T. Wright, *The Climax of the Covenant: Christ and the Law in Pauline Theology* (Minneapolis: Fortress, 1991), p. 129; Gordon D. Fee, *Pauline Christology: An Exegetical-Theological Study* (Peabody, Mass.: Hendrickson, 2007).

13. But recall the observations of the twentieth-century Jewish theologian Pinchas Lapide: "The Oneness of God, which could be called Israel's only 'dogma,' is neither a mathematical nor quantitative oneness . . . the difference between gods and the One God is indeed not some kind of difference in number — a more miserable understanding there could hardly be — but rather a difference in essence. It concerns a definition not of reckoning but of inner content; we are concerned not with arithmetic but rather with the inner heart of religion, for 'one' is not so much a quantitative concept as a qualitative one." *Jewish Monotheism and Christian Trinitarian Doctrine: A Dialogue by Pinchas Lapide and Jürgen Moltmann* (Philadelphia: Fortress, 1981), pp. 29-31.

14. On this see Michael C. Rea, "Polytheism and Christian Belief," *Journal of Theological Studies*, n.s., 87 (2006): 133-48. Rea's conclusion that Egyptian religion is not considered to be a version of monotheism by Egyptologists is not beyond challenge; see, e.g., Alan R. Millard, "Abraham, Akhenaten, Moses and Monotheism," in *He Swore an Oath: Biblical Themes from Genesis 12–50*, ed. R. S. Hess, G. J. Wenham, and P. E. Satterthwaite, 2nd ed. (Grand Rapids: Baker, 1994), pp. 119-29.

for more clarity on the exact particulars of this account, several things seem clear enough: *they* understood it to be real monotheism indeed, they understood it to be consistent with the monotheism they had inherited in the Shema, and they understood it to be monotheism that allowed for the worship of multiple divine agents who share in the divine identity. There is no doubting that this is a "radically novel development."[15] But it is one demanded by the earliest Christian experience of the risen Lord, and it is one that "did not require repudiation of the ways in which Jewish monotheism understood the uniqueness of God."[16]

B. Evaluating the Criticisms

Critics of ST such as Brian Leftow insist that "the Christian version of monotheism should complete, perfect, or fulfill its Jewish version"; he says the Christian version of monotheism "should be a monotheism that a Jew could accept as monotheistic, and a completion of Jewish monotheism." "Failing that," he goes on to say, "it should come as close to this as trinitarian orthodoxy permits."[17] In a similar vein, Daniel Howard-Snyder insists that "there are no monotheists unless traditional Jews are monotheists, and when *they* assert that there exists exactly one God, they affirm that there exists a certain number of Gods and the number is one."[18] He then argues that ST fails to meet the standard of monotheism laid down by Judaism, and he concludes that ST cannot count as a version of monotheism.

To these charges the defender of ST might argue that this is exactly what ST is doing: it is completing, perfecting, or fulfilling its Jewish predecessor and counterpart. It *is* a version of monotheism that a Jew could accept as monotheistic — at least it is if the Jewish monotheism on view is that of Paul and John's Second Temple inheritance. So long as it is the monotheism of John and Paul that is in view, there is no reason to think that ST violates it.

---

15. Bauckham, *God Crucified*, p. 4.

16. Bauckham, *God Crucified*, p. 4.

17. Brian Leftow, "Anti Social Trinitarianism," in *The Trinity: An Interdisciplinary Symposium on the Trinity*, ed. Stephen T. Davis, Daniel Kendall, S.J., and Gerald O'Collins, S.J. (Oxford: Oxford University Press, 1999), pp. 235-36.

18. Daniel Howard-Snyder, "Trinity Monotheism," *Philosophia Christi* 5 (2003): 401-2. Page references to this essay have been placed in the text.

Another major criticism is closely related to the foregoing. Howard-Snyder and Dale Tuggy both object that God is not *a* person in ST. Howard-Snyder points out that on the Moreland-Craig proposal, "the Trinity 'as a whole' is *not* absolutely identical with a particular person . . . in that case, the Trinity 'as a whole' — that is, God, on their view — is not absolutely identical with a particular person. God, that is, is not a person" (p. 399). He points out three deleterious implications of their view. First, he says that because God is not a person, then God did not — and indeed could not — create the heavens and the earth. This means that "the first sentence of the Bible expresses a necessary falsehood. Not a good start!" (p. 399). Secondly, he asserts that Judeo-Christian anthropology "will have to be remade," for if God is not a person then human persons cannot be said to be made in God's image (p. 400). Finally, he charges ST with promoting an "abysmally low" view of the divine nature, because "if God is not a person or agent, then God does not know anything, cannot act, cannot choose, cannot be morally good, [and] cannot be worthy of worship" (p. 401).

Tuggy's charges are similar in that they raise worries about what we are left with if God is not *a* person. In his interaction with Edward Wierenga, he points out an "important ambiguity" in Wierenga's case: "is God just a community or collection of divine individuals . . . or is God a composite individual, an individual thing as much as the divine persons, but composed of them?"[19] If ST takes the first horn of the dilemma, says Tuggy, then we are left with the conclusion that God lacks personal characteristics: "he, or rather, it, will not be conscious." Tuggy sees this as "a devastating problem for this kind of Social Trinitarianism," but not, he says, for any metaphysical reason. Rather, the problem is distinctly theological: it does not fit with Scripture. For "if scriptures tell us anything, they tell us that the God of the Old Testament is a personal being; hence, so is the God of the New Testament."[20] With respect to the second horn, Tuggy asks that "if we want to be theists at all," then "must we not say . . . that God is a divine person?"[21] He says as well that ST cannot believe (at least with any consistency) that God is divine: "whatever is divine in the primary sense, is

19. Dale Tuggy, "Tradition and Believability: Edward Wierenga's Social Trinitarianism," *Philosophia Christi* 5 (2003): 448.

20. Tuggy, "Tradition and Believability," p. 448.

21. Tuggy, "Tradition and Believability," p. 449.

a person, a personal being. But according to ST, God is *not* a person, but only a group of persons. What is not a person is not divine, not a divinity. Thus, God is not divine. Sadly, for all its lovely virtues, this seems to be the death of ST."[22]

Tuggy is convinced that ST's God is not a person. And he thinks that this is "a devastating problem"; it is nothing short of the "death of ST." Howard-Snyder would seem to agree wholeheartedly. But is it? Surely it is worth a closer look. And what a closer look shows is that Tuggy and Howard-Snyder alike move too quickly from the observation that ST's God is not *a* person to the conclusion that ST's God is not *personal*. But in response, ST's defenders could make a case that nowhere in Scripture is God said to be *a* person. Yes, God is depicted throughout the Old and New Testaments as having personal characteristics. But nowhere is it stated that this God is only *one* person, and Tuggy and Howard-Snyder move much too quickly from the (correct) observation that God is personal to the conclusion that God is *a* person. Scripture makes no explicit claim that God is a person, and Tuggy and Howard-Snyder have not yet shown that it is implied. As William Lane Craig points out, Howard-Snyder "cashes out" the observation that God is not a person "tendentiously as God's lacking the cognitive equipment sufficient for being 'a self-reflective agent capable of self-determination.'"[23] Craig complains that this is "very misleading, as though God were not on our view a personal being. But in fact on our view God has the cognitive equipment sufficient for personhood three times over and so is tri-personal."[24]

As Craig says, this is "part and parcel of Trinitarian orthodoxy." And surely he is right: the doctrine of the Trinity (which just *is* the Christian doctrine of God) holds that God is three persons, not one. With respect to Howard-Snyder's implications for ST, Craig responds by calling the objection from creation "fatuous," for "the Old Testament scriptures do not distinguish the persons of the Trinity," and "when they are finally distinguished in the New Testament, we find that God the Father is typically described as Creator, with Christ as his intermediary." As I have noted, here Craig is on solid theological ground. As for Howard-Snyder's objection

22. Dale Tuggy, "The Unfinished Business of Trinitarian Theorizing," *Religious Studies* 39 (2003): 168.

23. William Lane Craig, "Trinity Monotheism Once More: A Response to Daniel Howard-Snyder," *Philosophia Christi* 8 (2006): 104.

24. Craig, "Trinity Monotheism Once More," p. 105.

from theological anthropology, Craig retorts that "we are made in God's image because we are endowed with rational faculties sufficient for personhood even as God is so endowed, the only difference being that whereas we each have one set of faculties, God has three."[25] Again, Craig has sure theological footing here. While his account might usefully be nuanced to include discussion of relational as well as rational faculties, and where his statement that "the only difference" between us and God in this area concerns the number of sets of faculties might also be nuanced, his basic point holds. Unless Howard-Snyder (and Tuggy) can demonstrate that God must be only one person rather than three to be truly personal, these objections hold little water. Again, Howard-Snyder's third objection fails to be decisive. As Craig points out, Howard-Snyder is right that ST has an "abysmally low view of the divine nature" if and only if God cannot have personal properties unless God is *a* person. Once more, this has not been shown to be true, and Christian orthodoxy demands that God is three persons.

It seems that behind these objections is the conviction that to be a divine person just is to be a God. Thus if we have three divine persons, then we quite obviously have three Gods. Tuggy notes that Wierenga denies that whatever is a divine person is a God. He responds to Wierenga with this rhetorical question: "is this not a trivial truth?"[26] He apparently is convinced that if there is more than one divine person, then there is more than one God. Earlier we saw that he thinks that the Old Testament has only one divine person, thus he concludes that Scripture licenses belief in only one person. Now we see that he also thinks that multiple divine persons would be multiple deities. And since Christian orthodoxy is committed to monotheism, he concludes that it is inconsistent with the belief that there are multiple divine persons.

But Tuggy's argument seems theologically naive at both points. Tuggy's desire to connect analytic discussions of the doctrine with the biblical sources of Christian theology is admirable. Unfortunately, however, he seems to think the best way to understand those biblical sources is to interpret them according to what he calls "a principled, minimalist methodology" (he also refers to it as a "radical reformation approach"), which so far as I can see means that we are to interpret Scripture without reference either to the Christian tradition or to contemporary biblical scholar-

25. Craig, "Trinity Monotheism Once More," p. 105.
26. Tuggy, "Tradition and Believability," p. 451.

ship.[27] But to assume that the monotheism of Scripture prescribes belief in only one divine person while proscribing belief in multiple divine persons is painfully naive, and in light of the work of contemporary biblical scholarship such an assumption looks misguided indeed. Similarly, to conclude that the affirmation that there are multiple divine persons is equivalent to the affirmation that there are multiple deities is completely unwarranted in light of traditional Christian orthodoxy, and in doing so Tuggy comes perilously close to begging the question against ST.[28]

One of the most damning charges that Leftow makes against ST is his claim that it results in "Plantingean Arianism." Is Leftow right that the ascription of individual essences to the distinct persons (as in Plantinga's ST) leads straight into Arianism? Exactly what Leftow means by "Plantingean Arianism" is not clear; the closest thing to definition we get is that this "sort of Arianism" is "the positing of more than one way to be divine."[29] So far this is hardly informative or helpful, but I think Leftow's basic concern seems understandable enough. Does the ascription of individual essences to the distinct divine persons (as in Plantinga's ST) not obviously amount to a denial of the *homoousios*? Were the Arians right after all — at least would they have been if only they had our essentialism? Perhaps surprisingly, the answer is no. We can see this by taking a look at the central tenets of Arianism.[30]

Recalling our summary of the core beliefs of Arianism, we see the following points highlighted:[31]

---

27. Tuggy, "Tradition and Believability," p. 453.

28. Craig charges Howard-Snyder with begging the question, and with "evincing a disturbing proclivity toward unitarianism." "Trinity Monotheism Once More," pp. 105, 110.

29. Leftow, "Anti Social Trinitarianism," p. 208.

30. By "Arianism" I refer only to what is sometimes known as "early Arianism" (the Arianism of Arius) rather than "Homoian Arianism" or "neo-Arianism." For helpful accounts of these, see especially Richard Paul Vaggione, O.H.C., *Eunomius of Cyzicus and the Nicene Revolution* (Oxford: Oxford University Press, 2000); Thomas Kopacek, *A History of Neo-Arianism* (Cambridge, Mass.: Philadelphia Patristic Foundation, 1979); Michael E. Butler, "Neo-Arianism: Its Antecedents and Tenets," *St. Vladimir's Theological Quarterly* 36 (1992): 355-71; as well as Daniel H. Williams, "Another Exception to Fourth-Century 'Arian' Typologies: The Case of Germinius of Sirmium," *Journal of Early Christian Studies* 4 (1996): 335-57; and Lewis Ayres, *Nicaea and Its Legacy: An Approach to Fourth-Century Trinitarian Theology* (Oxford: Oxford University Press, 2004).

31. R. P. C. Hanson, *The Search for the Christian Doctrine of God: The Arian Controversy, 318-381* (Edinburgh: T. & T. Clark, 1988), pp. 20-23.

(A1) "God was not always Father; he was once in a situation where he was simply God and not Father."[32]

(A2) The Logos/Son is a creature who is created out of nothing.[33]

(A3) "The Logos is alien from the divine being and distinct; he is not true God because he has come into existence."[34]

(A4) "A Trinity of dissimilar hypostases exists."[35]

With this in view, it should be readily apparent that the mere affirmation that the divine persons have individual essences does not qualify as Arianism. Consider (A1). As Rowan D. Williams puts it, "to be Father is, *as it happens,* an identifying and thus inalienable characteristic of God, but it is not part of the 'essential' definition of God."[36] Or according to the summary of Robert C. Gregg and Dennis E. Groh, "Fatherhood and Sonship are thus neither absolute nor essentialist words in Arian vocabulary."[37] There is no reason to think that ST is Arian in this sense; indeed, on Plantinga's account, while "both kinds of essences unify," it is the "personal essences (that) relate each person to the other two" (and do so necessarily).[38]

Or consider (A2). In Arius's own words, (A2) says that the Son "is not God truly, but by participation in grace . . . he too is called God in name only."[39] Again, I can see no reason why the advocate of ST must be committed to this. For, as Plantinga says, "the generic essence assures that each person is fully and equally divine."[40] The common possession of the ge-

32. Hanson, *Christian Doctrine of God*, pp. 20-21. See also J. N. D. Kelly, *Early Christian Doctrines* (San Francisco: Harper and Row, 1978), p. 227; Aloys Grillmeier, *Christ in Christian Tradition,* vol. 1, *From the Apostolic Age to Chalcedon (451)* (Atlanta: John Knox, 1975), p. 227; Robert C. Gregg and Dennis E. Groh, *Early Arianism: A View of Salvation* (Philadelphia: Fortress, 1981), pp. 83-84; Rowan D. Williams, "The Logic of Arianism," *Journal of Theological Studies* 34 (1983): 61.

33. Hanson, *Christian Doctrine of God*, p. 20; Kelly, *Early Christian Doctrines,* pp. 227-28; Gregg and Groh, *Early Arianism,* p. 5; Rowan Williams, "The Logic of Arianism," p. 80.

34. Hanson, *Christian Doctrine of God*, p. 21; see also Gregg and Groh, *Early Arianism,* p. 91, and Rowan Williams, "The Logic of Arianism," p. 61.

35. Hanson, *Christian Doctrine of God*, p. 23; see also Kelly, *Early Christian Doctrines,* p. 229; Gregg and Groh, *Early Arianism,* p. 26.

36. Rowan Williams, "The Logic of Arianism," p. 61, emphasis in original.

37. Gregg and Groh, *Early Arianism,* p. 84.

38. Plantinga, "Social Trinity and Tritheism," p. 29.

39. Quoted in Kelly, *Early Christian Doctrines,* p. 229.

40. Plantinga, "Social Trinity and Tritheism," p. 29.

neric divine essence might not be enough to avoid tritheism, but it does not entail Arianism. At least not on this point.[41]

But what about (A3)? Williams summarizes the Arian position: "Father" and "Son" are titles that "name two individuals whose essential properties are different."[42] In the words of Gregg and Groh, the Father and Son are thus "foreign in essence, related in will."[43] According to individual-essence Trinitarianism, the divine persons in fact do have different essential properties, so maybe this is where the true allegiance of individual-essence Trinitarianism is revealed. But any similarity between Arianism and individual-essence Trinitarianism is superficial, and it should not be allowed to obscure the central point. For the Arians *denied* that there was a common nature[44] — but this is the very thing that Plantinga *affirms*. The individual-essence Trinitarian can easily deny that the Son has "come into existence"; she can just as easily deny the Arian premise that the Son is "not true God." Again, it should be clear that individual-essence Trinitarianism need not plead guilty.

The situation is similar with respect to (A4). Gregg and Groh are convinced that the "preserved utterances of Arius about the Trinity" illustrate well his main contention: "[T]here is a Triad not in equal glories; their subsistences *(hypostases)* are unmixed with each other, one infinitely more estimable in glories than the other. The essences *(ousai)* . . . are separate in nature, and are estranged, unconnected, alien, and without participation in each other."[45] Kelly's summary is apt: "the Three he [Arius] envisages are entirely different beings, not sharing in any way in the same nature or essence."[46] The central point here is that for the Arians, the Father and Son do not share the same nature or essence *in any way* — whether the divine essence is generic or not is hardly the point, for the Arians won't assent to *homoousios at all.* The Son is *not homoousios* with the Father! Yet the proponent of ST can readily affirm the *homoousios* of the generic divine na-

---

41. Of course, those theologians who agree with the Arians that "begat" is synonymous with "create" might wish to argue that Plantinga's account indeed *does* endorse (A2). But here Plantinga would seem to be no worse off than any other defender of the doctrine of eternal generation.

42. Rowan Williams, "The Logic of Arianism," p. 61.

43. Gregg and Groh, *Early Arianism,* p. 91.

44. See Hanson, *Christian Doctrine of God,* p. 104.

45. Gregg and Groh, *Early Arianism,* p. 98.

46. Kelly, *Early Christian Doctrines,* p. 229.

ture (as indeed does Plantinga), so she should not be deemed Arian on this point.[47] Nor should such versions of ST as that of Moreland and Craig, for they arguably have a much stronger claim to divine oneness than do the versions of ST offered by Plantinga and Swinburne.[48] Without further argument, it would be an unfortunate mistake to conclude that ST must be guilty of Arianism.[49]

C. Remaining Questions and Further Liabilities

ST does, however, still face some interesting and indeed difficult questions. Can it claim to fit within the tradition of Latin or Western Trinitarianism? Should Social Trinitarians rest content with their current accounts of divine oneness? Can they do more to ward off — or even finally put to rest — worries and charges of polytheism? The very fact that many defenders of ST apparently feel the pressure of such charges and the need to bolster their claims to "cling to respectability as monotheists" is intriguing; perhaps that fact alone tells us much about ST's weaknesses.[50]

With respect to the tradition of Latin Trinitarianism,[51] at this point it

47. This is a clear line between orthodox Christian versions of ST and what might be called "Mormon ST." In their discussion of ST, David Paulsen and Brett McDonald deny that there is any "metaphysical necessity" to the unity of the divine persons or that the oneness is "ontological." "Joseph Smith and the Trinity: An Analysis and Defense of the Social Model of the Godhead," *Faith and Philosophy* 25 (2008): 47-74.

48. In addition, Moreland and Craig see as an added benefit this feature of their view: it does not feature the doctrine of eternal generation (which they worry tilts toward subordinationism); see, e.g., *Philosophical Foundations for a Christian Worldview* (Downers Grove, Ill.: InterVarsity, 2003), p. 594.

49. In my "Social Trinitarianism and Tritheism Again: A Response to Brian Leftow," *Philosophia Christi* 5 (2003): 418-27, I respond to Leftow's other major criticisms of ST.

50. See Plantinga, "Social Trinity and Tritheism," p. 31.

51. I focus here on the Latin tradition because (a) its formulations of divine oneness are usually thought to be much more strict than those of the Eastern or Greek tradition, and (b) ST is generally not accused of running afoul of the Greek tradition. I do not mean to pit it *against* the Eastern tradition(s) of Trinitarian theorizing. David Bentley Hart is representative of a growing number of patristic scholars who are convinced that the common notion that "East" is to be pitted against "West" in some kind of Trinitarian theology all-star contest is simply wrong: "The notion that, from the patristic period to the present, the Trinitarian theologies of the Eastern and Western catholic traditions have obeyed contrary logics and have in consequence arrived at conclusions inimical each to the other — a particularly te-

seems safe to say that the jury is far from unanimous. On one hand, as I have pointed out elsewhere, themes that are often associated with (or sometimes taken to be characteristic of) ST may be found throughout the Latin tradition.[52] By way of example, it is not hard to see that Augustine's famous analogy of lover, beloved, and love itself employs something that is at least akin to a social analogy. Whatever lessons one might draw about the distinct personhood of the Holy Spirit from this analogy (who is portrayed as — some would say "reduced to" — the *vinculum caritas* between the Father and the Son), it nonetheless leaves us with at least two divine persons who love one another.[53] And when discussing his famous psychological analogies, Augustine insists that the Father remembers, wills, and loves; the Son remembers, wills, and loves; and the Holy Spirit remembers, wills, and loves.[54] He is prepared to say that Father knows all things "in himself" in one sense while knowing them through the Son in another sense.[55] Moreover, his interpretation of Genesis 18 is striking indeed, for he insists that Abraham's three mysterious visitors just *are* the three divine persons appearing in a theophany — leaving us to conclude that for Augustine, whatever exactly the distinction between the divine persons amounts to, it is a distinction that allows for the divine persons to reveal themselves in the form of three agents who are (apparently) distinct centers of consciousness and will.[56]

To cite another example, Richard of St. Victor is prepared to speak of the will of the Father *(voluntas paterna)* in a way that is distinct from the will of the Son and Spirit (the Father wills the existence of the Son as

---

dious, persistent and pernicious falsehood — will no doubt one day fade away from lack of documentary evidence." "The Mirror of the Infinite: Gregory of Nyssa on the *Vestigia Trinitatis*," *Modern Theology* 18 (2002): 541. Michel R. Barnes posits the genesis of this (mis)reading (or at least of its influence) in the work of Theodore de Régnon; see, e.g., "De Régnon Reconsidered," *Augustinian Studies* 26 (1995): 51-79. In her polemic against an "ST" reading of Gregory of Nyssa, Sarah Coakley notes that "it is ironic to find Lossky at points directly dependent on de Regnon on this issue, and Zizioulas on Prestige! To have the 'West' attacked by the 'East' on a reading of the Cappadocians that was ultimately spawned by a French Jesuit is a strange irony." "Re-Thinking Gregory of Nyssa: Introduction — Gender, Trinitarian Analogies, and the Pedagogy of *The Song*," *Modern Theology* 18 (2002): 434.

52. McCall, "Social Trinitarianism," pp. 407-17.
53. Augustine, *The Trinity* 15.12.
54. Augustine, *The Trinity* 15.28.
55. Augustine, *The Trinity* 15.23.
56. Augustine, *The Trinity* 2.20-21.

dilectus and the Spirit as *condilectus*).[57] This leads Nico den Bok to conclude that "it seems inescapable: Richard's conception of the divine *communion of love*, can only consistently be interpreted if we assume (a) there is *one thing willed* (in this sense: one divine will) and (b) that there are *three things willing* (three subjects of willing)."[58] Again, even Thomas Aquinas says that "it is not true that the Father, Son, and Holy Spirit are one speaker"; rather it is true that "each person understands and is understood."[59] This does not mean that these theologians of the Latin tradition were full-blown "Social Trinitarians," but it is enough to show that certain themes often associated with ST (and sometimes taken to be the antithesis of the Latin tradition) are to be found in the Latin tradition itself.[60] So whether or not there are Social Trinitarians to be found within the Latin tradition, it may be that theological desiderata dear to the hearts of ST's proponents *are* to be found in the Latin tradition. So it seems premature to conclude that all forms of ST are flatly inconsistent with the Latin tradition. It also seems wrongheaded to pit the entire tradition of Latin Trinity doctrine against all forms of ST. I am certainly not alone in making this assessment; Richard Cross, for instance, concludes that "Eastern and Western views of the divine essence are both consistent with social accounts of the Trinity."[61]

57. See the discussion by Nico den Bok, *Communicating the Most High: A Systematic Study of Person and Trinity in the Theology of Richard of St. Victor* (Paris: Brepols, 1996), p. 330.

58. Den Bok, *Communicating the Most High*, pp. 339-40.

59. Thomas Aquinas, *Summa Theologiae*, I, q.34, a.1.

60. The "covenant theology" prominent in seventeenth-century Reformed theology maintains that there is an eternal contract between the Father and the Son, thus seeming to imply at least two centers of volition and consciousness within the Trinity. This has been sharply criticized by Karl Barth, e.g.: "The conception of this inter-trinitarian pact as a contract between the persons of the Father and the Son is also open to criticism. Can we really think of the first and second persons of the triune Godhead as two divine subjects and therefore as two legal subjects who can have dealings with and enter into obligations with one another? This is mythology, for which there is no place in a right understanding of the doctrine of the Trinity as the doctrine of the three modes of the one being of the one God, which is how it was understood and represented in Reformed orthodoxy itself." *Church Dogmatics* IV/1, p. 65. For a markedly different reading of the Reformed orthodox, see Richard A. Muller, *Post-Reformation Reformed Dogmatics: The Rise and Development of Reformed Orthodoxy, ca. 1520 to ca. 1725*, vol. 4, *The Triunity of God* (Grand Rapids: Baker Academic, 2003), pp. 266-67.

61. Richard Cross, "Two Models of the Trinity?" *Heythrop Journal* 43 (2002): 288.

On the other hand, it seems very hard to square ST with some of the creedal and conciliar statements. Jeffrey E. Brower's criticisms of Edward Wierenga's ST regarding interpretation of the Athanasian Creed come to mind here. Brower explains Wierenga's interpretation of the creed: "when the Athanasian Creed states *'Ita deus Pater, deus Filius, deus Spiritus sanctus'* ('The Father is God, the Son is God, and the Holy Spirit is God'), [it] claims that 'the most plausible way to interpret it . . . is to take the first noun, *"deus,"* as expressing a property of the Father, the Son, and the Holy Spirit. That property is most naturally taken to be divinity, the property of being divine.'"[62] In response, Brower says that "even if we grant that the term *'deus'* or 'God' in such contexts expresses a property possessed by each of the Persons of the Trinity, it is extremely implausible to say that the property it expresses is *divinity,* where this is to be understood as a property distinct from *deity*. If there really were a distinction to be drawn between *divinity* and *deity,* and if the Creed writers really intended to be predicating *divinity* rather than *deity* of the Persons, wouldn't we have expected them to use the Latin term *'divinus'* rather than *'deus'?"*[63]

Brower's point is well taken. The most straightforward and plausible reading of the venerable *Quicunque Vult* is to understand *divinus* and *deus* to function similar to the way "human" and "man" function in English. As Brower points out, these terms "differ grammatically, and perhaps also in certain of their connotations; nonetheless, they express the same properties. To be human just is to be a man (in the gender neutral or archaic sense of the term)." And if this is right, says Brower, "then attributing a sharp distinction between *divinity* and *deity* to the individuals responsible for the traditional formulations of the Trinity is no more plausible than attributing a sharp distinction between *being human* and *being a man* to ordinary speakers of English."[64] Moreover, as Brower points out, Wierenga's ST fails to satisfy other aspects of this creedal statement: his version of ST is inconsistent with the claim that there are not three almighties or three eternals but only one almighty and one eternal.[65]

---

62. Jeffrey E. Brower, "The Problem with Social Trinitarianism: A Reply to Wierenga," *Faith and Philosophy* 21 (2004): 297.

63. Brower, "Problem with Social Trinitarianism," p. 297.

64. Brower, "Problem with Social Trinitarianism," p. 298.

65. Brower, "Problem with Social Trinitarianism," p. 298. Although it is Wierenga's version of ST that is in Brower's crosshairs, his criticism also applies to such proponents of ST as Timothy Bartel and Richard Swinburne; see, e.g., Timothy Bartel, "Could There Be More

Or consider the pronouncements of the Fourth Lateran Council. Here it is hard indeed to see how ST might cohere with the views of this council. According to the Fourth Lateran Council, a generic account of divine unity is not sufficient for monotheism. Nor will it suffice to say further that the unity of the Godhead is one of maximal cooperation.[66] Generic, perichoretic, and collective notions of divine oneness are not nearly enough for the theologians of this council, for they regarded this as a "dilution of the type of unity appropriate to the Trinity from a unity of essence to a mere collection, no more binding than the spiritual unity among the faithful as expounded in many passages in the Bible."[67]

Consider further the way the Fourth Lateran Council employs the doctrine of divine simplicity in the formulation of Trinity doctrine: "We . . . believe and confess . . . that there is one highest, incomprehensible and ineffable reality *(res)* which is truly Father, Son and Holy Spirit . . . each of the three Persons is that thing, that is, that divine substance, essence, or nature." As Cornelius Plantinga, Jr., recognizes, ST is simply inconsistent with this pronouncement: "Lateran IV apparently rules out the possibility that each person might be an *instance* of the essence, generically conceived, for then, God would be a quaternity of four things — an essence plus three exemplifications of it."[68] The result, then, is that "on this standard, social trinitarianism of the sort I have been proposing will have to plead guilty" to the charge of tritheism (p. 39). Plantinga rejects this doctrine of divine simplicity, and with it Lateran IV's account of the Trinity. He says that this doctrine of divine simplicity "cannot claim much by way of biblical support," is "clearly much more Western than Eastern," and renders such standards for orthodoxy "of very doubtful coherence" (pp. 39-40). Claiming that "simplicity theories are negotiable in ways that Pauline and Johannine statements are not" (p. 39), Plantinga concludes that "medieval simplicity doctrine is not so very much for the social trinitarian to worry about" (p. 42). Thus any doctrine of the Trinity that is compromised by a strong doctrine of divine simplicity is itself suspect, and at any rate should pose

---

Than One Almighty?" *Religious Studies* 29 (1993): 465-95, and Richard Swinburne, "Could There Be More Than One God?" *Faith and Philosophy* 5 (1988): 225-41.

66. As Plantinga insists, e.g., in "Social Trinity and Tritheism," p. 37.

67. Fiona Robb, "The Fourth Lateran Council's Definition of Trinitarian Orthodoxy," *Journal of Ecclesiastical History* 48 (1997): 22.

68. Plantinga, "Social Trinity and Tritheism," p. 39. Page references to this essay have been placed in the text.

no barrier to the acceptance of a robust ST. "Simplicity theory ends up complicating trinity doctrine quite needlessly. Its lease ought not to be extended" (p. 43).

Whether or not Plantinga should take this route is another issue; my point here is simply that the ST theorist should admit that Plantinga is right to recognize that ST is not consistent with what is said at Lateran IV. Plantinga makes much of the role played by the doctrine of divine simplicity (DDS) here, and surely he is right that ST is incompatible with the strongest versions of DDS. But there is more at stake here. Even if Lateran IV were shorn of its affirmations of DDS, we would still be faced with the stubborn fact that it insists that generic and collective notions of divine unity are not sufficient for monotheism. Versions of ST such as those of Swinburne and Plantinga are clearly inconsistent with such official "high-water mark" pronouncements of Latin Trinitarianism, and other theories such as those of Craig and Yandell likely are as well.

D. Conclusion

We should be in a position to see several things with clarity. First, on straightforward biblical grounds, ST emerges in good shape. It is able to make sense of the New Testament witness to the divinity and equality of the incarnate Son with his Father and their Spirit; it is able to make a strong case that it is consistent with the biblical portrayal of the real distinctness of the divine persons; and it is able to claim that it does so in a way that is consistent — or at least not obviously inconsistent — with the ways that the authors of the New Testament receive and adapt the monotheism of the Old Testament.

ST clearly avoids modalism as well.[69] Nor does it fall prey to the charge that it is a version of the archetypal version of polytheism in the Christian tradition: it is not a variety of Arianism. It does not — at least it need not — hold that the Son came into existence or that the Son is ontologically inferior to his Father. On the other hand, it offers a resounding affirmation that the Son and the Holy Spirit are *homoousios* with the Father. Again, some critics

---

69. E.g., Brower's comment on Wierenga's ST: Wierenga's account "avoids at least one of the standard Trinitarian heresies, namely, modalism." "Problem with Social Trinitarianism," p. 295.

will deny that the sense in which it understands the divine *ousia* is enough to safeguard monotheism. But even these critics should agree that if ST ends up being a kind of polytheism, it is not a polytheism of the *Arian* kind.

With respect to the Latin tradition of Trinitarian theorizing, however, the picture is not quite as rosy. While many themes that resound throughout the work of ST's proponents can also be found in the Latin tradition, and while some scholars of medieval theology say that ST is consistent with Latin views of the divine essence, we are nonetheless left with the conclusion that ST comes into at least apparent conflict with some major creedal statements of the Latin tradition.

The situation here raises a broader and very important methodological issue, one that too often goes unnoticed.[70] To what degree is the contemporary Trinitarian theologian constrained by the Latin tradition? To which creedal statements are analytic theologians accountable? I suspect that no single answer will draw anything close to unanimous approval, but at a bare minimum analytic philosophical theologians should give this matter careful consideration and be forthcoming about their conclusions.

Some of these theologians will doubtlessly feel constrained by the Latin tradition, and will see it as nonnegotiable. For them, any acceptable account of the Trinity will cohere well with the conciliar pronouncements of the Latin tradition (if not also with the formulations of major Latin theologians), any account that raises questions about its acceptability according to these standards will be viewed with suspicion and held at arm's length, and any theory that obviously conflicts with the Latin formulations will be rejected outright. Other theologians, however, make it clear that they view these Latin formulations with puzzlement, suspicion, or even outright hostility.

So if the Trinitarian theology of the historic Latin tradition is seen as unnecessary, it will likely also be seen as burdensome. In that case, the analytic theologian will likely agree with Craig that it need not detain us further. But if the tradition of Latin Trinitarian theorizing is viewed as important and helpful, then contemporary theologians will likely be concerned by ST. If the official Latin formulations are not negotiable, then they will be forced to reject ST outright. Either way, this issue deserves further discussion. Without further discussion of this, we will continue to talk past

---

70. Dale Tuggy notices the problem, and asks if the current analytic discussion takes place in "an inadequate genre." "Tradition and Believability," pp. 452-55.

one another. And we are unlikely to make much progress on the threeness/oneness problem if we are talking past one another.

Later I shall address these issues of theological prolegomena again, and I shall suggest that there are good reasons for Christian theologians — evangelical Protestants and Orthodox as well as Roman Catholics — to take seriously the tradition of Latin Trinitarian theorizing. If I am right, then we should hope for, and work toward, consistency with the Latin tradition (among other things). This would mean that we should work for as strong an account of divine oneness as is available to us.[71]

II. Revisiting Relative Trinitarianism

This brings us to Relative Trinitarianism (RT). How do the RT proposals fare in light of the theological desiderata? What are their strengths, and where do they raise theological worries?

A. *Theological Strengths*

One rather obvious strength of RT is its ability to account for the New Testament witness to the distinctness of the divine persons. In other words, it can — even though, as we shall see, it *may* be used to formulate a sophisticated version of modalism — account for the biblical data that speaks to the distinct identity of the Father, Son, and Holy Spirit in their relations. At least this is what some of the most prominent proponents of RT desire. Sir Peter Geach, for instance, understands "person" in a robust, straightforward way. As Brian Hebblethwaite notes, "Geach will have nothing to do with the suggestion that 'person' in trinitarian theology means something quite different from its normal use. Trinitarian theology supposes that there is mutual address in God: 'In the Scriptures "I" and "you" are used for the discourse of the divine Persons to one another.'"[72] Or as Peter van Inwagen puts it, "persons are those things to which personal pronouns are applica-

71. Of course, what "available to us" means will be contentious (and involves more consideration of issues in theological prolegomena that are beyond this discussion).

72. Brian Hebblethwaite, *Philosophical Theology and Christian Doctrine* (Oxford: Blackwell, 2005), pp. 78-79. Hebblethwaite quotes from Peter Geach, *The Virtues* (Cambridge: Cambridge University Press, 1977), p. 76.

ble: a person can use the word 'I' and be addressed as 'thou' . . . and it is evident that the Persons of the Trinity *are* in this sense 'persons,' *are* someones: if the Father loves us, then someone loves us, and if the Son was incarnate by the Holy Ghost of the Virgin Mary, then someone was incarnate by the Holy Ghost of the Virgin Mary."[73] So even though RT doesn't necessitate such a view of the distinctness of the divine persons, it is consistent with it.

RT also provides a stronger account of divine oneness than ST is able to muster. It avoids a merely generic or cooperative notion of unity, and it is able to do so without resorting to the view that the divine persons are parts of God. As Jeffrey Brower and Michael Rea put it, their version of RT is "consistent with the view that God is an individual rather than a society, and that the Persons are not parts of God."[74] Thus it holds out promise of consistency with the Latin tradition of Trinitarian theorizing; and at any rate, it does not run afoul of the pronouncements of such statements as are produced in the Athanasian Creed and by Lateran IV.

Furthermore, as Brian Hebblethwaite points out, the application of the logic of relative identity to the doctrine of the Trinity carries with the "corollary" that persons are not — and indeed cannot be — properly conceived of as isolated or autonomous individuals.[75] According to RT, what is ontologically basic is neither bare relations nor autonomous persons, it is persons-in-relation. "We have to think of persons in relation, not individuals, as basic. The individual is something of an abstraction. Maximal greatness cannot be modeled on such abstraction. It must include, essentially, interpersonal relation."[76] Trinitarian orthodoxy has long insisted on just this point, and it is reinforced admirably by RT.

B. Liabilities and Weaknesses

In addition to the strictly metaphysical worries raised about relative identity, there are several distinctly theological worries. As Rea has argued, the application of the logic of relative identity alone is beset with problems.

---

73. Peter van Inwagen, *God, Knowledge, and Mystery: Essays in Philosophical Theology* (Ithaca, N.Y.: Cornell University Press, 1995), pp. 264-65.

74. Jeffrey E. Brower and Michael C. Rea, "Material Constitution and the Trinity," *Faith and Philosophy* 22 (2005): 59.

75. Hebblethwaite, *Philosophical Theology*, p. 79.

76. Hebblethwaite, *Philosophical Theology*, p. 79.

Although it need not (and, as I have shown, in the hands of its most important defenders it does not) go in the direction of modalism, the use of the logic of relative identity does open the door to modalism. Indeed, in some cases this seems to be the result. Consider the examples used by John Macnamara, Marie La Palme Reyes, and Gonzalo E. Reyes. They ask us to consider an airline passenger Smith, who "makes three distinct trips with Canadian Airways in 1990, one in May, one in September, and still another in October."[77] They point out that "the company will correctly claim to have carried three passengers even though these three particular passengers are associated with only a single person. While every passenger is a person the number of persons is smaller than the number of passengers."[78] They adduce other examples: students in a university, patients of physicians and surgeons, diners in restaurants, and customers in shops. "A single person can at one and the same time major in philosophy and mathematics. The Department of Philosophy and Mathematics will separately include the student in their lists of majors and the university will add the lists and count two majors although only one person is involved. . . . A single person can simultaneously be the patient of a urologist and of a heart specialist: that is to be two patients. A person can be a professor in two universities. There are many such examples. They are particularly relevant because the Divine Persons, being eternal, are simultaneously one God."[79]

But these examples do not suffice to move us beyond modalism. If anything, they serve to illustrate modalism. They may show how a single person can be counted differently; they may even show that a single person *should* be counted as three students (or patients, etc.) in some circumstances. But the doctrine of the Trinity maintains that there are three divine persons who are really distinct, so illustrations that show (or purport to show) how one person might be referred to or counted differently in different situations do not offer much help. Moreover, the example of

77. John Macnamara, Marie La Palme Reyes, and Gonzalo E. Reyes, "Logic and the Trinity," *Faith and Philosophy* 11 (1994): 7. Although they explicitly distance themselves from relative identity (e.g., p. 5), John S. Feinberg interprets them in just this way. *No One Like Him: The Doctrine of God* (Wheaton, Ill.: Crossway, 2001), p. 496. In doing so, I take him to be offering a generous interpretation, for E. Feser has argued that relative identity is the only hope for their model. "Has Trinitarianism Been Shown to Be Coherent?" *Faith and Philosophy* 14 (1997): 90, 92-93.

78. Macnamara, Reyes, and Reyes, "Logic and the Trinity," p. 7.

79. Macnamara, Reyes, and Reyes, "Logic and the Trinity," p. 8.

Smith the airline passenger is worse. Not only does it fail as an analogy of the Trinity, it actually serves to illustrate modalism. The success of the analogy turns on sequence: Smith the May passenger is distinct from Smith the September passenger because his September travels come *after* his May travels. Furthermore, as Edward Feser points out, "the philosophy major and the mathematics major are both identical to the same student, so they are identical to each other, and thus are, in one sense, the same major; and the urologist's patient and the heart specialist's patient are both identical to the same person, so they are identical to each other, and thus are, in one sense, the same patient. The same thing, however, can only be said in the case of the Divine Persons and God on pain of Sabellianism . . . if he [God] 'underlies' them in the same way that one thing underlies another in the ordinary cases, then we must conclude that each Divine Person is identical to God, and thus that all of them are identical to each other."[80] But this only serves to illustrate classical modalism, and we are left to conclude that it is successful only as an analogy of modalism. Again, while RT *need not* embrace modalism, the application of relative identity to the doctrine of the Trinity may indeed go in this direction.

But other problems await. Recall Rea's distinction between "pure" and "impure" versions of RT. The pure version endorses both

(RTa)   some doctrine of relative identity is true;

and (RTb)   the words "is God" and "is distinct from" in Trinitarian formulations express relativized identity and distinctness relations rather than absolute identity and distinctness relations,[81]

while the "impure" version endorses (RTb) while remaining neutral on (RTa). Rea argues, as we have pointed out, that the "pure" version is open to modalism. But this is, he says, really a best-case scenario for pure RT; for the other possibility is antirealism: "the doctrine of relative identity seems to presuppose an antirealist metaphysic."[82] No wonder Rea says this strategy is "catastrophic" and "disastrous"![83]

---

80. Feser, "Has Trinitarianism?" p. 91.

81. Michael C. Rea, "Relative Identity and the Doctrine of the Trinity," *Philosophia Christi* 5 (2003): 437.

82. Rea, "Relative Identity," p. 442.

83. Rea, "Relative Identity," pp. 442-43.

But what about the impure versions (such as that of van Inwagen)? Despite his elegant statement of it, it is hard to call van Inwagen's account an unqualified success. As Craig and Moreland point out, van Inwagen "has no answer to the questions of how X and Y can be the same N without being the same P"; this leads them to conclude that "the ability to state coherently the trinitarian claims under discussion using the device of relative identity is a hollow victory."[84] Similarly, Rea points out that van Inwagen "leaves open the possibility that Father, Son, and Holy Spirit are absolutely distinct, and if they are absolutely distinct, it is hard to see what it could possibly mean to say that they are the same *being*."[85] So to this point RT faces a dilemma: either it endorses relative identity or it remains neutral about it. If it endorses it, RT should be prepared to face the charge that it is either modalist or antirealist (in addition to facing the more general metaphysical objections). If it does not endorse it, on the other hand, then surely more work needs to be done to show us why and how it might be a viable option.

The constitution view (CT) of Brower and Rea is meant to do just this work. They argue that their view carries no antirealist commitments in metaphysics, nor does it entail a denial of the view that classical (or absolute) identity exists. Moreover, it has the distinct advantages of being consistent with the view that God is an individual (rather than a society, or a complex entity made up of parts), and it does not conflict with a "natural" reading of either the Bible or the ecumenical creeds. Indeed, they are convinced that CT gives us a doctrine of the Trinity according to which the Father, Son, and Holy Spirit are divine individuals (in the full, robust sense of "person") — *and* there is exactly one divine individual! Does not this satisfy all the major theological desiderata?

But is this model successful? Does it fulfill its promise? The view is new enough (or perhaps long forgotten and thus new *again*) that a definitive answer is no doubt a bit premature, but the view is promising indeed.[86] As with the more generic versions of RT, the CT version *could* be

---

84. Moreland and Craig, *Philosophical Foundations*, p. 592.

85. Rea, "Relative Identity," p. 441.

86. I say "again" because there are possible antecedents within the Christian tradition; see, e.g., Jeffrey E. Brower, "Abelard on the Trinity," in *The Cambridge Companion to Abelard*, ed. Jeffrey E. Brower and Kevin Guilfoy (Cambridge: Cambridge University Press, 2004), pp. 223-57, and Michael C. Rea, "The Trinity," in *Oxford Handbook of Philosophical Theology*, ed. Michael C. Rea and Thomas P. Flint (Oxford: Oxford University Press, 2008), pp. 716-21.

taken to illustrate modalism. Indeed, this might be the most straightforward conclusion at which one might arrive. The lump of bronze, after all, is most plausibly understood to be *first* one statue, *then* melted down and composed into another. If so, this would serve to illustrate modalism.

But modalism is clearly not what Brower and Rea intend. And surely the analogy *need not* be taken this way — its defenders may cheerfully admit that this is one of the areas in which the analogy breaks down while still maintaining that it serves to illustrate numerical sameness without identity. So CT does not entail modalism, and surely it need not be taken that way. There remains some ambiguity on how the three divine persons are to be understood as agents or centers of consciousness and will on this view, but as it stands, the primary objections to the CT version of RT seem to be more metaphysical than theological.[87]

C. Conclusion

We are now in a position to make several concluding observations. First, proponents of RT should heed Rea's warning that "pure" versions of RT either fall into modalism or open the door to antirealism, while "impure" versions, on the other hand, need to tell a "supplementary story." As a supplementary story, the CT strategy might be taken in the direction of modalism. But it need not go in this direction, and its proponents need only take care to make clear that this is not what it intended and to guard against such interpretations. It would be good if CT's advocates could clarify for us how divine persons are analogous to the inanimate statues — or at least tell us that they cannot be, and why this is not a problem for the strategy. In addition, they should continue working to address the remaining metaphysical worries about "numerical sameness without identity." It is, however, a promising way forward, one that offers a very strong account of divine unity ("numerical sameness") while also offering the resources necessary to avoid modalism ("without identity") and allowing for a robust account of the distinctness of the divine persons.

---

87. E.g., William Lane Craig, "Does the Problem of Material Constitution Illuminate the Problem of the Trinity?" *Faith and Philosophy* 22 (2005): 77-86.

III. Latin Trinitarianism: A Closer Look

Brian Leftow's "Latin Trinity" proposal is an ingenious attempt to make sense of the tradition of Latin theorizing about the Trinity, and it is one that he intends to be genuinely monotheist and orthodox as well as coherent. How well does it fare in light of our theological desiderata?

A. The Analogy Briefly Reviewed

To review, Leftow suggests that we think of the Trinity as analogous to Jane, a performer with the Rockettes who simultaneously performs in three roles by the clever use of a time machine. Watching the Rockettes, you think you see three women dancing. But what you really see is Jane dancing in three roles, three events, three time streams that are distinct for Jane but that occur simultaneously for you. What you really see, says Leftow, "are many dancings of one substance." "Each Rockette," he explains, "is Jane. But in these many events, Jane is there many times over. She plays different causal roles, one (as the leftmost Rockette) supporting the second-from-left Rockette . . . etc. And she has genuine interpersonal relationships with herself in her other roles . . . [she is] one Jane in many *personae*."[88] Leftow explains how this serves as a model of the Trinity: "God always lives His life in three discrete strands at once, no event of His life occurring in more than one strand and no strand succeeding another. In one strand God lives the Father's life, in one the Son's, and in one the Spirit's. The events of each strand add up to the life of a Person. The lives of the three Persons add up to the life God lives *as* the three Persons. There is one God, but He is many in the events of His life, as Jane was in the chorus line: being the Son is a bit like being the leftmost Rockette."[89]

Initially, this may seem unpromising, for it raises worries about an area of critical ambiguity. What does it mean to refer to "leftmost Jane"? Isn't this a bit misleading, for surely *this* Jane is just plain Jane standing and dancing on the left? In fact, is she not just Jane-in-the-leftmost-position rather than something discrete enough to be "leftmost Jane"? This is where Leftow's use of the notion of "Locke-persons" (L-persons) is important. To

---

88. Brian Leftow, "A Latin Trinity," *Faith and Philosophy* 21 (2004): 308.
89. Leftow, "A Latin Trinity," p. 312.

recall, an L-person is someone who is "identical over time just as far as a single 'consciousness' exists"; L-persons begin to exist when a consciousness begins, and they cease to exist when this single consciousness ends.[90] To repeat Leftow's summary, "my Lockean 'mode'-based suggestion about the Trinity then, is this. Perhaps the triune Persons are event-based persons founded on a generating substance, God. . . . these streams are mental events, and each such stream is the life of a Locke-person. God never exists save *in* the Persons . . . there is just one God who generates and lives as the three Persons, by generating and living in three distinct mental streams."[91]

Leftow is clear about his views of the theological payoff: he is convinced that it allows consistency with the orthodoxy of the Latin tradition while also providing a coherent and genuinely monotheistic account of the Trinity. Importantly, the divine persons have but one trope of divinity. "While both Father and Son instance the divine nature (deity), they have but one trope of deity between them, which is God's."[92] Thus monotheism — what Leftow would say is *real* monotheism — is preserved.

B. Limits of the Analogy

Leftow is aware of the disanalogies; he says that while not all parts of Jane's life are on display in the chorus line, "every event in God's life is part of the Father-Son-Spirit chorus line; God does not live save as Father, Son, and Spirit." Jane's dance moves are sequential; "not so for God: God always lives in three streams. God's life always consists of three non-overlapping lives going on at once, none after the other."[93] Where the analogy seems to work because there is succession between events on the chorus line, Leftow says that "it's more basically the causal relations between her life segments."[94] Similarly, "as causal relations between the event-streams in the Jane case help make them streams within one life, we can suppose that causal relations do the like without succession in the Trinitarian case: that is, we can suppose that causal relations between the event-streams in-

90. Brian Leftow, "Modes without Modalism," in *Persons, Human and Divine*, ed. Peter van Inwagen and Dean Zimmerman (Oxford: Oxford University Press, 2007), p. 367.

91. Leftow, "Modes without Modalism," p. 374.

92. Leftow, "A Latin Trinity," p. 305.

93. Leftow, "A Latin Trinity," p. 312.

94. Leftow, "A Latin Trinity," p. 313.

volved are what make them all streams within one individual's life." So Leftow freely admits that there are limits to the analogy. But he also believes in its usefulness, and he presses on.

The analogy has other limits as well. The "causal relations" between leftmost Jane and center Jane, for example, are surely contingent, while the causal relations that obtain between the divine persons are necessary. Moreover, the story of Jane and the Rockettes gets off the ground only on the supposition that there is genuine temporal distinction between the event-streams of Jane's life, while for Leftow it is true that God is atemporal.[95] The issue is further complicated, and the analogy with Jane's time travel further weakened, by the fact that Leftow's model of the Trinity requires that the distinction between the divine persons is real in the sense that it is temporal — while there is not, and cannot be, any succession between the streams of events that make up the lives of the divine persons. But how are we to understand temporal distinctions that are not successive? Exactly how this works is left unclear, and we are left with the disappointing conclusion that the time-travel analogy is meant to shed light on this — even though this is one of the points where the time-travel analogy breaks down. In addition, LT needs the notion of "Locke-persons," but even Leftow does not argue that these exist (other than perhaps as the Father, Son, and Holy Spirit).[96] Meanwhile, all of this rides on the plausibility of an illustration of time travel.[97] Again, Leftow is aware of these limits. He does not claim that the analogy is perfect, but he is convinced that it is helpful nonetheless.[98]

C. Liabilities and Weaknesses

Despite any advantages, however (and despite the ingenuity of Leftow's proposal), we are left with some questions about some important issues.

95. E.g., Brian Leftow, *Time and Eternity* (Ithaca, N.Y.: Cornell University Press, 1991); Leftow, "The Eternal Present," in *God and Time: Essays on the Divine Nature*, ed. Gregory E. Ganssle and David M. Woodruff (Oxford: Oxford University Press, 2002), pp. 21-48; Leftow, "A Timeless God Incarnate," in *The Trinity: An Interdisciplinary Symposium on the Trinity*, pp. 273-99.

96. Leftow, "Modes without Modalism," p. 368.

97. Leftow addresses several of the more interesting and potentially problematic puzzles that arise in discussions of time travel (e.g., the "killing my earlier self" paradox). "A Latin Trinity," pp. 309-11.

98. Leftow, "A Latin Trinity," p. 313.

The first — and perhaps the most innocuous — question has to do with the claim to be a "Latin" model of the Trinity. Is "LT" really a version of Latin Trinitarianism? In what ways is it truly representative of medieval Latin doctrines of the Trinity? To what extent is it consistent with the Latin tradition? Answers to these questions are not readily available, but — despite Leftow's bestowal of the honorific title "LT" — there is reason to wonder just how well it represents and coheres with the Latin tradition.

A Latin Trinity?

Consider, for instance, the issue of how LT might fit with a doctrine of divine simplicity (DDS). At base, DDS claims that there are no divine parts or pieces; there is no composition within God. Some version or other of DDS was held by virtually every medieval theologian, and it was held by many patristic theologians as well.[99] Yet Leftow's LT requires God to be made up of parts. For Leftow these are *personal parts;* the relevant parts of God end up being the divine persons. Consider Leftow's claim that "God eternally has three parts of His life going on at once, without succession between them. One part is the Father's life, one the Son's, one the Spirit's."[100] So even though Jane has no temporal parts, the triune God does have parts.[101] Leftow does not say that these event-streams that add up to the life of a divine person are relevantly *like* temporal parts; he simply says they *are* parts. They are parts that "add up to the life of one God."[102] Again, for Leftow these are personal parts. It is the divine persons who are these parts, and they amount to temporal parts. But parts they are, and thus we are left to wonder how his doctrine might really be representative of the Latin tradition of Trinitarian theorizing. Indeed, we are left to wonder how consistent it might be with Latin formulations of the doctrine.

---

99. On patristic accounts of divine simplicity (still an underexplored area in modern patristic scholarship), see Basil Krivocheine, "Simplicity of the Divine Nature and the Distinctions in God, according to St. Gregory of Nyssa," *St. Vladimir's Theological Quarterly* 21 (1977): 76-104; Christopher Stead, "Divine Simplicity as a Problem for Orthodoxy," in *The Making of Christian Doctrine: Essays in Honor of Henry Chadwick,* ed. Rowan D. Williams (Cambridge: Cambridge University Press, 1989), pp. 255-69; and Katherin Rogers, "The Traditional Doctrine of Divine Simplicity," *Religious Studies* 32 (1996): 165-86.

100. Leftow, "Modes without Modalism," p. 374.

101. Leftow, "A Latin Trinity," p. 308.

102. Leftow, "Modes without Modalism," p. 375.

A Quaternity?

Consideration of the part-whole issue raises another area of concern for LT: this is the issue of Quaternity. If the personal parts add up to one God, then we are left to wonder how the one God (who is a whole) could be identical with any of the parts (much less with each of the parts).

This raises a dilemma for LT: either there is a fourth instance or exemplification of divinity, or there is not. Suppose we start by assuming that in LT there is a fourth of some sort. If there is, then it is either a divine person or it is not a divine person. Perhaps it is not a divine person. I suggest that this is a possible interpretation of LT, for one person is not plausibly understood to be a "part" of another person. Moreover, when three persons "add up to" something else, it is usually not another person. It is much more plausible to think that they "add up to" a society or community of persons, but to admit this would be to admit that LT is really only a version of ST (albeit an unusual version).[103] So just what is it that the three parts/divine persons amount to when joined together? The answer is less than obvious.

Whatever exactly they would amount to when the parts/divine persons are added up, it is pretty clear that to deny that God is *a person* is to lose more of the Rockettes analogy. After all, what gives the analogy any initial plausibility is the fact that we can conceive of Jane — as *a person* — entering and exiting the time machine to perform the different roles as leftmost Jane, center Jane, and rightmost Jane. To deny that God is *a person* would also be to open LT to the charges of Daniel Howard-Snyder, Dale Tuggy, and others that genuine monotheism must say that God is *a person*. Recall Howard-Snyder's charge that since God is not a person (as ST has it), then "God is not 'equipped with rational faculties of intellect and volition which enable it to be a self-reflective agent capable of self-determination,'"[104] and recall further his claims that because this God cannot act, God could not have created the heavens and the earth, that God could not have created humans in the divine image, and that "God does not know anything, cannot act, cannot choose, cannot be morally good, cannot be worthy of worship."[105]

In his response to Howard-Snyder, Craig has protested that these

---

103. William Hasker notes that "Leftow's view presents an intriguing combination of elements from both Social Trinitarianism and modalism." "A Leftovian Trinity?" *Faith and Philosophy* 26 (2009): 160.

104. Howard-Snyder, "Trinity Monotheism," p. 399.

105. Howard-Snyder, "Trinity Monotheism," p. 401.

charges are misleading, for according to Craig's own ST, "God has the cognitive equipment sufficient for personhood three times over and so is tripersonal."[106] Craig considers two different routes that are open for his ST: the Trinity can be thought of as a collection of individuals, or it can be thought of as an individual composed of individuals. Either way, concludes Craig, his version of ST avoids the charges brought by Howard-Snyder, and he leaves open both doors at this point. It may be that Leftow's LT could do likewise. But if his LT conceives of the Trinity as a collection of individuals, then surely it just becomes another version of the ST that he criticizes. On the other hand, if he takes the other route and holds that the Trinity is an individual made up of individuals, then his proposal offers no real advantages over Craig's ST. In addition, it suffers from several defects: it bears the burden of being committed to the notion of "L-persons" and is thus unnecessarily tied to another controversial position, it rests upon the possibility that temporal parts can be really distinct though simultaneous rather than successive, and it relies upon the notion that an atemporal God can have three temporal parts.

But perhaps the Trinity is *a person*. This is what the Rockettes analogy would seem to suggest; Jane is, after all, *a* distinct, individual person who plays three different roles in three different streams of events. But if we have three divine persons plus one Trinity who is also a person, we pretty plainly have four divine persons. And if this is not Quaternity, then it is hard to imagine what might be. So we would need another option.

One such possibility is this: there are three divine "Locke-persons" and one divine Person. While this might seem too close to a straight Quaternity to allow much theological comfort, a theologian sympathetic to Leftow's LT might insist that it is not exactly a Quaternity because we do not have four of the same entities: we have three "L-persons" and one "Person." If such a model could be defended (and a defender of LT would need to spell out just how a Person differs from an L-person), it would allow the proponent of LT to turn aside criticisms such as those of Howard-Snyder: God on this model would be, after all, *a* person, thus God would be able to create the world, create humans in the divine image, etc.

I find it doubtful, however, that an adequate defense of such a model could be pulled off. It might work for the story of Jane and the Rockettes, but it would do so by relying upon one of the points where the scenario ac-

---

106. Craig, "Trinity Monotheism Once More," p. 105.

tually breaks down as an analogy of the Trinity. For what it would explain is this: it would explain how one Person could have three distinct streams of events, and how each of these streams of events could be genuinely distinct while also simultaneous. But this part of the story of Jane works only on the supposition that there is more to Jane than all three Rockettes and that the streams of events (or the L-persons) are successive. In other words, it best explains those parts of the analogy that *don't* work for the doctrine of the Trinity.

At any rate, this account does not sit well with a natural reading of Scripture. The Father, Son, and Holy Spirit are depicted in the New Testament simply as *persons*. Although understanding the divine persons as L-persons *might* finally be consistent with the biblical depiction, it is surely not demanded by — nor even suggested by — the scriptural witness. If the triune God is a Person who underlies the L-persons, then there is a sense in which all the personal indexicals refer to the same Person. Consider such statements as that of the Father at the baptism of Jesus: "you are my beloved Son." Would it not be the case that here we would have *the* divine Person saying something close to "I just love myself when I do that"? Even if this is parsed as "I just love myself *as the L-person of the Son* when I do that," does this not lose touch with the personal indexicals as they are presented in the New Testament? Just how we should understand the personal indexicals of the New Testament on this model is far from clear.

There is a further concern here as well. Either the Person is omniscient, or the Person is not omniscient. If the Person is not omniscient, then (presumably) the Person is not divine, and thus is not the triune God after all. So we can safely rule out this option. Taking the other route, though, raises some puzzles. Either the Person is omniscient while the L-persons are *not* omniscient, or both the Person and the L-persons are omniscient. Again, if the L-persons are not omniscient, then presumably they are not divine. So presumably they are omniscient. But if they are omniscient, then we are faced with a puzzle. What distinguishes the minds of the L-persons from one another — and what distinguishes the minds of the L-persons from that of the Person? If they cannot be distinguished, then are they really distinct? It's not at all easy to see how they even could be. If we accept the Identity of Indiscernibles, then we are left to conclude that they are *not* really distinct.[107]

---

107. A defender of LT may respond that the Identity of Indiscernibles is not necessarily

Modalism After All?

All of this leads us to what is likely the biggest challenge facing LT: the menace of modalism. Leftow is aware of this challenge, and he works to distance his model from modalism. He begins his defense against modalism by saying that "it is no easy thing to say just what Modalism *was*, or exactly why it was rejected"; he then moves on to describe it as the view that "all distinctions between the Persons are impermanent and transitory," so that there is only a "Trinity of manifestation, not even a Trinity of economy, still less a Trinity of being."[108] He references various descriptions and definitions that can be found in theological dictionaries, and he argues that his view "seems comfortably far" from these depictions of modalism. He insists that "nothing in my account precludes saying that the Persons' distinction is an eternal, necessary, non-successive and intrinsic feature of God's life, one which would be there even if there were no creatures. If one asserts all this, one asserts a 'Trinity of being,' with no reference to actions *ad extra* or appearances to creatures. Further items on an anti-Modalist checklist: does the view set out here entail that the Father is crucified? No, although the God who is Father is crucified — at the point in His life in which He is not the Father, but the Son." Leftow goes on to ask if his view can deal adequately with the biblical texts. He responds that it indeed can do so: "on the present view, the Son cannot token truly 'I am the Father,' though he can token truly 'I am the God who is (at another point in His life) the Father.' Nor can the Son say truly that 'I am at one point in my life the Father and at another point the Son,' since at no point in the Son's life is He the Father."[109] Although the Son "can truly say that 'I am the God who is at one point in His life the Father and at another the Son,' he cannot say that 'I am the Father.'"[110]

Leftow works to explain further how we are to understand the use of personal indexicals. He recognizes that a "natural question" is this: "if the Son just *is* God, can't the Son use 'I' to refer to God, not to the Son, and if He does, can't He assert" that he is at one point in his life the Father and at another point the Son? Not exactly, says Leftow, for "if there is just one in-

---

true. Quite so, but it surely seems to be true, as a matter of fact, in the real world. See Max Black, "The Identity of Indiscernibles," *Mind* 61 (1962): 153-64.

108. Leftow, "A Latin Trinity," pp. 326-27.
109. Leftow, "A Latin Trinity," p. 327.
110. Leftow, "A Latin Trinity," pp. 327-28.

dividual, God, in the three Persons, then a purely referential 'I' would always contribute simply God to a sentence's content." This cannot be (apparently on pain of modalism), so on LT "God's 'I' always includes a mode of presentation, a sense under which a speaker conceives and refers to Himself. When the Son speaks as the Son, He presents Himself to Himself as the Son, and so the Father is never other than another 'I,' who as such has his own mind and will." This, concludes Leftow, "is enough to make sense of the texts, given the way my view guarantees the real distinctness of Father and Son."[111]

There is much here that is puzzling, and I find his conclusion less than adequate. Leftow summarizes his description of modalism by saying that the personal distinctions are impermanent and transitory,[112] and that "God is only temporarily Son and Spirit."[113] Surely this is true, but it is also true (as Leftow recognizes) that there is more to modalism. Notably, there are the versions that endorse or entail patripassianism. Leftow ponders the issue of patripassianism, but he again says his LT is not liable to it because it is only in the stream of events that constitute the life of the *Son* that God suffers and is crucified.

It is not, however, at all clear to me that Leftow can so easily defend his view. On Leftow's view, "when the Son speaks as the Son, He presents Himself to Himself as the Son." Unfortunately, the meaning of this is obscured by ambiguity. Who is the "He" here? Who is the referent of "Himself"? Does "He" refer to *the Son?* Or to *God?* "Himself" surely does not refer to the Father or the Spirit. But does it refer to *the Son?* Or does it refer to *God?* Is it an L-person presenting himself to the Person? Or is it the Person presenting himself as an L-person to himself as another L-person? It is hard to tell, and without being able to know the referent of this, it is difficult to judge either the coherence or the orthodoxy of Leftow's LT. But if it is the Person presenting himself, then are we left with the conclusion that the individual divine Person who is God is talking to himself (albeit perhaps as one L-person to another L-person)? If so, then we should not share Leftow's confidence that his LT can account for the biblical use of personal indexicals. And if whoever it is that suffers and dies on the cross just is the one divine Person (albeit as one L-person rather than another), then it is

111. Leftow, "A Latin Trinity," p. 328.
112. Leftow, "Modes without Modalism," p. 360.
113. Leftow, "Modes without Modalism," p. 374.

true that the one divine Person who is God suffers and dies on the cross. If so, then we should doubt very much that Leftow's LT avoids the kind of theopassianism that was ruled out in the rejection of modalism. Perhaps patripassianism itself is avoided, but only at the price of endorsing a model that entails theopassianism.

Not a Fourth?

Much of what Leftow says leads us to believe that there is a fourth instance of divinity — either a divine Person (in addition to the divine L-persons) or maybe even a collection of divine persons. As we have seen, the Rockettes analogy would suggest that there is — after all, Jane is *a* person who becomes (or becomes relevantly like) multiple L-persons. Leftow will also refer to the divine L-persons as "parts" of God. The invocation of a part-whole relation here seems telling indeed: wholes and parts have distinct properties, and if there is a whole then it cannot be identified with some or all of its parts. Moreover, Leftow refers to these parts as "parts of" *God's* life, and he distinguishes this from the lives of each of the three L-persons.[114]

Despite this, however, perhaps Leftow will deny that there is a fourth instance of divinity at all. Some of what he says surely leads us to conclude that there is not. He insists, for instance, that there is only one trope of deity. The analogy of Jane and the Rockettes would lead us to think that there is a fourth something that underlies the Rockettes, but Leftow appears to deny the parallel with Jane at this point, for "not all of Jane's life is on display in the chorus line. But every event in God's life is part of the Father-Son-Spirit chorus line."[115] So perhaps the way to interpret LT is as the denial that there is a fourth.

If we are to understand Leftow as denying that there is a fourth — either a fourth Person or a fourth collection — then we are left with three L-persons who are all divine. If so, then I am at a loss as to how to understand Leftow's language of parts. Of *what* are they parts? What do they "add up" to? Nor do I know what to make of his discussion of God's own life. Just *whose* life is it, if the L-persons are really distinct? And what makes this view superior to the most pluralistic versions of ST? Why

114. Leftow, "Modes without Modalism," pp. 374-75.
115. Leftow, "A Latin Trinity," p. 312.

would it not be liable to the criticisms that Leftow makes of "functional monotheism" that he has criticized in his assault on ST? For instance, if we have three divine centers of consciousness and will — all of which are distinct from the others — do we not need some kind of "group mind monotheism" to account for oneness? On the other hand, if the L-persons are *not* distinct, do we not have a version of modalism after all? Either way, Leftow's view needs clarification.[116]

The Meaning of "Is"

In this section I have raised several questions and worries. At the root of these is a fundamental area of ambiguity. Exactly what does Leftow mean when he says that "the Father is God" (and "the Son is God")?[117] Surely he does not mean merely the "is" of predication. This would mean a return to the ST that he so roundly criticizes, and it would weaken his claim that there is one and only one trope of divinity. But he can hardly mean the "is" of identity either. For to go this route is to welcome puzzles and problems. According to Leibniz's Law of the Indiscernibility of Identicals (InId), if the Father is identical with the triune God, then any property possessed by the Father is possessed by the triune God, and any property possessed by the triune God is possessed by the Father. So such properties as *being one L-person* and *being only one L-person* would be possessed by the triune God. Depending on our interpretation of LT, perhaps this might not be a problem for it. But it would also mean that such properties as *being a Person, being a Person who is composed of three parts that are L-persons,* and *being triune* would belong to the Father, as would such properties as *being the Son, knowing the contents of the mind of the Son,* and *being able to say "I am the Son."* The upshot of this should be plain enough: taking Leftow's "is" as the "is" of identity raises Leibniz's Law problems. And, as we have seen, it opens the door to the charge of modalism.[118]

Taking the "is" in statements such as "the Father is God" and "the Son is God" as the "is" of predication is to weaken LT's claim that there is but one trope of divinity. It would bring us back around to ST, and in doing so

---

116. Michael C. Rea also thinks that Leftow's model needs further work; see, e.g., "The Trinity," pp. 700-704.

117. E.g., Leftow, "A Latin Trinity," p. 305.

118. On this point see Hasker, "A Leftovian Trinity?" pp. 162-64.

would make Leftow's own LT liable to the criticisms he makes of ST. Taking the "is" as the "is" of identity, on the other hand, leads to InId problems. Barring an endorsement of a version of the logic of relative identity, the prospects for such an approach do not look good. Relativizing identity, on the other hand, would make Leftow's LT yet another version of RT. Leftow's model is underdeveloped, and he may be able to clarify — or modify — it so as to alleviate such concerns. My point is not that he *cannot* do so — it is rather that something needs to be done to make the position theologically viable. For as it stands, LT does not seem at all promising.

IV. Conclusion

In this chapter I have offered a theological assessment of the major extant views. Drawing upon my previous summary of the important theological desiderata, I have examined the various proposals for respective strengths and weaknesses. As we have seen, ST offers an illuminating account of the three persons that is obviously consistent with the New Testament witness to the divinity and distinctness of the persons. It is also able to do so in a way that is consistent with the monotheism that was the inheritance of Paul, John, and the other authors of the New Testament. Moreover, ST steers clear of both modalism and Arianism. On the other hand, the extent to which it coheres with the Latin tradition is questionable; while it may be consistent with the common Latin views of essence, it pretty clearly runs afoul of such major Latin statements as that of the Fourth Lateran Council. So those Trinitarians who are committed to the official statements of the Latin tradition will want to hold ST at arm's length, and those Trinitarians who are sympathetic to the Latin tradition will also want to look elsewhere.

I have argued that RT *can* lead to either modalism or antirealism, but I have argued further that it *need not* do so. The CT version leaves unanswered the question of just what the divine persons are on this analogy, but its proponents can cheerfully admit this while pointing out that what knowledge we have of this comes from beyond the analogy — it comes from divine revelation. What the analogy means to show, they can say, is how there might be three divine individual persons *and* exactly one God. But the payoff achieved is no mean feat: the analogy shows how three distinct persons can have numerical sameness without identity. So while some important questions about the metaphysics remain unanswered, the model shows theological promise.

LT, on the other hand, contains ambiguity at some critical points. By violating the doctrine of divine simplicity, it puts itself at odds with the Latin tradition. More importantly, however, it is threatened with either polytheism (of the type criticized by Leftow himself) or modalism. For if Leftow means by such statements as "the Father is God," "the Son is God," and "the Trinity is God" that the "is" is to be understood as the "is" of predication, then his view looks like ST of another kind. On the other hand, if the "is" in such statements is to be understood as the "is" of identity, then modalism looms if identity is not relativized. Either way, the future does not look bright for LT.

In conclusion, it seems clear that the Trinitarian theologian committed to biblical and ecumenical orthodoxy will want to avoid those versions of ST that depend upon merely generic or congregational notions of divine oneness or unity.[119] And it remains readily apparent why more is needed to ward off charges of tritheism. For if

(1) x is a man = x is a human substance

is plausible (which seems undeniable), then

(2) y is a god = y is a divine substance

would appear to be equally plausible. But if (2) is allowed, then

(3) polytheism = the view that there is more than one divine substance

is undeniable. Thus it is hard to deny that the social analogy — unmodified or unalloyed — invites the common charges of tritheism. Similarly, the theologian who wants to avoid modalism and antirealism will avoid both "pure" versions of RT and those "impure" versions that fail to tell a "supplementary" metaphysical story. And unfortunately, the problems facing LT seem severe indeed; it does not offer much promise.

This leaves us with the "constitution" version of "impure" RT and the

119. But see the spirited defense offered by Nathan Jacobs, "On Not Three Gods — Again: Can a Primary-Secondary Substance Reading of *Ousia* and *Hypostasis* Avoid Tritheism?" *Modern Theology* 24 (2008): 331-58.

modified versions of ST. Both offer models that cohere with the scriptural teaching that gave rise to the doctrine in the first place, and both can claim consistency with the major ecumenical councils. Both avoid Arianism and modalism. The CT model comes with an analogy that is initially helpful but also, as analogies go, potentially misleading. It can claim the benefits of ST, but clearly offers a much stronger account of divine oneness than either the generic, functional, or part-whole versions of ST. And it is an obvious advance beyond earlier RT accounts. The primary worries with it are mainly metaphysical, and critics will continue to protest either the very notion of relative identity or CT's employment of it.

We are in a similar situation with respect to the versions of ST that endorse complexity. Yandell's proposal comes with no handy-dandy analogy, but it addresses the threeness-oneness problem while not denying the doctrine of divine simplicity (at least not all versions of the doctrine). It achieves the "payoff" of ST: it can readily account both for the monotheism and for the personal distinctions demanded by an orthodox reading of Scripture. But it offers a much stronger account of divine oneness than mere appeal to "generic" oneness or functional unity, and it avoids the problems associated with part-whole Trinitarianism. Additionally, it does not bear the burden of being committed to any version of the doctrine of relative identity. It will likely draw charges of being unacceptably ad hoc due to its unusual account of complexity. But such objections are really metaphysical rather than theological (per se). Yandell might easily respond that perhaps we should not be too surprised if there are aspects of the metaphysics of the doctrine of the Trinity that are unusual — and he might say that responding to the common and serious charges by showing how the doctrine of the Trinity need not be either formally or informally inconsistent is a worthwhile exercise.

The Kingdom of the Trinity

"Whoever Raised Jesus from the Dead": Robert Jenson on the Identity of the Triune God

Robert W. Jenson is among the most important and influential contemporary Trinitarian theologians. Long recognized for his work as a Lutheran and ecumenical theologian, his recent *Systematic Theology* has garnered much attention and acclaim.[1] Even Jenson's sharpest critics laud this work. Oliver D. Crisp thinks that "Jenson's *Systematic Theology* is undoubtedly one of the most rich and forthright statements of ecclesial theology that has been produced in recent years." David Bentley Hart says that Jenson's attempt "to find in the story of Jesus, and all that attaches thereto, an essential narrativity in the identity of God" is "powerful and profound." Francis Watson does not shrink from dubbing Jenson "America's Theologian"; he opines that Jenson is "truly a scribe trained for the kingdom of heaven," and he concludes that "this is a work that deserves and requires patient, diligent, attentive readers, to whom it will demonstrate that the sheer oddity of the Christian faith is one of its chief glories and the clearest proof of its divine origin." And even George Hunsinger, who has raised some of the sharpest criticisms, calls this "the twentieth century's most accomplished systematic theology written in English." It has "few peers in any language," he says, and he goes on to point out that Jenson has "at his fingertips . . . an astonishing fund of citations and quotations from every period of theological history and every ecumenical tradition. Irenaeus, Cyril, Maximus and Palamas; Cyprian, Augustine and Aquinas; Luther,

---

1. Robert W. Jenson, *Systematic Theology, Volume 1: The Triune God* (New York: Oxford University Press, 1997), and *Systematic Theology, Volume 2: The Works of God* (New York: Oxford University Press, 1999), hereafter abbreviated *ST 1* and *ST 2*, respectively.

Melanchthon and Brenz; Jonathan Edwards; Ebeling, Pannenberg and Barth; not to mention lesser figures like Thomasius and Dorner; and many, many more, including the consensus documents of up-to-date ecumenical discussion — all are summoned, it seems, at just the right moment and for just the right effect. Besides being theologically deft, the work is also culturally, scientifically, and philosophically sophisticated."[2]

But with the lavish praise comes criticism of Jenson's theology.[3] Many of the areas of concern, it seems to me, come into sharper relief and are seen more clearly when we focus on his important notion of divine identity. In this chapter I take a close look at Jenson's account of the identity of God, especially as it relates to the God-world relationship. I make a case that if his theological proposal is taken in a fairly straightforward sense, then (on standard accounts of identity) it generates some puzzles and produces some problems. I argue that these problems are severe enough that they cripple his theology, but I suggest that with some modification his theology yields an important emphasis that should be taken seriously in contemporary Trinitarian theology. I conclude that while what I call the "Identity Thesis" is mistaken, the "Identification Thesis" is true and salutary.

I. Jenson on Divine Identity

Jenson is well known for his resolute insistence that the triune God of the Christian faith is "the one who raised Israel's Jesus from the dead."[4] God is

---

2. Oliver D. Crisp, "Robert Jenson on the Pre-existence of Christ," *Modern Theology* 23, no. 1 (2007): 30; David Bentley Hart, *The Beauty of the Infinite: The Aesthetics of Christian Truth* (Grand Rapids: Eerdmans, 2003), p. 160; Francis Watson, "'America's Theologian': An Appreciation of Robert Jenson's *Systematic Theology,* with Some Remarks about the Bible," *Scottish Journal of Theology* 55, no. 2 (2002): 215; George Hunsinger, "Robert Jenson's *Systematic Theology:* A Review Essay," *Scottish Journal of Theology* 55, no. 2 (2002): 161.

3. In addition to the criticisms of Crisp, Hunsinger, and Hart (many of which I heartily endorse), see also the engagement of Simon Gathercole, "Pre-existence, and the Freedom of the Son in Creation and Redemption: An Exposition in Dialogue with Robert Jenson," *International Journal of Systematic Theology* 7, no. 1 (2005): 38-51, and D. Farrow, D. Demson, and J. A. DiNoia, "Robert Jenson's *Systematic Theology:* Three Responses," *International Journal of Systematic Theology* 1 (1999): 89-104.

4. E.g., Robert W. Jenson, *The Triune Identity: God according to the Gospel* (Philadelphia: Fortress, 1982), p. 21. Characteristic of Jenson is his conviction that "the whole task of theology can be described as the unpacking of this sentence in various ways." See also Rob-

truly identified by — and *with* — the narrative of divine action in human history. To the people of Israel, God is "whoever rescued us from Egypt."[5] And to the question "Who is God?" the New Testament has "one new descriptively identifying answer: 'Whoever raised Jesus from the dead.'"[6] Seeing more exactly what Jenson means by this requires more careful exploration.

A. The Identification Thesis and the Identity Thesis

There is an important distinction between what I shall call the "Identification Thesis" and what we may term the "Identity Thesis." The Identification Thesis simply states that

(IdT1) God is to be identified by his revelatory speech and action;

while the Identity Thesis holds that

(IdT2) God is identical to his revelatory speech and action.

According to the Identification Thesis, the "is" used in such statements as "God is the one who rescued Israel and raised Jesus from the dead" is the "is" of predication. The point made here is simply that there is no God other than the deity revealed by Jesus Christ. While this is the traditional way to do theology, it has seen renewed emphasis in the twentieth century.[7]

The Identity Thesis, on the other hand, arguably is opposed to traditional understandings of the nature of God and of the God-world relation. Here "is" is not the "is" of predication but the "is" of identity. Here the reference is not to what is sometimes called "qualitative identity"; it is clearly not what is meant by phrases such as "the twins are identical." What is on

---

ert W. Jenson, "Second Locus: The Triune God," in *Christian Dogmatics: Volume 1,* ed. Carl E. Braaten and Robert W. Jenson (Philadelphia: Fortress, 1984), p. 99.

5. Jenson, *ST 1,* p. 44.

6. Jenson, *ST 1,* p. 44.

7. Prominent examples of this renewed emphasis can be found in the work of Karl Barth and Jürgen Moltmann (who in many ways radicalizes Barth's "Christocentrism" by focusing the "Christocentrism" on the cross, and indeed on the cry of dereliction, with his theology of the "Crucified God").

view here is numerical identity, according to which identity is normally understood to be *reflexive, transitive,* and *symmetric.* Identity is reflexive: for any object *x, x* is equal to *x.*[8] Identity is *transitive,* for if *x* is equal to *y,* and if *y* is equal to *z,* then *x* is equal to *z.*[9] Identity is *symmetric* because if *x* is related to *y,* then *y* is of course also related to *x.*[10] Furthermore, claims to identity will meet the requirement of Leibniz's Law of the Indiscernibility of Identicals:[11]

(InId) For any objects *x* and *y,* if *x* and *y* are identical, then for any property *P, x* has *P* if and only if *y* has *P.*[12]

Identity is thus an equivalence relation that satisfies (InId).[13]

B. Locating Jenson

Jenson offers a clear and ringing endorsement of the Identification Thesis. Underlying this contention is Jenson's suspicion of philosophical (especially "Greek" or "substance") metaphysics. As Crisp points out, "Jenson opposes any attempt to find the 'right' metaphysics with which to pursue the theological enterprise. Indeed, he appears to believe that any attempt to utilise the metaphysical tools on offer in the work of 'officially designated philosophers' is bound to end in a Babylonian captivity for theology."[14]

Indeed, Jenson is exercised to overcome what he sees as the disastrous influence of the Greek philosophical tradition (he refers to "Greece's theo-

---

8. $(x = x)$.

9. $(x = y \ \& \ y = z \Rightarrow x = z)$.

10. $(x = y \Rightarrow y = x)$.

11. This is not to be confused with the Identity of Indiscernibles (sometimes also called "Leibniz's Law"): "If any objects *x* and *y* share all of the same properties, then *x* and *y* are identical."

12. $(\forall x) \ (\forall y) \ [x = y \Rightarrow (\forall F) \ (F(x) \Leftrightarrow F(y))]$. As we shall see, to account for transworld identity, (InId) requires the appropriate world and time quantifiers; on this see Michael J. Loux, introduction to *The Possible and the Actual: Readings in the Metaphysics of Modality,* ed. Michael J. Loux (Ithaca, N.Y.: Cornell University Press, 1979), p. 42.

13. All entities that are identical will share an equivalence relation that satisfies (InId), but not all equivalence relations amount to identity. The statement "*x* and *y* are the same size" expresses an equivalence relation, but it makes no claims that *x* and *y* are identical.

14. Crisp, "Robert Jenson," p. 33.

logians"),[15] and he is especially motivated to rid Christian theology of its inheritance of the doctrines of timelessness and impassibility. "Mediterranean antiquity," he says, "defined deity by immunity to time, by 'impassibility'; offensively to this definition, the Gospel defines its God by temporal events of Exodus and Resurrection."[16] According to Jenson, "Hellenic theology was an exact antagonist of biblical faith."[17]

God is *not* to be identified first as a Perfect Being or Unmoved Mover (or by any other a priori notions), with the biblical account then pressed somehow to fit into this ready-made theology. Rather, God is to be identified by his saving action in human history: God is only truly known by his activity. God is "whoever raised Israel's Jesus from the dead." Jenson thus sees the triune name of God as a summary of this action, for "the phrase 'Father, Son, and Holy Spirit' is simultaneously a very compressed telling of the total narrative by which Scripture identifies God and a personal name for the God so specified."[18]

But Jenson goes beyond the Identification Thesis; he just as clearly (and just as ringingly) endorses the Identity Thesis. He points out the important "conceptual move" that he is making: it is the move "from the biblical God's self-identification *by* events in time to his identification *with* those events."[19] "Moreover," he says, the "whole argument of the work depends on this move." He "justifies" this move directly: "were God identified by Israel's Exodus or Jesus' Resurrection, without being identified *with* them, the identification would be a revelation other than God himself. The revealing events would be our clues *to* God, but would not *be* God."[20] Jenson will not countenance such results, for "it is precisely this distinction between the god and its revelation that the biblical critique of religion attacks. For the space normal religion leaves between revelation and deity is exactly the space across which we make our idolatrous projections . . . [thus] the doctrine of the Trinity is but a conceptually developed and sustained insistence that God himself is identified by and with the particular plotted sequence of events that make the narrative of Israel and her Christ."[21]

---

15. Jenson, *ST 1*, p. 9.
16. Jenson, *ST 1*, p. 16.
17. Jenson, "Second Locus," p. 115.
18. Jenson, *ST 1*, p. 46.
19. Jenson, *ST 1*, p. 59.
20. Jenson, *ST 1*, p. 59.
21. Jenson, *ST 1*, p. 60.

All this means that God's own identity is constituted in the story of Israel and her Jesus: "since the biblical God can truly be identified by narrative, his hypostatic being, his self-identity, is constituted in dramatic coherence."[22] And so we come to Jenson's conclusion that "the one God is an event; history occurs not only in him but as his being."[23] Jenson is of course aware that "events happen *to* something," and he goes on to say that "what the event happens to is, first, the triune persons." But he continues by fervently forwarding the Identification Thesis, for God is also "what happens to Jesus and the world. That an event happens to something does not entail that this something must be metaphysically or temporally prior to it. God is the event of the world's transformation by Jesus' love, the same love to which the world owes its existence."[24]

C. Toward Clarity: Jenson on the Meaning of Divine Identity

Jenson makes it obvious that any knowledge of God depends radically upon the self-revelation of God in the history of Israel and Jesus. God identifies himself *by* these events; God identifies himself *as* "whoever raised Jesus from the dead." But Jenson goes further. Indeed, he goes much further. God's own identity is bound up with these historical events: God *is* "whatever happens between Jesus and his Father in their Spirit."[25]

Exactly what any of this means is far from obvious, and as it stands, Jenson's attempt at "revisionary metaphysics" stands in need of conceptual clarification.[26] Indeed, standing alone and in such need of further clarification, his proposal of "revisionary metaphysics" is not obviously coherent. Crisp makes this point with reference to Jenson's account of divine temporality. According to Jenson, "God has a narrative-like life that is temporal, and which we may speak of in terms of past, present, and future. However, God's past is identical with the Father (who creates?) and his fu-

---

22. Jenson, *ST 1*, p. 64.

23. Jenson, *ST 1*, p. 221. Jenson here follows his earlier statement that "God is an event. The kind of reality that God has is like that of a kiss or an automobile accident." "Second Locus," p. 165.

24. Jenson, *ST 1*, p. 221.

25. Jenson, *ST 1*, p. 221.

26. Robert W. Jenson, "Response to Watson and Hunsinger," *Scottish Journal of Theology* 55, no. 2 (2002): 230.

ture is identical with the Spirit." Crisp notes that this is "very strange indeed," and he wants to know what this might mean: "why should we think that God's past is identical with the Father, or his future with the Spirit? What does that mean, exactly? In what sense is one person identical with a particular time in the life of God? Surely if all the persons of the Trinity are co-eternal (and necessarily so) it is meaningless to speak of the Father as identical with the past and the Spirit as identical with the future."[27] Jenson's view, in the absence of further clarification, flirts here with incoherence, but Crisp thinks it gets even worse. For Jenson also claims that God's temporality has no duration. According to Jenson, therefore, God "has infinite temporal extension across time, but no past, present or future that are past, present or future to God himself."[28] But how is this view supposed to work? Crisp points out that "it seems obvious that if something is temporal it moves through time from the past to the future via the present (however that is construed). But Jenson's God does not move through time, or at least, Jenson's God does not have a present in which certain things are past and certain things are future to him because nothing recedes into the past or comes to God from the future, according to Jenson. Finally, it seems intuitively obvious that no being that is temporal can constitute its own past and present from its future." This is, as Crisp concludes, "simply incoherent"; standing alone and in need of further clarification, it "makes no sense."[29]

And as with God and time, so also with divine identity. Again, Jenson's view seems to be either meaningless or obviously mistaken if taken on its own in the absence of further clarification. We can conceive quite clearly what it means to be identified *by* certain actions (e.g., God is whoever delivered Israel out of Egypt), but it is much more difficult to know what to make of claims that someone is identified *with* or *as* those actions. To borrow and extend Crisp's example, Jenson is identified *by* reference to his work. We know quite well what it means to say that "Robert Jenson is the author of *Systematic Theology, Volumes 1 and 2.*" But he is *not* to be identified *with* or *as* his work.[30] We simply have no idea of what it means to say "Robert Jenson? Oh, he *is Systematic Theology, Volumes 1 and 2.*" So I sug-

27. Crisp, "Robert Jenson," p. 36.
28. Crisp, "Robert Jenson," p. 42.
29. Crisp, "Robert Jenson," p. 42.
30. See Crisp, "Robert Jenson," p. 40.

gest that, for the sake of charity, we are not to understand Jenson to be saying that God *is* "what happened to Jesus and the world" or "what happens" to Jesus and his Father now; we are not to understand his Identity Thesis as the claim that God just *is* "what happens to Jesus and his Father in their Spirit" and "what happens to Jesus and the world." I suggest that we take such statements as a rhetorically-provocative way of making a slightly different point. Surely a more plausible interpretation of Jenson is this: the actions of God somehow constitute his very identity, and those properties had by "what happens to Jesus and his Father in their Spirit" and "what happens to Jesus and the world" are properties that belong to the identity of the triune God.

Recalling the principle of the Indiscernibility of Identicals,

(InId) For any objects x and y, if x and y are identical, then for any property P, x has P if and only if y has P,

we can see a bit more plainly that Jenson's doctrine of divine identity depends upon this (or something like it). In fact, it is hard to make sense of Jenson's claims without (InId). Reflection on (InId) also helps us see just what Jenson's view entails. If God's "identity is determined in his relation to others,"[31] then God has his identity — is who he is — only as this identity is constituted in and by these relations. If "God" is identical to "what happens to Jesus and his Father in their Spirit," then any and all properties possessed by "God" will also be possessed by "what happens between Jesus and his Father in their Spirit." And, of course, any and all properties possessed by "what happens between Jesus and his Father in their Spirit" will also be possessed by "God." Thus Jesus Christ is not who he is apart from the historical events that transpire between him and his Father; in exactly the same sense God is not God apart from the historical events that transpire between the man Jesus Christ and his Father.

To understand Jenson rightly, it is important to note what he refers to when he speaks of "Jesus." Jenson flatly rejects any notion of *logos asarkos*; when he says "Jesus" he means the historical son of Mary.[32] He does *not*

31. Jenson, *ST 1*, p. 75.

32. For excellent engagement with Jenson on the crucial issue of the preexistence of the Son, see Simon Gathercole, "Pre-existence, and the Freedom of the Son in Creation and Redemption," and Crisp, "Robert Jenson on the Pre-existence of Christ." It should be clear that my sympathies lie with Gathercole and Crisp on these matters.

use the name "Jesus" to refer to the eternal Son of God who became the human son of man in the womb of Mary (much as one might refer to George W. Bush as "a National Guard pilot"; even though we know that the one who was the forty-third president was not yet president while in the National Guard, we can readily and sensibly refer to an earlier temporal point in the life of the one who became president). The important point to be made here is that when Jenson refers to "what happens to Jesus and his Father in their Spirit," he does *not* make reference to some sort of eternal communion of blissful loving relationship. Instead he refers to what transpired in human history between the man Jesus and his Father.[33] So the identity of God is bound up with the identity of the man Jesus; God is not merely revealed or identified *by* Jesus Christ, God *is* whatever happens between *the man Jesus* and his Father. If "God" is identical to "what happens between Jesus and his Father in their Spirit," then all that happens to the man Jesus is part of the identity of God. Properties such as *being born in a shed, being betrayed by Judas Iscariot, being wrongly accused and unjustly sentenced, being beaten and tortured, being killed on a cross,* and *being raised from the dead* are thus (part of) the divine identity. Thus God, it seems, would not be God without them. Human sin — to the depths of its awful perversity, ugliness, and horror — is part of the history and identity of the triune God. Jenson's account of divine identity seems to presuppose (InId), but with this commitment evokes criticisms and worries about his theology.

II. Criticism of Jenson's Account

For Jenson, God's identity is determined by his history. And God's history is bound up with our own. God's history "with us," says Jenson, "is decisively shaped by our betrayal of the 'with us.'"[34] Creation, fall, redemption, and consummation are thus not only the crucial points of human history, somehow they are also the constitution of the divine identity.

---

33. Actually it is a bit more than the human history of the man Jesus; for Jenson, Jesus preexists his own birth in some sense in the people of Israel. Jenson also states that the Son's "eternal birth from the Father eternally precedes his reality as incarnate." *ST 1,* p. 141 n. 85. We have very little idea what this means, however, and understanding is made more difficult by Jenson's views of time and eternity.

34. Jenson, *ST 1,* p. 72.

Jenson's view raises some concerns. Colin E. Gunton worries that Jenson's theology brings us "dangerously near a Hegelian conception of self-realisation through the other."[35] Hunsinger is neither so cautious nor so diplomatic: he thinks Jenson's theology is obviously a version of panentheism, and he says Jenson "gives us a God whose baptism was administered by Hegel. It is Hegel, more than any other, who determines Jenson's view of the trinity."[36] For "although God is not identical with the world, he cannot be fully actual without it. The Hegelian idea that God is metaphysically conditioned by something other than himself, that God cannot be God without the world, that God must be conceived in fundamental dependence on his creation — this is Jenson's idea of a properly 'baptized' God."[37] Similarly, in commenting on Jenson's dalliance with Hegelianism, Hart warns that "we flirt here with calamity."[38]

Now there is good reason to associate Jenson with the metaphysics and philosophical theology of Hegel. For not only is Jenson fond of such statements as "God's being, 'into its furthest depths,' is historical,"[39] he also explicitly speaks of "Hegel's truth" and says that to "reclaim [it] for the gospel, we need only a small but drastic amendment: Absolute Consciousness finds its own meaning and self in the *one* historical object, Jesus."[40] But merely to link Jenson with Hegel does not take us very far toward an evaluation of his theology (unless we commit some form of the genetic fallacy), and at any rate Jenson tries to make it clear that God and creatures are truly distinct. The concerns, however, are deep enough to warrant further consideration.

35. Colin E. Gunton, *The Promise of Trinitarian Theology* (Edinburgh: T. & T. Clark, 1991), p. 135.

36. Hunsinger, "Robert Jenson's *Systematic Theology*," p. 175. Hunsinger adds that Jenson's view of the "cross is determined by Socinus and the 'incarnation' by a perfect inversion of Arius." He defines panentheism thus: "while God's being is not exhausted by the world, it is nonetheless in some sense constituted by the world . . . [it is] in some sense constituted by temporal events."

37. Hunsinger, "Robert Jenson's *Systematic Theology*," p. 176. The allusion to the "baptism of God" alludes to Jenson's *Unbaptized God: The Fatal Flaw in Ecumenical Theology* (Minneapolis: Fortress, 1992).

38. Hart, *Beauty of the Infinite*, p. 157.

39. Jenson, *ST 1*, p. 223.

40. Robert W. Jenson, "The Holy Spirit," in *Christian Dogmatics: Volume 2*, ed. Carl E. Braaten and Robert W. Jenson (Philadelphia: Fortress, 1984), p. 169.

A. The "Metaphysical" Problem

Jenson claims that the divine identity "must be constituted precisely in the integration of this abandonment" on the cross and the subsequent resurrection, that "the God of crucifixion and resurrection is one with himself in a moment of supreme dramatic self-transcendence or not at all," and that God "can have no identity except as he meets the temporal end towards which creatures live."[41] This leads some critics to wonder if such a God could possibly be a perfect being who is sovereign and *a se*. What is at stake here is sometimes referred to as the "Sovereignty-Aseity Conviction," the belief that "God is the one reality that exists *a se* (from and of himself) and is dependent on nothing outside himself for his essence and existence."[42]

Hart comes right to the point: if Jenson means "that history is the theater within which God — as absolute mind, or process, or divine event — finds and determines himself as God, there can be no way of convincingly avoiding the conclusion (however vigorously the theologian might deny the implication) that God depends upon creation to be God and that creation exists by necessity (because of some lack in God), so that God is robbed of his true transcendence and creation of its true gratuity."[43]

Jenson might simply reject this entire line of argument by decrying "Perfect Being Theology" as symptomatic of the very thought patterns that he is trying so creatively and desperately to overcome. He simply might admit that his theology cannot speak of divine perfection — and then simply shrug and say that since Scripture does not portray God in this way, he need not do so either.[44] But this would be unfortunate indeed: After all, what is the alternative? That we praise the triune God for being an *imperfect* Being? The doctrine of divine perfection is not dispensed with nearly

---

41. Jenson, *ST 1*, p. 65.

42. Jay Wesley Richards, *The Untamed God: A Philosophical Exploration of Divine Perfection, Simplicity, and Immutability* (Downers Grove, Ill.: InterVarsity, 2003), p. 33. Alvin Plantinga, who is well known for his criticism of the doctrine of divine simplicity, says that the "sovereignty-aseity intuition . . . must be taken with real seriousness." *Does God Have a Nature?* (Milwaukee: Marquette University Press, 1980), p. 34.

43. Hart, *Beauty of the Infinite*, p. 157.

44. Jenson states that "Aristotle himself regarded historical contingency as an ontological deficit. . . . But since God is identified by contingencies, Aristotle's prejudice need not hinder us. Why should not commitment in a history instead be an ontological *perfection?*" *ST 1*, p. 64. It seems to me that Jenson here (as elsewhere) conflates identification with identity and commitment with dependence.

so easily as is often supposed,[45] and at any rate it is not obviously opposed to the biblical faith.[46] As Hart argues, Anselm's "standard" is one "whose provenance may not exactly be biblical, but whose logic ultimately is, and that is a rule that teaches us to recognize when we are speaking of God and when we are speaking of a god, when we are directing our mind to the transcendent source of being and when we are fabricating for ourselves a metaphysical myth."[47]

The "metaphysical problem" looms large, and Jenson's theology needs adjustment to avoid outright self-contradiction. Either God really is "above all else sovereign and free," the being who is *not* dependent on creation and its sin, or he *is* dependent on the world for his identity.

As Hart sees things, the importance of this matter should not be underestimated. He draws out the contrast between the classical position (that God's being is truly *manifested* — but not *constituted* — by his action in history) and Jenson's revision: according to classical Christian theology, "God's infinitely accomplished life of love is that trinitarian movement of his being . . . [that is] an indestructible *actus purus* endlessly more dynamic than any mere motion of change could be. In him there is neither variableness nor shadow of turning because he is wholly free, wholly God as Father, Son, and Spirit, wholly alive, and wholly love" (p. 167). Even the cross of Christ, says Hart, "does not determine the nature of divine love but rather manifests it, because there is a more original outpouring of God that — without needing to submit itself to the order of sacrifice that builds crosses — always already surpasses every abyss of godforsakenness and pain that sin can impose between the world and God: an outpouring that is in its proper nature indefectible happiness" (p. 167). Only this, Hart argues, can ground both the sheer transcendence of God and the utter gratuity of creation, for

> the freedom of God from ontic determination is the ground of creation's goodness: precisely because creation is uncompelled, unneces-

---

45. Witness the return of the language of divine perfection in Moltmann's defense of Trinitarian panentheism. *The Trinity and the Kingdom: The Doctrine of God* (Minneapolis: Fortress, 1993), pp. 106-7.

46. In the interest of full disclosure, I here confess my sympathies to the view of Thomas V. Morris, *Anselmian Explorations: Essays in Philosophical Theology* (Notre Dame, Ind.: University of Notre Dame Press, 1987), pp. 10-25.

47. Hart, *Beauty of the Infinite*, p. 164. Page references to Hart have been placed in the text.

sary, and finally other than that dynamic life of coinherent love whereby God is God, it can reveal how God is the God he is; precisely because creation is needless, an object of delight that shares God's love without contributing anything that God does not already possess in infinite eminence, creation reflects the divine life, which is one of delight and fellowship and love; precisely because creation is not part of God . . . it is an analogy of the divine; in being the object of God's love without any cause but the generosity of that love, creation reflects in its beauty that eternal delight that is the divine *perichoresis* and that obeys no necessity but divine love itself. (p. 158)

God's identity as triune — as the utterly secure divine life of self-giving and receiving love — is what enables God to be maximally perfect while loving creation with a free, gracious, and steadfast love that reflects and reveals the love that God *is.* But as Hart sees things, Jenson's position undercuts this; his Identity Thesis renders God dependent upon creation for his own identity.

B. The "Moral" Problem

But there is yet another problem. Hart notes that "if, speculatively, Jenson's theology seems to fail Anselm's test, morally it seems to fail" as well (p. 165). The problem, according to Hart, is actually twofold: "the first problem with such a formulation is that, in depicting God as one who in any sense intends sin and evil, it reduces God to a being whose nature is not love (even if at the end of the day he turns out to be loving, having completed his odyssey of self-discovery, for a being can possess love only as an attribute); and one might justifiably wonder if a God who chooses himself . . . over against the creatures who suffer the adventure of his self-determination should evoke love in return" (pp. 164-65). And the second problem is at least as serious:

> if God's identity is constituted in his triumph over evil, then evil belongs eternally to his identity, and his goodness is not goodness as such but a reaction, an activity that requires the goad of evil to come into full being. All of history is the horizon of this drama . . . all of history *is* this identity: every painful death of a child, every casual act of brutality, all

war, famine, pestilence, disease, murder . . . all are moments in the identity of God, resonances within the event of his being, aspects of the occurrence of his essence: all of this is the crucible in which God comes into his elected reality. (p. 165)

C. The Christological Problem

Jenson's account of the preexistence of Christ, and his Christology more generally, have attracted much attention and drawn stout criticism. Some critics think his doctrine of the preexistence of Christ is of dubious coherence. Gathercole is convinced that "Jenson's system suffers from incoherence at this point,"[48] and Crisp concludes that "when we put Jenson's account of divine eternity side-by-side with what he says about the preexistence of Christ, we end up with a view of God, time, and Incarnation that is simply incoherent."[49]

Gathercole is convinced that Jenson's view "clearly suffers from a lack of *correspondence* as well — correspondence with the canonical witness."[50] Gathercole argues that Jenson's account falters badly here: it can account for neither an adequate interpretation of such passages as Philippians 2 or 1 Corinthians 8 nor the overall canonical witness to the freedom of the Son in creation, incarnation, and redemption. Anything less than real, personal preexistence is simply insufficient to account for the biblical data, and Jenson's theology does not quite affirm real, personal preexistence.

This leads to yet another concern: that of correspondence with creedal orthodoxy. Gathercole, for example, recognizes that Jenson flatly denies charges of Arianism, but he thinks nonetheless that "the plain sense of Jenson's language might imply that he is falling into Arianism."[51] Similarly, Hunsinger charges Jenson with exhibiting Monophysite, adoptionist, and Arian tendencies in his doctrine of the incarnation.[52]

---

48. Gathercole, "Pre-existence," p. 48.
49. Crisp, "Robert Jenson," p. 42.
50. Gathercole, "Pre-existence," p. 48.
51. Gathercole, "Pre-existence," p. 45.
52. Hunsinger, "Robert Jenson's *Systematic Theology.*"

III. Evaluating Jenson's Theses

Surely these are strong charges. What are we to make of them? Is Jenson's Identity Thesis really so problematic? And what are we to make of his Identification Thesis? Considering the latter first, I shall argue that we should accept with gratitude Jenson's insistence on the Identification Thesis, but that, without further modification (or perhaps only clarification), we should hold the Identity Thesis at arm's length.

A. The Identification Thesis Affirmed

Jenson's emphasis on

(IdT1) God is to be identified by his revelatory speech and action

should be welcomed and embraced. It is made with great rhetorical force by other Trinitarian theologians of the twentieth century.[53] And surely Crisp is correct that no "orthodox theologian" would deny Jenson's point "that the *biblical picture* should govern what we say about the divine life, not some prior metaphysical commitments."[54] But Jenson's point is nonetheless one that needs to be heard.

Recognizing the importance of Jenson's Identification Thesis does not entail that there is nothing of value to be gained from what is sometimes called "the Anselmian method." Ronald J. Feenstra points out how the Anselmian method and the Identification Thesis might be complementary. "The place to start," he says, "is Scripture, which describes God as unsurpassably great, powerful, all-knowing, sovereign over all creation (that is, not confined to certain localities), without beginning of days or end of life, dependent for existence on no one outside God, creator of every non-divine being, perfectly good, perfectly just, and more loving than the most gracious father or mother."[55] So where does the Anselmian

---

53. E.g., Karl Barth, "The meaning of His deity — the only true deity in the New Testament sense — cannot be gathered from any notion of supreme, absolute, non-worldly being. It can be learned only from what took place in Christ." *Church Dogmatics* IV/1 (Edinburgh: T. & T. Clark, 1956), p. 177.

54. Crisp, "Robert Jenson," p. 37.

55. Ronald J. Feenstra, "A Kenotic Christological Method for Understanding the Divine

method come in? Anselm "offers a helpful principle by which to express such attributes: God is that than which none greater can be thought. The Anselmian method, then, is to attribute to God great-making properties, that is, properties that it is better to have than to lack, and then to say that God has these properties to a superlative degree." And how does the Anselmian method fit together with the Identification Thesis? Anselmian theology attempts to summarize as well as develop the biblical depiction of God, thus it "describes God as the greatest possible being who possesses great-making properties such as maximal power (omnipotence), knowledge of every truth (omniscience), and perfect goodness. But Anselm's method can only be a guide, not the final word on the divine attributes."[56] In other words, the Anselmian method can be legitimate and indeed helpful, but it can also be misleading and even dangerous if it is not directed and corrected by what Thomas V. Morris calls "revelational control."[57] Jenson's insistence on the importance and centrality of the Identification Thesis is welcome indeed.

B. The Identity Thesis: The Central Issue Clarified

As we have seen, Jenson appears to presuppose (InId). And well he should. As Alvin Plantinga says, it is "a principle none sounder than which can be conceived."[58] But Jenson appears as well to assume that this commitment to (InId) must lead to the conclusion that if any of the properties related to divine action were different than they indeed are, then the divine identity would be different as well. In other words, he seems to conclude that (InId) entails what is sometimes called the "Theory of Worldbound Individuals" (TWI). This is not surprising; Richards points out that many philosophers who endorse (InId) "deny that individuals exist in more than one world."[59]

Attributes," in *Exploring Kenotic Christology: The Self-Emptying of God*, ed. C. Stephen Evans (Oxford: Oxford University Press, 2006), p. 163.

56. Feenstra, "A Kenotic Christological Method," p. 163.

57. Thomas V. Morris, *Our Idea of God: An Introduction to Philosophical Theology* (Downers Grove, Ill.: InterVarsity, 1991), p. 43; cf. Morris, *Anselmian Explorations*, p. 25.

58. Alvin Plantinga, "Transworld Identity or Worldbound Individuals?" in *The Possible and the Actual: Readings in the Metaphysics of Modality*, ed. Michael J. Loux (Ithaca, N.Y.: Cornell University Press, 1979), p. 150.

59. Richards, *The Untamed God*, p. 78.

It seems as though Jenson is following the move of the idealists who argued that all relational properties are essential to the things that have them.[60] As summarized by Plantinga, (TWI) states that

> For any object x and relational property P, if x has P, then for any object y, if there is a world in which y lacks P, then y is distinct from P.[61]

Now Jenson may not (or may) have a vested interest in whether or not this is true of just "any object," but much of what he says about divine identity would appear to endorse (TWI). "History occurs not only in him but as his being"; God is "what happens to Jesus and the world."[62] God "can have no identity except as he meets the temporal end towards which creatures live."[63]

As we shall see, Jenson's apparent endorsement of (TWI) is as unfortunate as it is understandable. But much of what Jenson says about divine identity appears to take this route; much of what he says seems to assume or presuppose (TWI). What are we to make of his account of divine identity in this light?

C. The Identity Thesis: The Metaphysical Problem Revisited

Hart charges that there is "no way of convincingly avoiding the conclusion (however vigorously the theologian might deny the implication) that God depends upon creation to be God and that creation exists by necessity (because of some lack in God), so that God is robbed of his true transcendence and creation of its true gratuity."[64] As we have seen, Hart states his criticisms with great rhetorical force. But what Hart says about the "metaphysical problem" is also appropriate, and understanding Jenson's claims in the light of a proper understanding of identity demonstrates this. Again, if the triune God truly is numerically identical with "what happens between Jesus and his Father in their Spirit," then all properties possessed by

---

60. On this see Alvin Plantinga, *The Nature of Necessity* (Oxford: Oxford University Press, 1974), p. 89. Plantinga refers here to the idealists of the late nineteenth and early twentieth centuries.

61. Plantinga, *The Nature of Necessity*, p. 90.

62. Jenson, *ST 1*, p. 221.

63. Jenson, *ST 1*, p. 65.

64. Hart, *Beauty of the Infinite*, p. 157.

"what happens between Jesus and his Father in their Spirit" are — *and must be* — possessed by the triune God. God's identity is, to use Jenson's word, "constituted" by these historical events.

For according to (TWI), all divine properties would be essential divine properties. Consider such properties as *being the Creator of the world in which Adam and Eve sin by eating the forbidden fruit,*[65] *being unjustly accused and sentenced, being tortured and killed on a cross,* and *forsaking and being forsaken on the cross.* If this is the correct interpretation of Jenson, God would not — and *could not* — be who he is if he did not have these properties. God would not be who he is if Adam and Eve had not sinned, if Judas had not betrayed Christ, if Christ had not been sentenced to such a grisly death and executed in such a horrific manner, or if he had not uttered the cry of dereliction from the cross. In Jenson's language, God is not only "what happens between Jesus and his Father in the Spirit," God is also "what happens to Jesus and the world."[66] If God's own identity is so constituted by this world, then we are left to conclude that God is in some strong sense dependent on it. For God would not — indeed God *could not* — be God without this world. And such a conclusion is, of course, hard to square with belief in divine perfection. As Hart concludes, "this means that this God fails the test of Anselm's *id quo cogitari nequit.*"[67]

(TWI) compromises divine perfection. Nor does Counterpart Theory offer any hope here. David Lewis makes clear his motivation for putting forth Counterpart Theory. It is an alternative to the theory of transworld identity: "the best thing to do, I think, is to escape the problems of transworld identity by insisting that there is nothing that inhabits more than one world." On Lewis's account, "something has for *counterparts* at a given world those things existing there that resemble it closely enough in important respects of intrinsic quality and extrinsic relations, and that resemble it no less closely than do other things existing there,"[68] and something has for "essential properties" those properties that it "has in common with all its counterparts."[69] For apart from the radically counterintuitive claim that

65. By "world" here I mean "possible world" in what I take to be a standard sense: a possible world is a maximally consistent state of affairs.

66. Jenson, *ST 1*, p. 221.

67. Hart, *Beauty of the Infinite*, p. 164.

68. David Lewis, "Counterpart Theory and Quantified Modal Logic," in *The Possible and the Actual*, p. 126.

69. Lewis, "Counterpart Theory," p. 127.

there in fact *are* counterpart gods in other possible worlds, Counterpart Theory itself is unable to avoid the conclusion that all properties are had essentially.[70] I cannot see how this might even possibly appeal to Jenson, so consideration of Counterpart Theory need not detain us further. It offers no way forward, and Jenson is left with the dilemma: either accept an alternative understanding of (InId), or come to grips with what I've laid out as the metaphysical problem.

To his credit, Jenson does want to protect divine freedom and sovereignty while also insisting that the world really matters to God's own identity. But as things stand, it is not clear that he can have his cake and eat it too. If God really is free to choose between worlds or to refrain from actualizing a world with creatures, then God's identity as such cannot be constituted by divine action (in this world). If God is free in any robust sense, then Jenson's Identity Thesis collapses. If God is not free, however, then God is dependent upon creation to be who he is. Neither way looks all that promising for Jenson's theology.

Even if this move were to help Jenson, however, he could not make it with consistency. For to allow divine freedom to this extent would be to deny the Identity Thesis. Hart points out that the assertion that God could have been the very God he is sans creatures

> calls attention to an instability in Jenson's system: it is simply prima facie false that if God achieves his identity in the manner Jenson describes, he could have been the same God by other means, without the world. The logic of such a proposition can never span the gulf between either and or, because in this case the gulf is absolute: if God *could* be God otherwise, then he already *is* God otherwise; this is who God is, which history can manifest but never determine. If, however, the particular determinations of history are also determinations of God — as he "chooses" to be God — then there can be no identity of God as *this* God apart from the specific contours of *this* history.[71]

Once again, reflection on the standard account of identity shows that Hart is correct in his assessment. For if the triune God already has a stable identity, then *this* identity is *not* constituted in "what happens between Jesus and his Father in their Spirit" and "what happens to Jesus and the

---

70. For the argument see Plantinga, *The Nature of Necessity*, pp. 98-120.
71. Hart, *Beauty of the Infinite*, pp. 162-63.

world."[72] If, on the other hand, the divine identity in fact *is* so constituted, then *this* identity could not have been otherwise. Recalling again (InId), we can see that if the triune God has such a property as "possibly not being what happens to Jesus and the world," then "what happens to Jesus and the world" must also have this property. But "what happens to Jesus and the world" just *is* the divine identity. And it is hard indeed to know how even to make sense of such a statement as "'what happens to Jesus and the world' has the property of 'possibly not being what happens to Jesus and the world.'" Either such properties as "being the Creator of the world in which Adam and Eve sin by eating the forbidden fruit," "being unjustly accused and sentenced," "being tortured and killed on a cross," and "forsaking and being forsaken on a cross" are essential divine properties, or they are not. According to (TWI), such properties indeed are essential divine properties. According to traditional orthodoxy, they are not. But they are either one or the other; they are not both at once.

D. The Identity Thesis: The Moral Problem Again

Hart claims that the God of Jenson's theology is not worship-worthy, for "if God's identity is constituted in his triumph over evil, then evil belongs eternally to his identity, and his goodness is not goodness as such but a reaction, an activity that requires the goad of evil to come into full being."[73] Surely Hart is making some very strong claims here. But a moment's reflection on the nature of identity shows that his criticisms, however strongly worded, are on target. Again, if the triune God is numerically identical with "what happens to Jesus and the world," then any properties had by "what happens to Jesus and the world" must also be had by the triune God. If every horrific event (and the properties associated with such events) — every "painful death of a child, every casual act of brutality, all war, pestilence, disease, [and] murder" — is part of "what happens to Jesus and the world," then these horrific events are also part of the triune God (p. 165). They are part of the divine identity; they are essential divine properties. God would not be — and *could* not be — God without them. God is thus dependent on the vicissitudes and vio-

---

72. Recall Jenson's denial of *logos asarkos*.
73. Hart, *Beauty of the Infinite*, p. 165. Page numbers have been placed in the text.

lence of this world to be who he is — the divine identity itself is forged in the fires of sin and death.

Hart reminds us that classical Christian theology holds that "within the plenitude" of the divine life "no contrary motion can fabricate an interval of negation, because it is the infinite possibility of every creaturely motion or act; no pathos is possible for God because a pathos is, by definition, a finite instance of change visited upon a passive subject, actualizing some potential, whereas God's love is pure positivity and pure activity. His love is an infinite peace and thus needs no violence to shape it, no death over which to triumph" (p. 167). But once again, we see that Jenson's Identity Thesis will not allow such an affirmation. Thus we are left with the conclusion that God "is love" only in the contingent history of "what happens between Jesus and his Father in their Spirit" — God "is love" only in the violence of human history that culminates in the cry of dereliction from the cross of Calvary. We then are left with the conclusion that God "is love" only contingently. His "goodness is not goodness as such but a reaction, an activity that requires the goad of evil to come into full being."

Hart is right to point out that "Jenson says and intends none of this" (p. 166). Jenson does not state that the divine identity is constituted as love only contingently; he does not say that evil belongs to the being of God. But Hart is also right to insist that "we must ask of him and every theologian . . . whether, when the logic of their theology is pressed on toward its ultimate ends, it can arrive at any other end" (p. 166). What I have argued here is that, when analyzed in terms of identity conditions and understood to endorse (TWI), Jenson's theology cannot arrive at any other end.

E. The Identity Thesis: The Christological Problem Examined

What are we to make of the criticisms of Jenson's Christology? Consider what is perhaps the most serious of the charges against Jenson on this point: the worry that his theology is Arian. If indeed Jenson's account of divine identity presupposes (InId) (as surely seems to be the case), and if this is taken to entail (TWI) (as much of what Jenson says seems to indicate), then the problems with Jenson's Christology are even worse than Gathercole, Crisp, and Hunsinger make them out to be.

If the Son is a worldbound individual, then the Son has all of his properties essentially. Since he has the property of "being incarnate," then he has this property essentially. This seems to cohere fairly well with Jenson's views of the *communicatio idiomatum* and of the identity of Jesus. But if this is true, then the Son has this property — and has it essentially — while the Father does not have it. And surely it is true that if the Son has essential properties that differ from those of the Father, then the Son is of a different essence than the Father. Thus the direct denial of *homoousios* is entailed by Jenson's doctrine.

But the problem is even worse. Again, if the Son is a worldbound individual, then the Son has all of his properties essentially. Given the fact (authorized by the canonical witness) that Jesus Christ is subordinate to the Father in this world, we are left to conclude that the Son is essentially subordinate to the Father. The Son has the property *being subordinate to the Father*, and the Son has this property essentially. But the Father, of course, does not have this property. So not only would it be true that the Son is of a different essence than the Father; it would also be true that the Son is essentially *subordinate to* the Father.

In conclusion, it should be clear that the worries about Arianism are well grounded. If Jenson's doctrine of divine identity is to be understood as entailing or endorsing (TWI), then the Father and Son just *are* of different essences, and the Son just *is* essentially subordinate to the Father. Is this not a version of Arianism? Indeed, what else could it be? We are left to hope that, despite appearances, Jenson does not endorse (TWI).

F. The Identity Thesis Once More

Jenson's Identity Thesis,

(IdT2) God is identical to his revelatory speech and action,

is, I have argued, beset with both ambiguities and problems. But perhaps there is a way to rework it so that the desiderata that motivate Jenson's theology may be satisfied without encountering the problems that beset his Identity Thesis. Perhaps he need not be interpreted as endorsing (TWI).

For, as we have seen, Jenson does want to insist upon some element of divine freedom, and he makes it clear that this is important to him. Despite the fact that he does not tackle it head-on, Jenson does seem to see that there might be some sort of problem lurking here. Thus he says that "presumably God could have been himself on different terms, established in his identity without reference to us or the time he makes for us, and so without confronting the death which closes our stories in that time."[74] Or "it might not have been so. God might have been the God he is without this world to happen to."[75] Taken this way, to understand his affirmation that "in the present connection we may also say: God is what happens to Jesus and the world," we must interpret the "in the present connection" merely to refer to the way that things actually have worked out in the actual world. Perhaps things could have been different and God could still have been the triune God, but in the actual world in which we find ourselves, this is indeed the way things have worked out.

Now it is hard to know just how to take Jenson here. On one hand, he seems to recognize the need to preserve a more robust account of divine freedom and sovereignty: God is "above all free and sovereign."[76] But on the other hand, he has very little patience with such considerations. "But of this possibility," he says, "we can assert only the sheer counterfactual; about *how* God would then have been the same God as we now know, we can say nothing whatever."[77] For having answered such "contrary-to-fact questions themselves, we must resolutely say no more. About *how* God could as the same God have been other than *Jesus* the Son and *his* Father and *their* Spirit, or about what that would have been like, we can know or guess nothing whatsoever."[78] Jenson appears to see the need to preserve some notion of divine freedom, but he is also rather dismissive of any further considerations.

A possible reading is this: Jenson means to say that God could have chosen to actualize a different (but near) possible world. Maybe God is not restricted to *this* possible world; perhaps there is a galaxy of possible worlds any of which are feasible for God and that are relevantly similar: they all have the requisite amount of sin and grace needed for God's identity to be what it is. If this is what Jenson intends to say, then it is not at all clear that he can say this with any consistency. For if the identity of God really is bound up with the history of the world in the way that Jenson seems to think it is, then the divine identity is different if the history of the world

74. Jenson, *ST 1*, p. 65.
75. Jenson, *ST 1*, p. 221.
76. Jenson, *ST 1*, p. 75.
77. Jenson, *ST 1*, p. 65.
78. Jenson, *ST 1*, p. 141; see also p. 221.

varied at all. Nor is it obvious that the situation is improved (nor is it clear that he avoids Hegelianism by such a move).[79] For God would still be dependent on a world of creatures and sin to be who he is, so the charge of panentheism still stands. The fact that God is not dependent on *this* world is not very comforting; if God's identity depends at all upon creatures and their sin and redemption for its constitution, then God is nonetheless dependent on creation to be who he is. But at least Jenson wants to maintain some notion of divine freedom and sovereignty, and perhaps there is another way forward.

Recall an important motivating factor for Jenson's theses. He wants to insist upon the sheer goodness and reliability of God: God protects us from our idolatrous imaginations and projections, and he does so by the revelation of himself in the life of Israel's Jesus. The "true God" knows we project our values onto himself and so conceive him idolatrously, and is unmoved by this childishness. He is intent on giving us new values and contravening our idolatry.[80] It is this concern that leads Jenson from the Identification Thesis to the Identity Thesis, for "if God were identified by Israel's Exodus or Jesus' Resurrection, without being identified *with* them, the identification would be a revelation ontologically other than God himself. The revealing events would be our clues *to* God, but would not *be* God."[81] And this, of course, leaves an opening for idolatry: "it is precisely this distinction between the god and its revelation that the biblical critique of religion attacks. For the space normal religion leaves between deity and itself is exactly the space across which we make our idolatrous projections."[82] But God loves us

---

79. According to Brian Leftow, according to Hegel "the existence of God strongly depends on the existence of *some* world, but weakly depends on the existence and precise nature of *this* world." "God and the World in Hegel and Whitehead," in *Hegel and Whitehead: Contemporary Perspectives on Systematic Philosophy,* ed. George R. Lucas, Jr. (Albany: State University of New York Press, 1986), p. 262. Hunsinger cites this passage and comments further on Hegel's view: "although God is not identical with the world, he cannot be fully actual without it." "Robert Jenson's *Systematic Theology,*" p. 176. It seems that this is exactly what the proposed interpretation of Jenson would amount to.

80. Jenson, *ST 1,* p. 53. His antipathy toward (what he sees as) speculative theology that is divorced from revelation is evidenced in his negative comments on "Reinvigorated English-language 'theism,' (which is) often somewhat oddly related to the Christian faith it claims to defend." *ST 2,* p. 8 n. 35. Jenson labels Richard Swinburne's *The Christian God* (Oxford: Oxford University Press, 1994) a "truly bizarre case."

81. Jenson, *ST 1,* p. 59.

82. Jenson, *ST 1,* p. 59.

far too much to leave us prey to our idolatrous imaginings, so he delivers us from them by his revelation of himself. God reveals himself as the one who rescues his people from oppression, as the one who is incarnate, and as the one who raises Jesus from the dead. There simply is no other God.

Jenson's reminder that God is gracious to deliver us from the idolatry to which we are so prone is well taken. Unfortunately, however, he weakens his case by overstatement. He makes it seem as though on one hand we would be left with only "clues" or "pointers" to God while on the other hand we have God truly identical with his "personal self-introduction."[83] But this seems to be a false dilemma; it does not follow from the fact that revelation is God's "personal self-introduction" either that God is some-how strictly identical *to* the action of introducing himself or that the prop-erty of "introducing himself personally to Moses" is an essential divine property. Moreover, it is glaringly obvious that idolatry continued in the life of the people whom God rescued in the exodus (and in life today), and it is less than obvious to know how we are to account for this depressing fact if Jenson is correct in insisting that God's "personal self-introduction" delivers the people of God from such a threat.

But perhaps there is a way to accommodate (at least much of) Jenson's concern without resorting to the Identity Thesis. Many metaphysicians and logicians recognize that Leibniz's Law of the Indiscernibility of Identicals,

> (InId) For any objects x and y, if x and y are identical, then for any property P, x has P if and only if y has P,

can be interpreted in a way that is extremely restrictive. In fact, such an in-terpretation is overly restrictive. It cannot account either for the reality of change through time or for transworld identity, and, as we have seen, to give up transworld identity causes all sorts of theological problems.

But the problem is even worse. For even if Jenson were able to defuse the worry about transworld identity, there would be an additional worry. (InId) requires Jane to have the same properties at t_1 (time 1) as she does at t_2. But this clearly rules out change through time; if Jane has different properties at t_2 than she did at t_1, then the Jane of t_2 is not identical to the Jane of t_1. As Jay Wesley Richards puts it, if (InId) "were necessary to preserve the identity of

83. Jenson, *ST 1*, p. 60.

individuals, then change through time, no matter how trivial, would destroy identity . . . the proponent (of (InId)), then, seems committed not only to world-bound individuals, but to 'instant' or time-bound individuals as well."[84] Central to Jenson's doctrine of God is his claim that God is temporal, so the challenge looms large. If "whoever rescued Israel from Egypt at t1" has different properties than "whoever raised Jesus from the dead at t2," then "whoever raised Jesus from the dead at t2" is *not* identical to "whoever rescued Israel from Egypt at t1." And this, of course, is exactly *not* what Jenson wants to say. Holding to (InId) would mean compromising the Identity Thesis, while rejecting (InId) out of hand would make it hard to know how Jenson's claims about divine "identity" might be interpreted.

But there is yet reason to be optimistic: (InId) need not be taken in this overly restrictive way. What if we were to qualify (InId) to account for identity across time and worlds? Michael J. Loux and others have suggested that we qualify (InId) to

(InId*) For any objects x and y, if x and y are identical, then for any property, P, any world, W, and any time, t, x has P in W at t if and only if y has P in W at t.[85]

Adopting (InId*) (rather than (InId)) avoids the criticisms of transworld identity. As Loux concludes, "identity across worlds turns out to be no more problematic than the idea of identity across times."[86] When we add the insight that some properties are "world-indexed," we are armed with what we need to move forward.[87]

Jenson could say that God has transworld identity; he could easily say that the triune God has essential divine properties. As essential properties, these are properties possessed by God in all possible worlds. God possesses the divine attributes essentially; in all possible worlds God is omnipotent, omniscient, omnibenevolent, etc.[88] Jenson might also say that God has

---

84. Richards, *The Untamed God*, p. 78.

85. Loux, introduction to *The Possible and the Actual*, pp. 42-43.

86. Loux, introduction to *The Possible and the Actual*, p. 43.

87. Socrates has the property of being-snubnosed-in-W; he also has the property of being-not-snubnosed-in-W^*. These properties are "world-indexed"; the former is indexed to W, while the latter is indexed to W^*. See Plantinga, *The Nature of Necessity*, pp. 62-65.

88. Or, to accommodate doubt in ontological arguments, we might say that God has these divine attributes in all possible worlds in which he exists.

some properties accidentally; for instance, perhaps such properties as "being the Creator of the world in which Adam and Eve sin by eating the forbidden fruit" and "being tortured and killed on a cross" are had by God in some possible worlds but not in others. They are world-indexed properties, and there are possible worlds in which they are not possessed by God.

Jenson might worry that this would violate his commitment to the faithfulness and goodness of God — what, he might ask, are we to make of those worlds in which people are oppressed but where God does not intervene? What are we to make of those worlds in which there is sin but no salvation? But while I appreciate such a concern, I think it is misplaced here. For we could readily affirm, say, that the divine Son has the property *being the incarnate mediator for the sins of W* (where *W* is the actual world). And although the divine Son is actually incarnate only in *W* (and in the galaxy of worlds in which there are sinful humans in need of a mediator), the Son has the property of "being-the-incarnate-mediator-in-*W*" in all possible worlds.[89] But, the defender of Jenson might persist, are there not possible worlds in which God abandons his creatures to oppression, evil, and suffering? Perhaps this is true in the broadly logical sense, but even if it were, all one would need to do to avoid the undesirable conclusion would be to draw a distinction between possible worlds and feasible worlds, and then say that some galaxies of possible worlds are broadly logically possible while other galaxies are feasible, and then include the galaxies of possible worlds in which God *does* take action on behalf of his creatures in the realm of those that are feasible for God.[90] Thus armed, we could affirm that God is essentially good (thus satisfying a fairly obvious desideratum for Jenson) while also protecting belief in the Sovereignty-Aseity Conviction (thus satisfying a desideratum that unfortunately is not so obvious in Jenson but that I have argued should be).

IV. Conclusion

A defender of Jenson might respond that these criticisms are simply inappropriate for Jenson's project. Jenson states forthrightly that "the whole of

---

89. I here assume actualism.

90. For helpful discussion of these matters, see Thomas P. Flint, "The Problem of Divine Freedom," *American Philosophical Quarterly* 20 (1983): 255-64; Flint, *Divine Providence: The Molinist Account* (Ithaca, N.Y.: Cornell University Press, 1998), pp. 51-59.

my systematics is one aspect of an effort of revisionary metaphysics, aimed at allowing one to say things about God that scripture seems to require but that inherited metaphysics inhibits. The attempt is to revise certain inherited deep patterns of thought, partly by explicit proposal and partly by treating the material topics within the emerging new patterns."[91] Jenson is aware that there is a "risk" involved in such an attempt: "some readers will not allow the project on its own terms but will simply carry on in the assumption that their inherited construal of reality is the only one possible and so must after all be that of the writer; or, if they notice deviations will assume that these must derive from some — undesirable — variant of the same inherited construal, and must be classifiable as 'Hegelian' or 'existentialist' or whatever." Perhaps the defender of Jenson would charge that this is exactly what my criticisms amount to, for to analyze and judge Jenson's account of identity according to classical identity (as I have done) is to miss the point.

But I hope not. I appreciate Jenson's concern to give priority to theological concerns and his insistence that we must say what "scripture seems to require" (even if this is made difficult by "inherited metaphysics"), and I am quite sympathetic to his goal of "revising certain inherited deep patterns of thought."[92] But to say that one is attempting a revisionary project does not obviously serve as a shield that insulates the project from analysis, scrutiny, or critique. I am simply trying to make sense of what Jenson is proposing, and since he does not offer full explanations of what he means, I am using the tools that are available.

So what are we to make of Jenson's proposals? Are they, as some critics have charged, at best entirely meaningless and incoherent? At worst is his theology home to numerous nefarious theories long held at arm's length or even deemed heretical by the church catholic?[93] There is still something puzzling about the aims and goals of Jenson's project: on one hand, he presents his work as a seriously ecumenical theology, one that is consonant with the deep and rich heritage of the church catholic. On the other hand,

---

91. Jenson, "Response," p. 230.

92. Jenson, "Response," p. 230.

93. Hunsinger, for example, charges Jenson with drifting to(ward) a Socianian doctrine of the atonement; with exhibiting Monophysite, adoptionist, and Arian tendencies in his doctrine of the incarnation; with somehow managing to advance both modalistic and tritheistic as well as subordinationist tendencies; and with promoting Hegelian panentheism in general. "Robert Jenson's *Systematic Theology.*"

however, he claims to be offering something that is metaphysically revolutionary. If Gathercole's claims that Jenson's theology does not correspond to the canonical narrative are correct, and if the criticisms of Hunsinger and Crisp that Jenson's work does not cohere well with the broad Christian tradition are sound, then just what does Jenson's theology have going for it? If his view is so ontologically revolutionary (and virtually the entire Christian tradition erred at the most crucial points), then he should give up his claims to classical orthodoxy. Or if his views really are in line with Scripture and tradition, then he has some explaining to do.

Despite this puzzlement, however, we have gained some ground through reflection on Jenson's account of divine identity. While I appreciate Jenson's insistence on the Identification Thesis, in this chapter I have argued that Jenson's account of divine identity is beset with problems and truly in need of help. If Jenson's doctrine of divine identity is taken to endorse (TWI) — as in many places it appears to (e.g., God "can have no identity except as he meets the temporal end toward which creatures live")[94] — then it makes God dependent upon creation, makes evil a necessary element both of this world and of God's own life, and produces a Christology that compromises the doctrine of *homoousios*. I have argued further that Jenson need not endorse (TWI) in order to account for divine identity (and do so in a way that is consistent both with (InId) and his admirable desire to insist on the utter reliability and faithfulness of God). Clarification may be forthcoming, and modification is surely possible. But in the absence of such midcourse correction, I conclude that, as it stands, Jenson's account of divine identity is fatally flawed. We should be grateful for Jenson's insistent reminders about the priority of divine revelation, but we should reject the Identity Thesis.

---

94. Jenson, *ST 1*, p. 65.

CHAPTER FIVE

Moltmann's Perichoresis:
Either Too Much or Not Enough

J ürgen Moltmann is a towering figure in contemporary Trinitarian theology. John Cooper says he is "probably the most widely known and
popular contemporary Protestant theologian." Veli-Matti Kärkkäinen refers to him as a "key figure in the recent renaissance of trinitarian doctrine." Stanley J. Grenz and Roger E. Olson think he "has done more than
anyone since Karl Barth to revitalize the doctrine of the Trinity in contemporary theology," and they call him the "best known expositor" of this re-
newal of Trinitarian theology in "the English-speaking world."[1]

Central to Moltmann's theological vision is the concept of perichoresis. Perichoresis, as Oliver Crisp notes, often serves as something of a
"theological black box."[2] Initially employed in discussions of the hypostatic union, it later became used for the ontology of the Trinity. It is now
widely used — some would say *abused* — in contemporary theology.[3]
Thomas F. Torrance notes that, after its initial use in christological discussions, it "was then applied to speak of the way in which the three divine

---

1. John W. Cooper, *Panentheism: The Other God of the Philosophers; From Plato to the
Present* (Grand Rapids: Baker Academic, 2006), p. 237; Veli-Matti Kärkkäinen, *The Doctrine
of God: A Global Introduction* (Grand Rapids: Baker Academic, 2004), p. 158; Stanley J. Grenz
and Roger E. Olson, *Twentieth Century Theology: God and the World in a Transitional Age*
(Downers Grove, Ill.: InterVarsity, 1992), pp. 185, 172.

2. Oliver D. Crisp, *Divinity and Humanity: The Incarnation Reconsidered* (Cambridge:
Cambridge University Press, 2007), p. 1.

3. E.g., Randall Otto, "The Use and Abuse of Perichoresis in Recent Theology," *Scottish
Journal of Theology* 54 (2001): 366-84; Karen Kilby, "Perichoresis and Projection: Problems
with Social Doctrines of the Trinity," *New Blackfriars* 81 (2000): 432-45.

Persons mutually dwell in one another and coinhere or inexist in one another while nevertheless remaining other than one another and distinct from one another."[4] It thus "expressed the truth that the Father, the Son and the Holy Spirit are distinctive Persons each with his own incommunicable properties, but that they dwell *in* one another, not only *with* one another, in such an intimate way . . . that their individual characteristics instead of dividing them from one another unite them indivisibly together."[5] Catherine Mowry LaCugna says,

> *Perichoresis* means being-in-one-another, permeation without confusion. . . . While there is no blurring of the individuality of each person, there is also no separation. There is only the communion of love in which each person comes to be (in the sense of *hyparxeos*) what he/she is, entirely with reference to the other. Each person expresses both what he/she is (and, by implication, what the other two are), and at the same time expresses what God is: ecstatic, dynamic, vital. *Perichoresis* provides a dynamic model of persons in communion based on mutuality and interdependence.[6]

The notion of perichoresis is vitally important to Moltmann's theology; he applies it to a wide range of issues. Both his doctrine of the Trinity and his panentheistic account of the God-world relation depend upon it. Unfortunately, however, his employment of the concept is so broad that it runs risks on several fronts. After surveying the uses of perichoresis in Moltmann's theology, I argue that it either does "not enough" or does "too much." If, contrary to Moltmann's critics, perichoresis really does secure divine unity, then it also ties God too closely to the cosmos. In this chapter I make a case that, as it stands, Moltmann's doctrine of perichoresis either fails to exonerate him from the charges of tritheism or else produces pantheism rather than the desired panentheism. Despite these problems, however, I conclude that Moltmann captures an important insight, and I suggest that recent work in analytic philosophical theology might offer a way forward for Moltmann.

---

4. Thomas F. Torrance, *The Christian Doctrine of God: One Being, Three Persons* (Edinburgh: T. & T. Clark, 1996), p. 102.

5. Torrance, *Christian Doctrine of God*, p. 172.

6. Catherine Mowry LaCugna, *God for Us: The Trinity and Christian Life* (New York: HarperSanFrancisco, 1993), p. 271.

I. Moltmann's Doctrine of Perichoresis

It would be difficult to overstate the importance of perichoresis for Moltmann's theology. Perichoresis functions as the overarching and underpinning motif that holds his theology together. It is central to his understanding of the God-world relation, and it is basic to his understanding of theological anthropology and the doctrine of creation. God is in the world, and the world is in God.[7]

And the theological "archetype of this dialectical movement is to be found in the Godhead itself. . . . Through the concept of perichoresis, the social doctrine of the Trinity formulates the mutual indwellings of the Father, the Son, and the Holy Spirit, and the eternal community that is manifested through these indwellings."[8] Thus the "starting point" for Moltmann "is that all relationships which are analogous to God reflect the primal, reciprocal indwelling and mutual interpenetration of trinitarian perichoresis: God *in* the world and the world *in* God; heaven and earth *in* the kingdom of God, pervaded by his glory; soul and body united *in* the life-giving Spirit to a human whole, woman and man *in* the kingdom of unconditional and unconditioned love, freed to be true and complete human beings."[9]

This leads Cooper to conclude that "for Moltmann, all things consist in a vast perichoretic network. Perichoresis is the structural dynamic of all reality. It functions as Moltmann's implicit ontology: to be is to be perichoretically related."[10] Notably, perichoresis functions as the divine unity that holds the three divine persons together so as to render them "one," and it functions as the relation between God and the world.

A. Perichoresis as Divine Unity

Moltmann makes obvious his dissatisfaction with the accounts of divine unity prominent both in the theological tradition and in modern (nineteenth- and much twentieth-century) theology. He criticizes notions of divine unity as "supreme substance" and "absolute subject." The culprits of the former approach include Thomas Aquinas and (especially) the neo-

7. Jürgen Moltmann, *God in Creation* (San Francisco: Harper & Row, 1985), p. 17.
8. Moltmann, *God in Creation*, p. 16.
9. Moltmann, *God in Creation*, p. 17.
10. Cooper, *Panentheism*, p. 252.

Thomists; while much of the blame for the latter approach can be laid at the feet of Hegel (after the groundwork was laid by Descartes, Kant, and Schleiermacher): "ever since Hegel in particular, the Christian Trinity has tended to be represented in terms belonging to the general concept of the absolute subject: *one subject — three modes of being*."[11] Moltmann especially targets the concept of divine unity put forth by Barth and Rahner. Barth's "Idealist heritage," charges Moltmann, "finally betrays itself here" (p. 142), the result being that Barth's emphatic insistence that there is only *one* divine subject and center of consciousness constitutes "a late triumph for Sabellian modalism" (p. 137). Rahner's theology is similar: "Sabellian modalism — or, to be more precise, Idealistic modalism — is what Rahner himself is in danger of, like Schleiermacher and Barth" (p. 144).

In place of either traditional notions of substance or idealist notions of subject, Moltmann offers perichoresis as a way of understanding divine unity. Starting not with philosophical notions of monotheism but with the biblical witness to the distinct divine persons, Moltmann concludes that "the concept of God's unity cannot in the trinitarian sense be fitted into the homogeneity of the one divine substance, or into the identity of the absolute subject either; and least of all into one of the three Persons of the Trinity. It must be perceived in the *perichoresis* of the divine Persons" (p. 150). In fact, Moltmann thinks, commitment to orthodoxy compels us to conclude thus: "if the unity of God is not perceived in the at-oneness of the triune God, and therefore as a *perichoretic* unity, then Arianism and Sabellianism remain inescapable threats to Christian theology" (p. 150). Thus the "unity of the divine tri-unity lies in the *union* of the Father, the Son and the Spirit, not in their numerical unity. It lies in their *fellowship*, not in the identity of a single subject" (p. 95).

Moltmann explains a bit further what he means by "perichoretic unity." He says that

> the Father exists in the Son, the Son in the Father, and both of them in the Spirit, just as the Spirit exists in both the Father and the Son. In virtue of their eternal love they live in one another to such an extent, and dwell in one another to such an extent, that they are one. It is a process of most perfect and intense empathy. Precisely through the personal characteristics that distinguish them from one another, the Father, the

11. Jürgen Moltmann, *The Trinity and the Kingdom: The Doctrine of God* (Minneapolis: Fortress, 1993), p. 17. Page numbers for this discussion have been placed in the text.

Son and the Spirit dwell in one another and communicate eternal life to one another. In the perichoresis, the very thing that divides them becomes the very thing that binds them together. . . . The doctrine of the perichoresis links together in a brilliant way the threeness and the unity, without reducing the threeness to the unity, or dissolving the unity in the threeness. The unity of the triunity lies in the eternal perichoresis of the divine persons. (p. 175)

Whether or not this is sufficient as an account of divine unity is debatable, but one thing should be clear indeed: Moltmann thinks it is.[12]

B. Perichoresis as the God-World Relation

So the perichoretic relationship within the life of God the Holy Trinity is the basis and "archetype" of the God-world relation for Moltmann. This leads him directly to what has been called "perichoretic panentheism."[13] Moltmann consistently expresses his dissatisfaction with pantheism as well as with more traditional doctrines of the God-world relation. As early as *The Crucified God,* Moltmann distanced his view from pantheism while also endorsing panentheism. He says that "a trinitarian theology of the cross perceives God in the negative element and thus the negative element in God, and in this dialectical way is panentheistic."[14] This theme continues throughout Moltmann's work. In *The Trinity and the Kingdom* he quotes Nicholas Berdyaev to make the point that "creative and suffering love has always been a part of his love's eternal nature. 'The creation of the world . . . is a moment of the deepest mystery in the relation between God the Father and God the Son.' Creation is part of the eternal love affair between the Father and the Son."[15] He says that "the relationship between God and the world has a reciprocal character," for the world is a "counterpart" to God.[16]

---

12. Although Moltmann also talks of an "eschatological unity," e.g., in *Trinity and the Kingdom,* p. 149. Moreover, it is not always clear that Moltmann wants to *replace* essentialism with perichoresis; in some places it looks as though perhaps he only wants to supplement or refine it.

13. E.g., Cooper, *Panentheism,* chapter 10.

14. Jürgen Moltmann, *The Crucified God* (San Francisco: Harper & Row, 1974), p. 277.

15. Moltmann, *Trinity and the Kingdom,* p. 59. The quotation from Berdyaev is taken from *The Meaning of History,* p. 48.

16. Moltmann, *Trinity and the Kingdom,* pp. 98-99.

The consequence of this, he thinks, is that in the presence of God in the eschaton "everything ends with God's being 'all in all' (1 Cor. 15:28 AV). *God in the world and the world in God* — that is what is meant by the glorifying of the world through the Spirit. That is *the home of the Trinity*."[17] Linking monotheism with deism, Moltmann places his panentheism "between" monotheism and pantheism: "the trinitarian concept of creation integrates the elements of truth in monotheism and pantheism. In the panentheistic view, God, having created the world, also dwells in it, and conversely the world he has created dwells in him."[18] As part of his effort at interpreting world religious history in a messianic light, he says that "the interpretation of the world which emerges right down the line, from the symbol of the World Mother to the symbol of the redeeming cosmic human being, Christ, is the panentheistic understanding of the world as the sheltering and nurturing divine environment for everything living: 'in him we live and move and have our being' (Acts 17:28)."[19] The evidence is clear enough that Cooper concludes that Moltmann "offers the most fully articulated, explicitly panentheistic Christian theology in history. It is panentheistic because the perichoretic mutuality of God and the world is ontologically constitutive for both."[20]

Definitions of panentheism vary, so perhaps it will help to try to understand with more precision just what Moltmann intends in his affirmation of panentheism. Standard definitions of panentheism tell us that it is literally "all-in-God-ism,"[21] and that its basic meaning is that "the Being of God includes and penetrates the whole universe, so that every part exists in Him, but His Being is more than, and not exhausted by, the universe."[22] While helpful, such definitions only take us so far. What is more interesting and more important is to discern what Moltmann means when he uses the term.

Without attempting to be exhaustive, it is clear that Moltmann means at least this much in his employment of the term: God is affected by the

---

17. Moltmann, *Trinity and the Kingdom*, p. 105, emphasis in original.

18. Moltmann, *God in Creation*, p. 98.

19. Moltmann, *God in Creation*, p. 300.

20. Cooper, *Panentheism*, p. 257.

21. Cooper, *Panentheism*, p. 26. Cooper says Karl Krause (1781-1832) coined the term, and that Charles Hartshorne popularized it in the mid–twentieth century.

22. Cooper, *Panentheism*, p. 27. Cooper quotes from *The Oxford Dictionary of the Christian Church*, ed. F. L. Cross and E. A. Livingstone (Oxford: Oxford University Press, 1997), p. 1213.

world, creation is necessary for God, and the world is a part of God. That God is affected by the world is a cornerstone of Moltmann's theology; instead of asking only *"just what God means for us human beings in the cross of Christ,"* he also asks *"what this human cross of Christ means for God."*[23] We are not only to ask "*how do I experience God?* What does God mean for me? How am I determined by him? We must ask the reverse questions: *how does God experience me?* What do I mean for God? How is he determined by me?"[24] Surely the passion of God is central to Moltmann's theology.

Moltmann is also clear that creation is necessary for God. He criticizes the traditional doctrine of divine freedom in creation, according to which "God need not have created the world."[25] Moltmann rejects the traditional doctrine because such a "fictitious suggestion of arbitrariness within God leaves behind it a residue of despotism in the concept of God."[26] He contrasts this "despotic theology" with his own preferred panentheism, and he justifies the move to panentheism by appealing to what can only be described as a form of "Perfect Being Theology." It is "impossible," he says, "to conceive of a God who is not a creative God. A non-creative God would be imperfect compared with the God who is eternally creative."[27] This does not mean that divine freedom is abridged, for "in God necessity and freedom coincide; they are what is for him axiomatic, self-evident."[28] Creation is necessary for God because God is perfect.

Moltmann's panentheism goes a step further: the world is included in the divine being. Creation is not coextensive with God; it is not all that there is to God. Moltmann denies that creation is divine, but he insists nonetheless that it "acquires a share in the inner life of the Trinity itself."[29] This will be completed in the eschaton, for only then will the "mutual indwelling" of God and the world take place. But when it does, it will result

---

23. Moltmann, *The Crucified God*, p. x, emphasis in original.

24. Moltmann, *Trinity and the Kingdom*, p. 3, emphasis in original.

25. Moltmann, *Trinity and the Kingdom*, p. 105. For a recent articulation of the traditional view, see Colin E. Gunton, *The Triune Creator: A Historical and Systematic Study* (Grand Rapids: Eerdmans, 1998); cf. Colin E. Gunton, "The Doctrine of Creation," in *The Cambridge Companion to Christian Doctrine*, ed. Colin E. Gunton (Cambridge: Cambridge University Press, 1997), pp. 141-57.

26. Moltmann, *Trinity and the Kingdom*, p. 106.

27. Moltmann, *Trinity and the Kingdom*, p. 106.

28. Moltmann, *Trinity and the Kingdom*, p. 107. Moltmann's conception of divine freedom is thus compatibilist (see especially pp. 52-56). See also Cooper, *Panentheism*, p. 29.

29. Moltmann, *Trinity and the Kingdom*, p. 113.

in cosmic *communicatio idiomatum*. For then we will share in a kind of "cosmic perichoresis of divine and cosmic attributes."[30]

Moltmann explicitly affirms panentheism, and he understands this to be a direct consequence of his doctrine of perichoresis. God is affected by the world due to his reciprocal relations with it. The creation of the world is necessary for God. And the world is included in the divine being. Moltmann makes obvious the motivation for his panentheism. Apart from the aforementioned conviction that the concept of a Perfect Being itself requires creation and thus entails panentheism, Moltmann is concerned to articulate a theology "after Auschwitz." In particular he is exercised to understand the love of God, and his reflections on divine love lead him to endorse panentheism. Thus when we affirm with 1 John 4 that "'God is love,' we mean that he is in eternity this process of self-differentiation and self-identification; a process which contains the whole pain of the negative within itself."[31] The cosmos "is part of the eternal love affair between the Father and the Son," and such a relationship of love requires suffering.[32] For "in order to be completely itself, love has to suffer."[33] Again, "a God who cannot suffer cannot love either."[34] True love, understood perichoretically, requires suffering. One might object that, on Moltmann's own "social" doctrine of the Trinity, the eternal love of the three divine persons for one another would be enough to satisfy the Johannine dictum. But Moltmann disagrees, for "this inner-trinitarian love is the love of like for like, not love of the other."[35] And since genuine love is love for what is truly other, something "other" is necessary for genuine love. Therefore the creation of a world to be the theater of suffering and redemption is necessary.

II. Either Too Much or Not Enough

Moltmann presents us with a grand theological vision. God's own life is an interpersonal relationship of perichoresis, and the life and destiny of all creatures is — or at least will be — one that shares in this divine

30. Jürgen Moltmann, *The Coming of God* (Minneapolis: Fortress, 1996), p. 295.
31. Moltmann, *Trinity and the Kingdom*, p. 57.
32. Moltmann, *Trinity and the Kingdom*, p. 59.
33. Moltmann, *Trinity and the Kingdom*, p. 33.
34. Moltmann, *Trinity and the Kingdom*, p. 38.
35. Moltmann, *Trinity and the Kingdom*, p. 106.

perichoresis. But is it successful? Does it offer an adequate account of divine oneness or unity? And if it does, does it also work for the God-world relation? As we shall see, it is far from clear that perichoresis can do the work Moltmann needs it to do.

A. Not Enough for Divine Triunity

Many critics worry that Moltmann has not done enough to ward off charges of polytheism. Cooper complains that Moltmann's use of perichoresis "does not provide a strong ontological account of essential divine unity," and he concludes that "it is doubtful whether Moltmann's idea of essential triunity is an adequate account of God's oneness."[36] John J. O'Donnell is willing to leave open the question of whether or not Moltmann is a tritheist, but he worries that this is a "key vulnerability in Moltmann's core conception."[37] John Thompson says Moltmann's theology "borders on tritheism."[38] George Hunsinger comments that "despite the evident scorn with which he anticipates such a charge, *The Trinity and the Kingdom* is about the closest thing to tritheism that many of us are ever likely to see."[39] Even so sympathetic a theologian as Wolfhart Pannenberg argues that "the unity of the persons in mutual perichoresis" does not give "us the thought of the unity of the three persons. Perichoresis presupposes another basis for the unity of the three persons. It can only manifest this unity."[40] How are we to evaluate such criticisms?[41] What is to be done with such concerns?

36. Cooper, *Panentheism*, p. 251.

37. John J. O'Donnell, *Trinity and Temporality: The Christian Doctrine of God in the Light of Process Theology and the Theology of Hope* (Oxford: Oxford University Press, 1983), pp. 153-54.

38. John Thompson, *Modern Trinitarian Perspectives* (Oxford: Oxford University Press, 1994), p. 51.

39. George Hunsinger, "Review of Jürgen Moltmann, *The Trinity and the Kingdom*," *Thomist* 47 (1983): 131.

40. Wolfhart Pannenberg, *Systematic Theology*, vol. 1 (Grand Rapids: Eerdmans, 1991), p. 334. Pannenberg further rejects the notion that the three divine persons are "mere specimens of a common genus or species" (p. 336).

41. Interestingly, Paul D. Molnar also charges Moltmann with *modalism*. *Divine Freedom and the Doctrine of the Immanent Trinity: In Dialogue with Karl Barth and Contemporary Theology* (London: T. & T. Clark, 2002), p. 232.

Perhaps it will help to disambiguate the notion of perichoresis itself a bit further. Oliver Crisp offers a helpful clarification here when he suggests that we understand the perichoresis of the persons of the Trinity along these lines. With slight modification:

(P): For any *x* and any *y* (in this case the Persons of the Trinity), *x* and *y* are perichoretically related if and only if *x* and *y* share all their properties in a common essence apart from those properties that serve to individuate *x* and *y*, or that express a relation between only *x* and *y*.[42]

(P) would appear to be consistent with the Christian tradition.[43] As Torrance notes, according to the historic concept of perichoresis the divine persons share "all but the incommunicable properties which differentiate them from one another as Father, Son and Holy Spirit."[44] It may be somewhat more restrictive than Moltmann intends; if anything, such an account of divine oneness is likely too strong for Moltmann. For as he puts it, "perichoresis is not just something existing between like and like in the Trinity; it exists too between the unlike natures of God and human beings."[45] But for the sake of charity, let us proceed on the assumption that it would be acceptable.

Now back to the worries about Moltmann's use of perichoresis. Recall Brian Leftow's sharp criticisms of Social Trinitarianism; he argues that the perichoretic indwelling and cooperation of three morally perfect beings fall far short of genuine monotheism. Although he does not focus directly on the concept of perichoresis (the real problem is Social Trinitarianism

---

42. Crisp, *Divinity and Humanity*, p. 31.

43. If we agree with the classical tradition that any of the divine persons could have become incarnate (see Richard Cross, *The Metaphysics of the Incarnation: Thomas Aquinas to Duns Scotus* [Oxford: Oxford University Press, 2002], p. 179), then (depending on our view of such properties) we might need to modify (P) to account for one-owner properties that are world-indexed, e.g., "being incarnate in W" (which is possessed by the Father) and "being incarnate in W*" (which is possessed by the Son). But the basic idea should be obvious enough for our present purposes.

44. Torrance, *Christian Doctrine of God*, p. 175.

45. Jürgen Moltmann, "The World in God or God in the World?" in *God Will Be All in All: The Eschatology of Jürgen Moltmann*, ed. Richard Bauckham (Minneapolis: Fortress, 2001), p. 39. See also Jürgen Moltmann, "Perichoresis: An Old Magic Word for a New Trinitarian Theology," in *Trinity, Community, and Power: Mapping Trajectories in Wesleyan Theology*, ed. M. Douglas Meeks (Nashville: Kingswood Books, 2000), pp. 117-18.

with its three divine minds, and perichoresis is only one strategy of defense), surely Leftow has something like it in mind when he compares Social Trinitarianism to Greek paganism and concludes that "it is hardly plausible that the Greek paganism would have been a form of monotheism had Zeus and Co. been more alike, better behaved, and linked by the right causal relations."[46] Leftow might argue that (P) is of little help here; he might continue to say that just as we should be skeptical of the claim that Zeus and his brood were really one God just because they shared all properties other than those "personal" properties that served to differentiate them, so also should we be suspicious of perichoresis as an account of divine unity in Christian theology.

Admittedly, Moltmann's debt to Hegel does not help him here.[47] Nor does his criticism of "monotheism."[48] Nor yet does his rather flippant response to these criticisms and worries; merely saying that the danger of tritheism is nothing to worry about is simply not helpful, nor is it adequate merely to assert that "there has never been a Christian tritheist."[49] Nor (worse yet) does it help him to retort that every German theologian is a Lutheran and a Hegelian — as if that provides an excuse to dismiss "the responsibility to be metaphysically clear."[50] But even if Moltmann's theology were purged of its Hegelianism (which admittedly would be a massive revision — likely more than Moltmann would want), it is not clear that (P) offers enough to stake a claim to monotheism.[51] Many interlocutors will think that something more robust is needed.

46. Brian Leftow, "Anti Social Trinitarianism," in *The Trinity: An Interdisciplinary Symposium on the Trinity*, ed. Stephen T. Davis, Daniel Kendall, S.J., and Gerald O'Collins, S.J. (Oxford: Oxford University Press, 1999), p. 232.

47. E.g., his famous interpretation of the cry of dereliction, his insistence that "God is revealed in his opposite: godlessness and abandon by God," and his language of "a rebellion in God himself." *The Crucified God*, pp. 27, 227; see also *Trinity and the Kingdom*, pp. 76-83.

48. E.g., Moltmann, *Trinity and the Kingdom*, pp. 129-48. Pannenberg defends Moltmann here; he says Moltmann only inveighs against *political* monotheism and thus is only guilty of a "wrong terminological decision." *Systematic Theology*, 1:336 n. 217.

49. Moltmann, *Trinity and the Kingdom*, p. 243 n. 43.

50. Marilyn McCord Adams, *Christ and Horrors: The Coherence of Christology* (Cambridge: Cambridge University Press, 2006), p. 106 n. 67.

51. I am not convinced that Leftow's arguments are devastating to Social Trinitarianism, but surely Social Trinitarians should not rest content with mere assertions. See Tom McCall, "Social Trinitarianism and Tritheism Again: A Response to Brian Leftow," *Philosophia Christi* (2003): 405-30.

B. Too Much for the God-World Relation

But at any rate, a bit of reflection makes it obvious that (P) does too much for the God-world relation. As we have seen, Moltmann wants to offer perichoretic panentheism as a *via media* between theism and pantheism. Clearly he wants to avoid the shoals of pantheism as much as he desires to avoid the rocks of theism; he wants to insist that God and the world are ontologically distinct even though reciprocally and perichoretically related. But here lies a problem: any version of perichoresis that is strong enough to be plausible as an account of monotheism will provide a similar account of the God-world relation.

For according to (P), God and the world would be perichoretically related if and only if they share all but their individuating and personal/relational properties in common. According to (P), then, God and the world would share such properties as "being finite" and "suffering the results of evil." Moltmann might find this satisfactory, but if we accept (P), then it is also true that God and the world would share such properties as "being infinite," "being omnipotent" (where omnipotence is understood, as Moltmann understands it, as "the almighty power of suffering love"),[52] "being omnibenevolent," and "necessarily being omnibenevolent."[53] Perhaps such a view has its attractions. Unfortunately, however, it suffers from the defect of obviously being untrue — it cannot be true that some entity called "God and the world" is both finite and infinite, both evil and necessarily omnibenevolent. Moreover, if we accept (P), then God and the world share all these properties in a common essence. Thus we — and the entire cosmos — would be *homoousios* with the Trinity! We would all be members of the Godhead, for we would all be related to the Father and Spirit as is the Son. There seems to be no way around it: if (P) is sufficient for monotheism, then it also entails monism.[54]

---

52. E.g., Moltmann, *Trinity and the Kingdom*, p. 31. Here Moltmann is describing the view of C. E. Rolt, but so far as I can see he is offering an unqualified endorsement of Rolt's position.

53. Recall Moltmann's view of the way that "necessity and freedom coincide" for God, e.g., in *Trinity and the Kingdom*, pp. 106-7.

54. Much of what William Lane Craig says about the panentheism of Wolfhart Pannenberg and LeRon Shults is appropriate for Moltmann as well. "Pantheists in Spite of Themselves: God and Infinity in Contemporary Theology," in *For Faith and Clarity: Philosophical Contributions to Christian Theology*, ed. James K. Beilby (Grand Rapids: Baker Academic, 2006), pp. 135-56.

III. Toward Resolution

But surely monism is not what Moltmann intends. One option would be to weaken (P) to avoid such disastrous entailments, but weakening (P) would also weaken the account of divine unity or oneness. As we have seen, however, Moltmann likely has an uphill climb to persuade his critics that (P) is adequate as it stands, so weakening it does not look at all promising. Perhaps what is needed is a distinction between Trinitarian perichoresis and what I shall call creational and soteriological perichoresis.

A. Trinitarian Perichoresis

Crisp has noted that perichoresis is often used as a theological "black box."[55] Surely he is right, and just as surely there will remain much that is mysterious about the concept. But to admit this is not to say that progress is impossible. And here we get help from an unlikely source: Keith Yandell's metaphysical structure for the doctrine of the Trinity. Yandell and Moltmann may seem like strange theological (not to mention philosophical) bedfellows, but Yandell has much to say that is directly relevant to Moltmann's dilemma. And while Yandell does not set out to mount an explicit defense of perichoresis, he recognizes that his view "could be read as an interpretation of that notion" that Jesus and the Father are in a perichoretic "relation of mutual profound love."[56]

Recall that Yandell argues that God is a complex being — albeit not one who is composed of parts.[57] In Yandell's technical sense of "complex," "X is complex if and only if there is a Y and a Z such that Y is not numerically identical to Z, it is logically impossible that Y exist and Z not exist, and Y and Z *together* are numerically identical to X in the sense of their together composing X."[58] When applied to the doctrine of the Trinity,

---

55. Crisp, *Divinity and Humanity,* p. 1.

56. Keith E. Yandell, "An Essay in Particularist Philosophy of Religion: A Metaphysical Structure for the Doctrine of the Trinity," forthcoming, p. 10.

57. Brian Leftow is among those who find Yandell's earlier claims problematic: "his definitions of these terms create problems . . . every composite depends for its existence on its proper parts, and no composite is identical with any of its proper parts." "Anti Social Trinitarianism," p. 209 n. 29. As we shall see, Yandell denies that these are "*proper* parts."

58. Yandell, "An Essay," p. 5. Page references to this essay have been placed in the text.

Yandell carefully spells out just what it is that the Trinity is complex in virtue of: it is three fully divine persons, each of whom are conscious, rational agents (p. 9).

God is complex. But according to Yandell, this complex God has no parts. On his understanding of parts (really, "proper parts"), "if Y is a part of X, then Y can exist whether X exists or not. Further, if Y and Z are parts of X, then Y can exist without Z existing and Z can exist without Y existing" (p. 6). Put a bit differently, "X is a *part* of Y if and only if X exists, Y exists, X plus something else is all of Y, X is not all of Y, and it is logically possible that X exist and Y not exist or Y exist and X not exist (or both)" (p. 8). Yandell denies that the divine persons are parts of God: it is logically impossible that any of the divine persons exist without the others. He says something is what he calls "simple(i)" if and only if it has no parts, and he affirms that this is necessarily true of the Trinity (p. 8). He draws a distinction between this and what he calls "simplicity(ii)," according to which an entity is simple just in case it is not complex. Not surprisingly, he affirms that the triune God is necessarily simple(i) and necessarily not simple(ii).

The fact that the triune God is triune but necessarily not simple(ii) means that God is necessarily complex. But the fact that the triune God is necessarily simple(i) means that God is not composed of parts or pieces. The divine persons are "necessarily strongly internally related," thus the triune God is "necessarily particularly strongly internally complex" (p. 21). This requires some explaining.[59] The triune God is *necessarily* complex if and only if the triune God exists, the triune God is complex (in the sense specified), and necessarily, were the triune God not complex then God would not exist. The triune God is *particularly* complex if and only if the triune God exists, is complex, and necessarily could not be complex in any other manner than that in which he is complex. And the triune God is *internally* complex if and only if the triune God exists, the triune God is complex, and it is logically impossible that that in virtue of which the triune God is complex exist other than that in virtue of which the triune God is complex, and it is logically impossible that anything in virtue of which the triune God is complex exist without everything else in virtue of which the triune God is complex existing.

Yandell is convinced that this account avoids the charge of tritheism. He defines tritheism as "the view that there are three distinct omni-

59. For the following see Yandell, "An Essay," pp. 6-8.

competent beings," and he concludes that "the Trinity has *being trinitarian* as an essential property and that it is logically impossible that any trinitarian person exist and any other trinitarian person not exist."[60]

This brings us to a place where we can summarize (TP) as

(TPa) The divine persons are perichoretically related in virtue of the fact that they share all their properties in a common essence apart from those properties that serve to individuate them or express a relation between two of them;[61]

(TPb) The divine persons are perichoretically related in virtue of the fact that they are necessarily strongly internally related; and

(TPc) The divine persons are perichoretically related in virtue of their relationships of loving communion.

Perhaps this is what Moltmann's doctrine needs. Armed with this account of perichoresis, he could insist that the triune God is exactly *one* complex being, and what make the triune God complex are three fully divine persons who are necessarily strongly internally related — that is, three fully divine persons who indwell one another in the eternal divine communion of love, three divine persons who could not exist apart from this indwelling, three fully divine persons whose life and love are found in one another. With such clarification, Moltmann could say that the divine persons are numerically distinct, he could affirm that they each possess all the essential divine attributes, and he could also insist that there is only *one* God.

B. Creational and Soteriological Perichoresis

But more work remains. For if the foregoing account of perichoresis were to be applied to the God-world relation, then once again pantheism would result (the one God would turn out to be a great deal more complex than Trinitarians had thought him to be). So a distinction must be drawn between Trinitarian Perichoresis (TP) and what I shall refer to as Creational/Soteriological Perichoresis (CSP).

60. Yandell, "An Essay," p. 21.

61. Again, (TPa) might need modification to account for one-owner properties that are world-indexed.

(TP) affirms that the divine persons are necessarily particularly strongly internally related, but (CSP) must deny much of this with respect to the God-world relation. (CSP) must deny that God and the world are *particularly* related, for there is no reason to think that we must be related to God exactly as we in fact are related. Nor is there reason (outside of the commitments that lead to monism, on one hand, or a certain confusion on the other hand) to think that God must have the exact relationship to us that he in fact does have.

Similarly, (CSP) should deny that God and the world are *internally* related. There is no reason to think that this is true, and to avoid pantheism we must deny both that God and the world compose a greater complexity and that these relations are internal. After all, what could be greater than God? Furthermore, it is absurd to think that God could not exist without everything else in virtue of which God and the world would be complex — which would be *everything* that exists — also existing.

(CSP) could affirm, on the other hand, that to be a creature just *is* to be related to God. At one level, of course, this is merely a confession of the fact that we are creatures. But it could go much further; it could affirm that the intention of the triune God is that his creatures be rightly related to him; it could affirm that God desires that all of creation find its destiny by glorifying, enjoying, worshiping, and loving God while being loved and enjoyed by the Father, Son, and Holy Spirit.[62] (CSP) could readily and gladly affirm that the prayer of Jesus in John 17 — that his believers would be "in" the life of the triune God — reveals the design and intention of the triune God as well as the destiny of those who are rightly related.[63] In this way, Moltmann could insist that the inter-Trinitarian life shared by the Father, Son, and Holy Spirit is one of perichoretic love and communion, and he could also hold fast to the beliefs that we are created for an analogue of that life, that part of what it means to be redeemed is to share in the recovery of this life as it is shared together (John 17:21) — and indeed, that the love we are made to know and enjoy as creatures is the same love shared within the life of the triune God (17:23).

We might summarize (CSP) as:

62. I leave aside such important issues as how the rest of creation is related to those creatures who alone are said to bear the *imago Dei*, how the rest of the cosmos might be affected by human sin, and how the rest of creation is related to the triune God.

63. I here leave aside as well the question of *who* is included. Moltmann's belief in the universal scope of salvation is well known; see, e.g., *The Coming of God*, p. 251.

(CSPa) Human persons are created for the purpose of knowing, enjoying, and sharing the love of the Father, Son, and Holy Spirit;[64] and

(CSPb) The triune God works in redemption and salvation to restore human persons and bring them to this destiny (which will reach its terminus in the eschaton).

Now I readily admit that this amounts to a rather drastic revision of Moltmann's theology. What began as an apparent attempt at clarification has become a complete overhaul. But it does, I think, satisfy Moltmann's primary desideratum. Recall his forceful insistence on the primacy of the love of God: he wants to insist on the ultimacy of perichoretic love, and he is exercised to reject all suggestions that God's love is at all arbitrary or capricious.[65] I happily confess my sympathies with Moltmann at this point; I am convinced that divine love *is* essential to God. I believe that holy love is of the essence of God. But I think this is accounted for and grounded in the Trinity. In the words of John D. Zizioulas, "the expression 'God is love' (1 John 4:16) signifies that God 'subsists' as Trinity. . . . Love is not an emanation or 'property' of the substance of God . . . but is constitutive of his substance, i.e., it is that which makes God what He is, the one God. Thus love ceases to be a qualifying — i.e. secondary — property of being and becomes the *supreme ontological predicate*."[66] God's love for the world is grounded in and issues from the life shared by the Father, the Son, and the Holy Spirit, but this love itself is infinite and inexhaustible. It cannot be diminished — nor can it be added to or supplemented. Therefore the triune God does not need me or my sin — or any creatures with their sin and suffering — in order to *be* love. And it is the same love that is extended to the world. As Torrance puts it, "When we turn to the First Epistle of Saint John we learn that 'God is Love,' and that this Love is defined by the Love that God bears to us in sending his Son to be the propitiation for our sins, and indeed for the sins of the world. That is to say, the very Being of God as Love is identical with his loving, for he is himself the Love with which he loves."[67]

---

64. Again I leave aside questions of how the nonhuman creation is included (not because it is unimportant, but because it is not vital for present purposes).

65. E.g., Moltmann, *Trinity and the Kingdom*, pp. 105-7.

66. John D. Zizioulas, *Being as Communion: Studies in Personhood and the Church* (Crestwood, N.Y.: St. Vladimir's Seminary Press, 1985), p. 46, emphasis in original.

67. Torrance, *Christian Doctrine of God*, p. 165.

But Moltmann apparently thinks the revised view offered here does not satisfy his primary desideratum, and as a rejoinder he might repeat once again his claim that genuine love *requires* suffering. Unfortunately, however, Moltmann has given us no *reasons* to think that this must be true; he offers no arguments for this assertion. He moves quickly — much too quickly — from "God *can* suffer" to "God *must* suffer." But surely such an important claim deserves an argument, and in the absence of one we have little motivation to find Moltmann's view compelling.

Moltmann might dig in his heels by insisting on his denial that the divine persons are distinct enough for what is shared between them to count as genuine or authentic love.[68] This would be unfortunate, for again Moltmann gives us not the slightest reason to think that this is — or even might be — true. On his view the divine persons are numerically distinct, and each is a center of consciousness and will. Surely this is enough! But more importantly, if Moltmann is correct then we are left with the conclusion that the divine persons do not love each other at all — thus the only true love of the triune God would be the love extended to the world. Is not this an outright denial of Moltmann's primary desideratum — does he not want to insist that the love shared between the divine persons is the same love extended to the world?

I concur with Moltmann that the love that is essential to the triune God is the same love with which he loves us. With Moltmann, I am convinced both that "God is love" and that "God loves the world." But I see no reason to think that this conviction should take us beyond (CSP) to a confusion of (TP) with the God-world relation. And I conclude that Moltmann's dictum that "God loves the world with the very same love which he himself is in eternity" is not threatened at all by the revisions I have proposed here.[69]

IV. Conclusion

Much of what I have said about Moltmann's doctrine of perichoresis could also be said about many other contemporary theologians. For instance, Catherine Mowry LaCugna notes that both Patricia Wilson-Kastner and

68. E.g., Moltmann, *Trinity and the Kingdom*, p. 106.
69. Moltmann, *Trinity and the Kingdom*, p. 57.

Leonardo Boff follow Moltmann in using perichoresis to account for divine unity.[70] Like Moltmann, such theologians have work ahead of them. I have argued that perichoresis does either too much or not enough — either it fails as an acceptable notion of divine unity, or it links God and the world too closely to gain the desired panentheism. As it stands, Moltmann's doctrine is in rather desperate need of clarification and modification. It risks either incoherence, polytheism, or monism.

But I have suggested further that Moltmann is right to uphold the doctrine of the Trinity, and he is correct to insist that we understand the God-world relation in a way that is consistent with a Trinitarian doctrine of God. I have argued that Moltmann's account of perichoresis stands in need of adjustment or repair, but I have also suggested a way forward. If the Trinitarian theologian is willing to distinguish between intra-Trinitarian perichoresis and an analogous sense in which the notion might be used for the God-world relation, then perhaps the concept is serviceable and helpful. Suggesting that we understand the former along the lines of Yandell's notion of one God of three persons who are necessarily strongly internally related, while taking the latter to affirm God's loving and gracious purposes in creation and redemption, I conclude that the doctrine of perichoresis is — despite the criticisms of its detractors and the abuses of its defenders — an important aspect of Trinitarian theology.

70. LaCugna, *God for Us*, pp. 270, 275.

CHAPTER SIX

"Eternal Functional Subordination": Considering a Recent Evangelical Proposal

R ecent evangelical theology has witnessed the rise of a doctrine sometimes called the "Eternal Functional Subordination of the Son" (hereafter EFS). Some influential evangelical theologians want to deny "ontological" or "essential" subordination while also insisting that the Son's
functional (or "economic") subordination is eternal.[1] Some evangelicals
have received this proposal with enthusiasm; others have expressed grave
concern about it.

To this point, much of the debate has centered on such issues as the
purported biblical basis for the doctrine, the extent to which it reflects (or
departs from) the tradition, and its compatibility (or lack thereof) with
creedal orthodoxy.[2] Much has been said along these lines, and surely much

---

1. Some of the most influential recent theologians making these claims are Wayne
Grudem, *Systematic Theology: An Introduction to Biblical Doctrine* (Grand Rapids:
Zondervan, 1994), pp. 248-52; Grudem, *Evangelical Feminism and Biblical Truth* (Sisters,
Oreg.: Multnomah, 2004); Bruce A. Ware, "How Shall We Think about the Trinity?" in *God
under Fire: Modern Scholarship Reinvents God*, ed. Douglas S. Huffman and Eric L. Johnson
(Grand Rapids: Zondervan, 2002), pp. 269-77; and Ware, *Father, Son, and Holy Spirit: Rela-
tions, Roles, and Relevance* (Wheaton, Ill.: Crossway, 2006).

2. In addition to the work of Grudem and Ware, see Stephen D. Kovach and Peter R.
Schemm, Jr., "A Defense of the Doctrine of the Eternal Subordination of the Son," *Journal of
the Evangelical Theological Society* 42 (1999): 461-76. In personal correspondence, Grudem re-
minded me that he thinks that such luminaries as Charles Hodge, A. H. Strong, and B. B.
Warfield teach this doctrine as well. For examples of criticisms, see Gilbert Bilezikian,
"Hermeneutical Bungee-Jumping: Subordination in the Godhead," *Journal of the Evangelical
Theological Society* 40 (1997): 57-68; Millard Erickson, *God in Three Persons: A Contemporary
Interpretation of the Trinity* (Grand Rapids: Baker, 1995), pp. 291-310; Kevin Giles, *The Trinity*

more will be said (and likely needs to be said). In this essay, however, I work to clarify some conceptual issues. I believe that the current discussion and debate would benefit from some metaphysical analysis. I argue that, given some eminently plausible metaphysical assumptions, such analysis shows that if EFS is understood one way, then it is straightforwardly true and should not even be controversial. Taken another way, however, EFS entails the direct denial of creedal orthodoxy.

I. Eternal Functional Subordination: A "Soft" Account

According to orthodox Christianity, the Son is subordinate to the Father during his incarnate earthly career. In other words, in the economy of salvation the Son "humbles" himself for us and our salvation (Phil. 2:5-11); the fully divine Son of God, without in any way or for any time ceasing to be divine, is able to truthfully and freely say "the Father is greater than I" (John 14:28). The Son has full ontological and essential equality, and this continues unabated even as he is functionally and temporally subordinate. In fact, without recourse to such a distinction, it is doubtful that the pro-Nicenes could have prevailed against "Arian" exegesis.[3] Perhaps EFS is only recognizing and emphasizing this point.

One way of understanding the claim that the Son is "eternally functionally subordinate" is what I shall term the "soft" account. On this understanding, the claim made here is simply something like "in this possible world it is everlastingly true that at times $t - tn$ the Son is incarnate and thus functionally and temporally subordinate."[4] The Son is functionally

---

and *Subordinationism* (Downers Grove, Ill.: InterVarsity, 2002); and Giles, *Jesus and the Father: Modern Evangelicals Reinvent the Doctrine of the Trinity* (Grand Rapids: Zondervan, 2006).

3. On this debate see Lewis Ayres, *Nicaea and Its Legacy: An Approach to Fourth-Century Trinitarianism* (Oxford: Oxford University Press, 2004), and R. P. C. Hanson, *The Search for the Christian Doctrine of God: The Arian Controversy, 318-381* (Edinburgh: T. & T. Clark, 1988).

4. Alternatively, the claim might be that "it is timelessly true that at times $t - tn$ the Son is incarnate and thus functionally and temporally subordinate." I'm confident that, *mutatis mutandis,* the outcome would be the same, but I work with the former formulation because it is more straightforward and easier to handle. Indeed, some proponents of divine temporality think that the doctrine of the incarnation itself is decisive against timeless or atemporal doctrines of God, e.g., Nicholas Wolterstorff, "Unqualified Divine Temporality," in *God and Time: Four Views,* ed. Gregory E. Ganssle (Downers Grove, Ill.: InterVarsity, 2001), pp. 209-10.

subordinate to the Father during the time of his incarnate and redemptive work, and this is true at all times.

If this is what the EFS claim amounts to, then it is hard to see what might be objectionable about it. If it is true at all that the Son is functionally subordinate at time t (or times $t — tn$), then it is always true. Barring an unfortunate confusion of temporal with logical modalities, it is hard to see a problem here. For the modal status of a proposition does not change: the proposition *the incarnate Son is functionally subordinate at times t — tn*, if contingently true, is always contingently true.[5] It was contingently true at time *t-1*, it is contingently true now, and it will remain contingently true.[6] And surely it is not worth all the controversy.

II. Eternal Functional Subordination: A "Hard" Account

But perhaps the proponents of EFS intend more than what I've called the "soft" account. It may be that they mean to say more than that the Son is functionally subordinate in this possible world.[7] Perhaps EFS is a statement about what God is *ad intra;* maybe it is a description of the interior of the divine life. Perhaps it is a claim about the "immanent Trinity." Bruce A. Ware seems to think that "the eternal and inner-Trinitarian Father-Son relationship" is "indicative" of "some eternal relationship of authority within the Trinity itself."[8] Similarly, Wayne Grudem appears to think that the very doctrine of the Trinity is at stake here: "if we do not have economic subordination, then there is no inherent difference in the way the three persons relate to one another, and consequently we do not have the three divine persons existing as Father, Son, and Holy Spirit for all

---

5. For brief but helpful discussion of this, see Keith E. Yandell, *Philosophy of Religion: A Contemporary Introduction* (London and New York: Routledge, 1999), pp. 337-38; Yandell, *The Epistemology of Religious Experience* (Cambridge: Cambridge University Press, 1993), pp. 358-60.

6. A characteristic axiom of S5 supports this claim: $\Diamond p \supset \Box \Diamond p$. For a helpful account of S5 (and its antecedents), see Kenneth Konyndyk, *Introductory Modal Logic* (Notre Dame, Ind.: University of Notre Dame Press, 1985); see also Michael J. Loux, "Introduction: Modality and Metaphysics," in *The Possible and the Actual,* ed. Michael J. Loux (Ithaca, N.Y.: Cornell University Press, 1979), pp. 15-64.

7. I take "possible worlds" to be what Alvin Plantinga describes as maximally consistent states of affairs. *The Nature of Necessity* (Oxford: Oxford University Press, 1974).

8. Ware, "How Shall We Think?" p. 270.

eternity. For example, if the Son is not eternally subordinate to the Father in role, then the Father is not eternally 'Father' and the Son is not eternally 'Son.' This would mean that the Trinity has not eternally existed."[9]

So perhaps the proponents of EFS intend it as a pronouncement about the inner being of the triune God. If EFS is a statement about the immanent Trinity — if it is a statement about the essence of divinity — then it is a statement about what God is of necessity. On this understanding of EFS (what I call "Hard" EFS), the Son is functionally subordinate to the Father in all time segments in all possible worlds; there are no time segments in any possible worlds in which the Son is not subordinate to the Father.[10] If this indeed is the proper understanding of EFS, then we are faced with some hard questions and a serious problem.

A. Some Questions for Hard EFS

What *is* this functional subordination in all these possible worlds? What *are* these functions? What *could* they be? A possible world containing no sin needs neither Judge nor Savior. A possible world with no creation needs no Governor. In fact, it is hard to even conceive of "functional subordination" in a possible world in which only God exists — in which there is only the triune communion of holy love. It is also hard to imagine what the motivation might be for holding to such a view.

EFS's advocates might respond that there just are no such possible worlds; they may insist on a doctrine of "eternal creation" or, more precisely, a doctrine of the necessity of creation in all possible worlds. They could take this route, and in doing so they could argue that some kind of creation is necessary so that the divine persons can really be distinct. But apart from the sheer dubiousness of such a claim, it is not easy to think that the current proponents of EFS (even if they are to be understood as promoting Hard EFS) would take this route. For in doing so they would both court panentheism and lose all claims to robust doctrines of divine sovereignty and aseity.[11] Surely this would be a stiff price to pay.[12]

9. Grudem, *Systematic Theology*, p. 251.

10. I here assume for the sake of convenience that God is in some sense temporal.

11. Ware stoutly affirms the doctrine of divine aseity, e.g., in "How Shall We Think?" pp. 255-56.

12. Alternatively, they could deny that God has transworld identity; they could opt in-

B. The Problem for Hard EFS

However tough these questions might be for the proponent of Hard EFS, in the end they are just that: questions. There is, however, a real problem with the position. It is this: Hard EFS entails the denial of the *homoousion*. To see this spelled out, consider the following:

(1) If Hard EFS is true, then the Son has the property *being functionally subordinate in all time segments in all possible worlds.*[13]

(2) If the Son has this property in every possible world, then the Son has this property necessarily. Furthermore, the Son has this property with *de re* rather than *de dicto* necessity.[14]

(3) If the Son has this property necessarily *(de re)*, then the Son has it essentially.[15]

---

stead for a theory of worldbound individuals. But to do this would be to make all of God's properties essential divine properties, and I doubt that anyone committed to the doctrines of divine freedom and aseity would see this as much of a bargain. Moreover, in this case the Son just would have different essential properties than the Father (e.g., properties such as "becoming incarnate" would belong to the Son alone, and they would belong to the Son essentially), and the Son would be essentially subordinate (since the Son has the property of "being subordinate" in this world, the Son would have this property essentially). In addition, such a move would raise the question of whether or not there are counterpart Gods. For a lucid discussion of the theory of worldbound individuals, see Alvin Plantinga, *The Nature of Necessity,* pp. 88-120.

13. Or, if God's existence (or existence *as triune*) is contingent, the Son has the property *being functionally subordinate in every possible world in which the Son exists.*

14. Alvin Plantinga notes that "although the distinction between *modality de re* and *modality de dicto* was the stock in trade of every medieval graduate student in philosophy, it was disastrously lost in the modern repudiation of all things medieval; it was painfully re-won during the present century." "Essence and Essentialism," in *A Companion to Metaphysics,* ed. Jaegwon Kim and Ernest Sosa (Oxford: Blackwell, 1995), p. 138.

15. According to Alvin Plantinga's summary, something "has a property essentially if and only if it has it and could not possibly have lacked it. Another way to put the same thing is to say that an object *x* has the property *P* essentially if and only if *x* has it in every possible world in which *x* exists." "Essence and Essentialism," p. 138. For further discussion see E. J. Lowe's account (which he offers in comparison with a weaker version): "an essential property of an object is a property which that object always possesses and which it could not have failed to possess — in other words, in the language of possible worlds, it is a property which that object possesses at all times in every possible world in which it exists." *A Survey of Metaphysics* (Oxford: Oxford University Press, 2002), p. 96.

(4) If Hard EFS is true, then the Son has this property essentially while the Father does not.

(5) If the Son has this property essentially and the Father does not, then the Son is of a different essence than the Father. Thus the Son is *heteroousios* rather than *homoousios*.

C. Some Possible Responses

Proponents of EFS might attempt to take refuge in something like the "Social Trinitarianism" of Cornelius Plantinga, Jr. Plantinga distinguishes "personal from generic essence and posits three of the former and one of the latter in God."[16] Plantinga says that "each of Father, Son, and Holy Spirit possesses the whole generic divine essence"; he also says that each possesses "a personal essence that distinguishes that person from the other two."[17] Advocates of Hard EFS might try to adopt this strategy; they might claim "Social Trinitarianism" as a way to hold onto the *homoousios* (of the generic divine essence).[18]

However, going the "Social Trinity" route will be difficult for EFS. For Plantinga's "personal essences" are not simply what are often called "individual essences."[19] They are strongly internally-related properties (thus giving the Social Trinitarian tools with which to attempt to fend off charges of tritheism);[20] these personal essences amount to "a derivation or

16. Ronald J. Feenstra and Cornelius Plantinga, Jr., introduction to *Trinity, Incarnation, and Atonement: Philosophical and Theological Essays*, ed. Ronald J. Feenstra and Cornelius Plantinga, Jr. (Notre Dame, Ind.: University of Notre Dame Press, 1989), p. 7.

17. Cornelius Plantinga, Jr., "Social Trinity and Tritheism," in *Trinity, Incarnation, and Atonement*, p. 29.

18. As J. Scott Horrell might be doing; see his "Toward a Biblical Model of the Social Trinity: Avoiding Equivocation of Nature and Order," *Journal of the Evangelical Theological Society* 47, no. 3 (2004): 399-421.

19. Graeme Forbes defines individual essence as follows: "an individual essence of an object x is a set of properties I which satisfies the following two conditions: every property P in I is an essential property of x, and it is not possible that some entity y distinct from x have every member of I." *The Metaphysics of Modality* (Oxford: Clarendon, 1985), p. 99; Forbes, "Essentialism," in *A Companion to the Philosophy of Language*, ed. Bob Hale and Crispin Wright (Oxford: Blackwell, 1997), p. 516.

20. On internal properties see J. P. Moreland's "General Ontology and Theology: A Primer," in *For Faith and Clarity: Philosophical Contributions to Theology*, ed. James K. Beilby (Grand Rapids: Baker Academic, 2006), pp. 59-60.

origination relation" (i.e., generation and procession).[21] But if Ware and Grudem deny the doctrines of generation and procession (as it appears they might), then this route would not be open to them.[22] They might want to hold both to a generic divine essence (the attributes of omniscience, omnipotence, etc.) and to individual or personal essences that are functional (i.e., the Father's individual essence is made up of properties such as *having authority over,* while the Son's individual essence is made up of such properties as *being subordinate*), but it is not obvious that they can do even this.

For in addition to the hard questions raised earlier, several additional challenges face such a move. First, on this account the Son just would be essentially subordinate to the Father, and this is the very thing that most EFS proponents want to deny.[23] Furthermore, such functional properties are not the stuff of strongly internally-related properties (as Plantinga's doctrine has), nor do they bring us to a Father-Son relation (a Master-Servant relation would capture this authority structure at least as well). So Hard EFS has a long way to go if it wants to take refuge in Social Trinitarianism.[24]

More troubling yet, however, is the concern that Hard EFS would struggle mightily to hold on to even a generic divine essence. Recall that Ware worries that without EFS we have no reason for the Father to send the Son (rather than the Father being sent by the Son).[25] Grudem insists that "these roles could not have been reversed or the Father would have

---

21. Cornelius Plantinga, Jr., "Social Trinity and Tritheism," p. 28.

22. Ware says these doctrines are "highly speculative and not grounded in biblical teaching." *Father,* p. 162 n. 3. While this is not an outright denunciation, it falls somewhere short of a ringing endorsement of the venerable doctrine. John Feinberg quotes Grudem (from an unpublished footnote) as taking the same approach. *No One Like Him: The Doctrine of God* (Wheaton, Ill.: Crossway, 2001), pp. 490-91, but Grudem has indicated to me (in personal correspondence) that he does not deny these venerable doctrines.

23. An exception would be John V. Dahms, who affirms essential subordination. "The Subordination of the Son," *Journal of the Evangelical Theological Society* 37, no. 4 (1994): 351-64.

24. Furthermore, even the Social Trinitarianism of theologians such as Plantinga (who have a stronger claim to monotheism than Hard EFS currently does) is on trial for charges of tritheism; see, e.g., Brian Leftow, "Anti Social Trinitarianism," in *The Trinity: An Interdisciplinary Symposium on the Trinity,* ed. Stephen T. Davis, Daniel Kendall, S.J., and Gerald O'Collins, S.J. (Oxford: Oxford University Press, 1999), pp. 203-49. While I do not find these criticisms of Social Trinitarianism to be devastating to all versions of Social Trinitarianism, I do think the criticisms raise some important concerns that should be addressed.

25. Ware, "How Shall We Think?" p. 275.

ceased to be the Father and the Son would have ceased to be the Son."[26] Now unless we strictly equate the "economic Trinity" with the "immanent Trinity," there is no reason to think that this is the case.[27] To the contrary, many theologians in the tradition are of the opposite conviction — Thomas Aquinas, for example, insists that any of the divine persons could have become incarnate.[28]

Nor is it hard to see why much of the classic Christian tradition has insisted on this, for if only the Son can become incarnate we run into even more theological problems. If only the Son has the property *possibly being incarnate* (and has it essentially), then the Son again has an essential property that the Father does not have. So once again we are faced with a Son who is not *homoousios* with the Father. In addition, it seems that the Father and Son are not even of the same generic divine essence on this account. For if the defense of Hard EFS goes in this direction, then the Father and Son do not share the property of *omnipotence:* on this account the Father would be limited in his abilities to perform actions that are logically possible (i.e., becoming incarnate), even actions that are possible for a morally perfect being — thus the Father would be less than omnipotent.[29] And if the Father does not have the property or attribute of omnipotence, then surely the Father does not have the whole generic divine essence. Thus the Father and the Son are not *homoousios* — even with respect to a generic divine essence.

A drastic response from the proponents of Hard EFS would be simply to deny essentialism. But then we are left to wonder why they would bother to defend *homoousios* at all. A somewhat less drastic response would be to deny essentialism *as it is commonly understood.*[30] But in this case they

---

26. Grudem, *Systematic Theology,* p. 250.

27. On this see Randal Rauser, "Rahner's Rule: An Emperor without Clothes?" *International Journal of Systematic Theology* 7 (2005): 81-94, and Fred Sanders, *The Image of the Immanent Trinity: Rahner's Rule and the Theological Interpretation of Scripture* (New York: Peter Lang, 2005).

28. E.g., *Summa Theologiae,* 3a, q.1-3. Richard Cross argues that this view is held by virtually everyone in medieval Christology; see, e.g., *The Metaphysics of the Incarnation: Thomas Aquinas to Duns Scotus* (Oxford: Oxford University Press, 2002), p. 179.

29. This would seem to result in the Son having less authority than the Father (as Grudem makes clear, e.g., in *Evangelical Feminism,* p. 410), while it is the Father — oddly enough — who is less than omnipotent.

30. Other contemporary ways of understanding essential properties do not seem promising. Baruch A. Brody takes essential properties to be those properties that an object

would need to supply an alternative metaphysics. For the proponents of Hard EFS are making some strong claims about divine ontology, and it is they who owe us a coherent alternative. In the absence of such an alternative account, such a dismissive response should not be appealing.

III. A Biblical Basis?

Proponents of EFS might respond that their position is mandated by a proper interpretation of Scripture. Such a response could take several different forms. Grudem seems to think that the very identity of the divine persons is at stake here. He says that "authority and submission between the Father and the Son, and between Father and Son and the Holy Spirit, is a fundamental difference (or probably *the* fundamental difference) between the persons of the Trinity."[31] Otherwise, he says, we would have only "Person A and Person B and Person C before Christ came to earth"; thus the personal relationships themselves require the subordination of the Son (p. 406). He asserts that "the very names 'Father' and 'Son' attest" to the authority of the Father over the Son (p. 413). He is exercised especially to combat claims that there is mutual submission within the Trinity: "if the Father also submitted to the authority of the Son, it would destroy the Trinity, because there would be no Father, Son, and Holy Spirit, but only Person A, Person A, and Person A" (p. 433). This is indeed a strong claim, and he explains it further by stating that "the differences in authority among Father, Son, and Holy Spirit are the only interpersonal differences that the Bible indicates exist eternally among the members of the Godhead. . . . These differences, in which there is authority and submission to authority, seem to be the means by which Father, Son, and Holy Spirit differ from one another and can be differentiated from one another" (p. 433).

We might wonder why Grudem would make such a claim. Unless one begs the question here (i.e., assuming that personal distinctions equate or entail a hierarchical authority structure and then arguing that, since there are genuine distinctions among the divine persons, these differentiations

---

has always possessed and that it cannot cease to possess without thereby ceasing to exist. See, e.g., *Identity and Essence* (Princeton: Princeton University Press, 1980), pp. 81ff. and 116ff. Surely applying this account to Hard EFS would result in the conclusion that the divine persons just are of different essences.

31. Grudem, *Evangelical Feminism,* p. 47. Page references have been placed in the text.

obviously amount to a hierarchical structure), it is less than clear what might motivate this claim. Grudem says that "if we did not have such differences in authority in the relationships among the members of the Trinity, then we would not know of any differences at all, and it would be unclear whether there are *any* differences among the persons of the Trinity" (p. 433).

But surely the personal distinctions of the Trinity do not depend upon human recognition of them for their existence. It may be an interesting fact about *us* that we might not know much (or perhaps anything) about the personal distinctions other than by the revelation that we have, but such an admission says nothing about the nature of the triune God.

At any rate, however, it is not at all clear why someone skeptical of Hard EFS and unconvinced by Grudem's claim might not simply appeal to the personal properties. Traditionally, properties such as "being generated," "being ingenerate," or "being spirated" belong to the distinct persons and are thus called "personal properties." These belong eternally to the divine persons, and each is possessed by only one of the divine persons. The Father, Son, and Spirit are personally distinct in their relations, and they are so eternally. Given this, why would we need to appeal to functional properties to account for genuine distinction?

More promising for EFS is the direct appeal to the scriptural witness to the subordination of the Son. Advocates of EFS sometimes appeal to the plethora of passages that speak of the Son's subordination to the Father in his incarnate ministry, but these do little to support the contention that this functional or economic subordination is eternal. And they get us nowhere near Hard EFS. In the incarnation, Jesus Christ is submissive to the will of his Father. Surely this is beyond dispute. But to say this is not to say that there is some sort of eternal hierarchical authority structure, and it surely is not to say that the Son is subordinate to the Father in all possible worlds.

Despite this, however, one passage does seem to indicate clearly that the Son is subordinate to the Father into the eschaton. 1 Corinthians 15:28 tells us that after death, our last enemy, is destroyed, "the Son himself will also be subjected to him who put all things in subjection under him, that God may be all in all." Grudem comments that

> in 1 Corinthians 15:28, Scripture shows us the beginning of the eternal state with the Son subject to the Father. Unless there is strong evidence

in Scripture showing a later change in that situation (which there is not), the passage leads us to think that that situation will continue for eternity. Prior to the foundation of the world, the Son was eternally subject to the Father. When He returned to sit at the Father's right hand, the Son was subject to the Father. As today He intercedes for us, the Son is subject to the Father. When the last enemy, death, is finally destroyed, the Son will be subject to the Father. The relationship between Father and Son has always been that way, and it will be that way forever. (p. 414)

But surely 1 Corinthians 15:28 underdetermines the issue. So far as I can see, it does not push us in the direction of either Soft EFS or Hard EFS. What is clear is that the Son will be subject after the last enemy is destroyed. If we take "will also be subjected to" to imply functional subordination (as seems reasonable enough), then we should conclude that the functional subordination of the Son will continue. Even after our final enemy is destroyed, the Son will be "subjected to" the Father. As Grudem recognizes, just how long this will continue is not made explicit; surely it may (due to the continuing incarnation of Christ) be permanent or everlasting. But this in no way implies either that it is timelessly eternal or backwardly everlasting.[32] More importantly, however, this passage gets us nowhere close to Hard EFS. It tells us only of what *is* and *will be* — it does *not* tell us what *must be*. It does not tell us that the Son is subordinate necessarily; i.e., it does not tell us that the Son is subordinate in all possible worlds.

Again, it seems clear that this passage underdetermines the issue at hand. I have argued that, given common understandings of essentialism, Hard EFS entails the denial of *homoousios*. If I am right, and if it is true (as I believe) that affirmations of *homoousios* are themselves grounded in scriptural revelation, then we would be well advised not to read 1 Corinthians 15:28 in a way that entails such a denial.

What is striking in this discussion is the lack of distinctly *christological* reflection. The patristic theologians who wrestled with heretical challenges

32. Grudem appeals to such passages as John 3:16-17; 4:34; 8:42; Gal. 4:4; 1 Cor. 8:6; Heb. 1:2; Rom. 8:29; Eph. 1; and Rev. 13:8 to support his claim that "the Son was subject to the Father before He came to live on earth" (*Evangelical Feminism*, pp. 406-7). It is worth noting that his arguments only attempt to show that at some point prior to the incarnation the Son is subordinate to the Father. In other words, his exegetical arguments do not even begin to make the stronger modal claims of Hard EFS (again, if Grudem doesn't mean to endorse Hard EFS, this may be exactly what Grudem intends).

were concerned to keep both the humanity and the divinity of Christ in sight: the two natures of Christ subsist in one person, and they do so without either separation or confusion. When considering Jesus' statements of fear, weakness, growth, ignorance, or subordination, the patristic theologians were generally prone to predicate these of the humanity of Jesus.[33] If these are predicated of his divinity, game over: the Arians win. On the other hand, if such properties are attributed to the humanity of Christ (or, a bit more precisely, to the Son according to his human nature), then the biblical arguments of the Arians are turned aside. Interestingly, however, the discussion of passages speaking of the submission of the Son to the Father by the proponents of EFS makes little use of this sort of interpretive strategy. For while the proponents of EFS do not wish to predicate this exactly of the *divinity* of Christ, they do not predicate it of his humanity either.

But just what are we to make of the biblical witness to the subordination of the incarnate Son? Should we predicate the subordination of the Son to his divinity — that is, to *his* divinity? If so, then the divinity of the Son is different from the divinity of the Father, and Arian polytheism (or something approaching it) is correct after all.[34] Should we simply attribute this subordination to *"the Son"* while forbidding any mention of essence at this point? If so, then how does this differ from the strategy of the Homoian Arians? Or should we join the majority tradition in attributing this subordination to the humanity of the incarnate Son whose two distinct natures are joined in one person?[35]

---

33. E.g., Athanasius, *Contra Arianos* 28.43-48; Ambrose, *Of the Christian Faith*, 2.7-10. On the other hand, the "Homoian Arians" are known for predicating the subordination of the person of the Son (while avoiding mention of the divine essence), e.g., the Council of Sirmium as recorded in Athanasius, *De Synodis* 28-29. For more on Homoian Arianism, see Hanson, *Christian Doctrine of God*, pp. 579-97; Daniel H. Williams, "Another Exception to Fourth-Century 'Arian' Typologies: The Case of Germinius of Sirmium," *Journal of Early Christian Studies* 4 (1996): 335-57.

34. I say "something approaching it" because the proponent of Hard EFS need not be committed to the full Arian view; the defender of Hard EFS could, for example, consistently deny that the Son is created (and no doubt many other items on the Arian checklist). This important point, however, remains: Hard EFS would leave us with distinct divine persons who are of different essences and who are hierarchically structured.

35. I am aware that the traditional way of predicating properties to the distinct natures (or, more precisely, to the *person* according to one or another of the distinct natures) is not without its challenges. For a sampling of the discussion of these, see Marilyn McCord Adams, *Christ and Horrors: The Coherence of Christology* (Cambridge: Cambridge University

IV. Conclusion

The debates over EFS seem to this point to have generated as much heat as light.[36] What strikes me as particularly unfortunate is the way these discussions have become so closely tied to debates over the subordination of women. The waters of Trinity doctrine are deep enough that it is hard to see very far even when they are clear — and it is much harder when they are muddied needlessly. And needlessly they are, for (so far as I can tell) these discussions are not tied together.[37] One could be both a "complementarian" with respect to male-female relations and hold Hard EFS at arm's length;[38] while one could also be both an "egalitar-

---

Press, 2006), pp. 108-43; Thomas V. Morris, *The Logic of God Incarnate* (Ithaca, N.Y.: Cornell University Press, 1986); Edwin Chr. Van Driel, "The Logic of Assumption," in *Exploring Kenotic Christology: The Self-Emptying of God,* ed. C. Stephen Evans (Oxford: Oxford University Press, 2006), pp. 265-90; Thomas D. Senor, "Incarnation, Timelessness, and Leibniz's Law Problems," in *God and Time: Essays on the Divine Nature,* ed. Gregory E. Ganssle and David M. Woodruff (Oxford: Oxford University Press, 2002), pp. 220-35; Douglas K. Blount, "On the Incarnation of a Timeless God," in *God and Time,* pp. 236-48; Eleonore Stump, "Aquinas' Metaphysics of the Incarnation," in *The Incarnation: An Interdisciplinary Symposium on the Incarnation of the Son of God,* ed. Stephen T. Davis, Daniel Kendall, S.J., and Gerald O'Collins, S.J. (Oxford: Oxford University Press, 2002), pp. 197-218; Brian Leftow, "A Timeless God Incarnate," in *The Incarnation,* pp. 273-99; Ronald J. Feenstra, "Reconsidering Kenotic Christology," in *Trinity, Incarnation, and Atonement,* pp. 128-52; Stephen T. Davis, *Christian Philosophical Theology* (Oxford: Oxford University Press, 2006), pp. 172-92; Cross, *The Metaphysics of the Incarnation.*

36. Grudem's comment about egalitarianism's supposed lack of affection for God comes to mind: "And when we begin to dislike the very idea of authority and submission — not distortions and abuses, but *the very idea* — we are tampering with something very deep. We are beginning to dislike God Himself." *Evangelical Feminism,* p. 48.

37. As Keith Yandell has pointed out to me, if the doctrine of the Trinity is so closely tied to gender relations, and if Hard EFS is true, then it is also possible to mount an argument directly parallel to my argument against Hard EFS to the conclusion that women and men are *not* equal in essence. In other words, if Hard EFS is true, and if this doctrine has direct entailments for gender issues, then it would be true that women are of a different essence than men.

38. If the analogy with Trinitarian relations is that direct, then the "complementarian" might continue to appeal to the inter-Trinitarian relations to support his claim that submission and subordination in role may be consistent with equality of essence. As Grudem himself puts it: "if we were to limit ourselves to those passages of Scripture that speak of Christ's obedience to His Father during his earthly ministry (and there are many such passages), it still proves that two persons can be equal in value and in their very being, and one can still

ian" and (alas) a theologian who denies the full equality of the Son with the Father.[39]

I am not sure whether Grudem and Ware (or others) intend to defend Hard EFS or merely remind us of Soft EFS. While they make statements that could be taken to support Hard EFS, they also clearly affirm *homoousios* and just as clearly deny Arianism. As Ware puts it: "the Father, Son, and Holy Spirit each possesses fully the identically same one and undivided, infinite, and eternal divine nature. I fully reject the Arian view (period). . . . I reject this unequivocally."[40] How someone might coherently affirm both *homoousios* and Hard EFS is far from obvious, and to say that such a position is internally strained is to put it rather mildly. But perhaps Grudem and Ware will clarify (or modify) their views, or maybe they will access an account of essence that allows for both consistency and orthodoxy. My point here is *not* that they *cannot* do so; it is simply that they need to do so (if indeed they intend to promote and defend Hard EFS).

In this essay I have suggested that a bit of modal analysis might bring some helpful clarity to the debate. I have pointed out that EFS is open to various readings. If its proponents mean only to affirm what I have called Soft EFS, then there seems to be no good reason to oppose what they are saying and reasons aplenty to make such affirmations with them. On the other hand, Hard EFS, understood along the lines of contemporary essentialism, flatly entails the denial of the *homoousion,* and with it an unfortunate departure from creedal orthodoxy. Hard EFS does not merely tend toward a denial of the *homoousion,* nor does it merely "smack of" it.[41] If I am right, it simply entails the direct denial of the *homoousion,* and thus should be resisted by Christians who hold to creedal orthodoxy.

---

be subordinate to the authority of the other. Thus it still proves a parallel to a husband and wife who are equal in the image of God but different in roles in marriage, and it still disproves the egalitarian claim that equality in the image of God cannot exist along with the idea that a husband has authority over his wife." *Evangelical Feminism,* p. 425.

39. Grudem identifies the "fundamental egalitarian objection" as this: "if different, then not equal, and if equal, then not different." *Evangelical Feminism,* p. 411. Whether or not Grudem is correct in his belief that this is the "fundamental egalitarian objection," I certainly have no interest in defending it (or, for that matter, egalitarianism) here.

40. Bruce A. Ware, personal correspondence, 18 September 2006. Ware also says that my argument is "simply wrong," but to this point he has not indicated where he thinks the problems lie.

41. Bilezikian says that talk of subordination "smacks of the Arian heresy." "Hermeneutical Bungee-Jumping," p. 67.

CHAPTER SEVEN

Holy Love and Divine Aseity
in the Theology of John Zizioulas

The Trinitarian theology of John D. Zizioulas is often recognized as one
that is suggestive and profound, and theologians who engage it are
finding it fertile soil for further developments in theological anthropology
and ecclesiology.[1] It has also, however, generated a fair amount of controversy, not the least of which concerns Zizioulas's faithfulness to the Greek
patristic tradition.[2] In this chapter I do not focus directly on the historical
issues; instead I address some *conceptual* issues raised by Zizioulas's Trinitarian theology. After introducing and explicating two major themes in his
theology, I argue that these themes do not fit together comfortably. In fact,
they appear to collide. I then suggest a possible resolution to this conundrum, and I address several further possible objections.

---

1. E.g., Miroslav Volf, *After Our Likeness: The Church as the Image of the Trinity* (Grand
Rapids: Eerdmans, 1998), and Catherine Mowry LaCugna, *God for Us: The Trinity and Christian Life* (New York: HarperCollins, 1991).

2. E.g., Lucian Turcescu, "'Person' versus 'Individual,' and Other Modern Misreadings
of Gregory of Nyssa," *Modern Theology* 18 (2002): 527-639; see also his very helpful explica-
tion of Gregory of Nyssa in his *Gregory of Nyssa and the Concept of Divine Persons* (Oxford:
Oxford University Press, 2005), and the response to Turcescu's criticisms by Aristotle Papa-
nikolaou, "Is John Zizioulas an Existentialist in Disguise: Response to Lucian Turcescu,"
Modern Theology 20 (2004): 601-7.

I. "Being as Communion" and the "Sovereignty-Aseity Conviction"

Many contemporary theologians find Zizioulas's theology to be rich indeed; it is brimming with insights and proposals. Two themes, however, stand out above all others in his doctrine of God. These are what I shall call (with some explanation) the "Sovereignty-Aseity Conviction" (SAC) and (more conventionally) the "Being as Communion" thesis (BAC).[3]

A. Persons in Relation: Zizioulas on Being as Communion

Central to his Trinitarian theology is Zizioulas's contention that to be a person is to be in relation to other persons. For him, there is no such thing as an individual person. As he understands it, a crucial insight of patristic theology is that "the being of God could be known only through personal relationships and personal love. Being means life, and life means communion."[4] This insight entails the radical conclusion that "the being of God is a relational being: without the concept of communion it would not be possible to speak of the being of God." Thus the doctrine of the Trinity is a "*primordial* ontological concept and not a notion which is added to the divine substance or rather which follows it . . . the substance of God, 'God,' has no ontological content, no true being, apart from communion." Zizioulas sees this as a repudiation by the patristic theologians of the individualism of Aristotle. Because "communion becomes an ontological concept in patristic thought," personal identity is always relative: "nothing in existence is conceivable in itself, as an individual, such as the τόδε τι of Aristotle, since even God exists thanks to an event of communion" (p. 17).[5]

---

3. On the sovereignty-aseity thesis in the thought of Aquinas, see Alvin Plantinga, *Does God Have a Nature?* (Milwaukee: Marquette University Press, 1980); see also Jay Wesley Richards, *The Untamed God: A Philosophical Exploration of Divine Perfection, Simplicity, and Immutability* (Downers Grove, Ill.: InterVarsity, 2003).

4. John D. Zizioulas, *Being as Communion* (Crestwood, N.Y.: St. Vladimir's Seminary Press, 1985), p. 16. Page references have been placed in the text for this discussion.

5. Does this entail the logic of relative identity? For a careful and elegant defense of the doctrine of the Trinity employing the logic of relative identity, see Peter van Inwagen, "And Yet They Are Not Three Gods but One God," in *Philosophy and the Christian Faith*, ed. Thomas V. Morris (Notre Dame, Ind.: University of Notre Dame Press, 1988), pp. 241-78; see also the helpful discussion by Michael C. Rea, "Relative Identity and the Doctrine of the Trinity," *Philosophia Christi* 5 (2003): 431-45.

Zizioulas thinks that the early apologists such as Justin Martyr and the early academic "Alexandrian catechetical theologians" such as Clement and Origen largely missed this crucial theological insight (pp. 16, 84). Instead, "pastoral theologians such as Ignatius of Antioch and above all St Irenaeus and later St Athanasius" pioneered this insight (p. 16; cf. p. 84). Athanasius in particular is applauded for his contribution; his insistence that the Son is of the substance of God "implies that substance *possesses almost by definition a relational character*" (p. 84). But with Zizioulas's obvious appreciation for the brilliance and helpfulness of Athanasius comes some criticism. First, Zizioulas notes that Athanasius still tends to conflate *ousia* and *hypostasis;* Zizioulas's second concern is that Athanasius continues to succumb to the temptation to prioritize substance over persons as he champions the *homoousion* against the Arians (pp. 83-88). As Zizioulas sees it, the Cappadocians were the theologians to articulate the distinction between *ousia* and *hypostasis;* they grasped the crucial insight, latent in Trinitarian thought all along, that "being is communion."

My purpose here is not to pass judgment on Zizioulas's reading of patristic theology, but it should be clear that he works to read the tradition both carefully and critically. Important for our purposes is his insistence that the Cappadocian insight into the priority of the person of the Father is a significant advance over the earlier, and especially Athanasian, formulations. As he sees it, patristic theology has delivered for us the absolutely central insight that the doctrine of the Trinity teaches us that "there is no true being without communion. Nothing exists as an individual, conceivable in itself." The result is clear: "communion is an ontological category" (p. 18).

This does not, as far as I can see, commit Zizioulas to a rejection of essentialism. To reject essentialism would be to deny and abandon the *homoousion,* and Zizioulas surely does not take this route. After all, it was the "Homoian Arians" of the fourth century who insisted that no mention should be made of *ousia,* and it is hardly conceivable that Zizioulas would side with them against the Cappadocians.[6] Nor does it enlist him in the

6. By "Homoian Arianism" I mean the theology set forth and defended by such theologians as Akakius of Caesarea, Eudoxius, Valens of Mursa, Ursacius of Singidunum, Ulfilas, Palladius, and Germinius of Sirmium, and enshrined in the Second Creed of Sirmium (357) and the Creed of Nike (360). See R. P. C. Hanson, *The Search for the Christian Doctrine of God: The Arian Controversy, 318-381* (Edinburgh: T. & T. Clark, 1988), pp. 579-97. Daniel H. Williams argues that Germinius does not fit Hanson's neat categorization. "Another Excep-

forces of those who ride forth to battle against the dreaded evils of "ontotheology."[7] Instead, he seems to want to *rehabilitate* the concept of substance. But this is not the same as to deny it or "overcome" it. No, on his account the divine substance just *is* the communion of holy love shared by the Father, Son, and Holy Spirit. Commenting on the Johannine affirmation that "God is love" (1 John 4:16), Zizioulas states that "love is not an emanation or 'property' of the substance of God — this detail is significant in light of what I have said so far — but it is *constitutive* of his substance, i.e., it is that which makes God what he is, the one God."[8]

The results of this are profound for Zizioulas; there are implications both for *personhood* and for our understanding of the *being* or *essence* of God. Zizioulas recognizes the implications for our understanding of the divine essence: "Thus love ceases to be a qualifying — i.e. secondary — property of being and becomes the *supreme ontological predicate*. Love as God's mode of existence 'hypostasizes' God, *constitutes* his being" (p. 46). Thus the divine *persons* are "concrete, unique, and unrepeatable" entities who exist only in communion. As Zizioulas puts it, "the mystery of being a person lies in the fact that here otherness and communion are not in contradiction but coincide. Truth as communion does not lead to the dissolving of the diversity of beings into one vast ocean of being, but to the affirmation of otherness in and through love" (p. 106). God's *being*, the triune life and love given and shared between the Father, Son, and Holy Spirit, is "identical with an act of communion" (p. 44). The persons have their identity only in communion, and the one divine essence is now to be identified with the communion of holy love shared by the Father, Son, and Holy Spirit.

---

tion to Fourth-Century 'Arian' Typologies: The Case of Germinius of Sirmium," *Journal of Early Christian Studies* 4 (1996): 335-57.

7. Examples of theological opposition to "ontotheology" abound; surely among the most important are Jean-Luc Marion, e.g., *God without Being*, trans. Thomas A. Carlson (Chicago: University of Chicago Press, 1991), and John Milbank, *The Word Made Strange* (Oxford: Blackwell, 1997); "Only Theology Overcomes Metaphysics," *New Blackfriars* 76 (1995): 325-42. James K. A. Smith notes that Milbank extends Marion's critique of Scotus; where Marion recognizes "Scotus' idolatry with respect to God but fails to acknowledge Scotus' idolatry toward creatures," Milbank has no such failure. *Introducing Radical Orthodoxy: Mapping a Post-Secular Theology* (Grand Rapids: Baker Academic, 2004), p. 98. For a quite different reading of Zizioulas, see Wayne Hankey, "Theoria versus Poesis: Neoplatonism and Trinitarian Difference in Aquinas, John Milbank, Jean-Luc Marion, and John Zizioulas," *Modern Theology* 15 (1999): 387-415.

8. Zizioulas, *Being as Communion*, p. 46. Page references have been placed in the text.

B. The Priority of the Father: Zizioulas and the Sovereignty-Aseity Conviction

Zizioulas states clearly that "discussion of the being of God leads patristic thought to" the two main theses under consideration in this chapter (p. 18). As we have seen, the first is the "Being as Communion" (BAC) thesis: "communion is an ontological category" (p. 18). The second thesis is that of the priority of the Father. Where the BAC thinks of the Holy Trinity as a "primordial" ontological concept that raises communion to ontological status (and supreme ontological status at that), the SAC insists on the absolute priority of the person of the Father. Zizioulas is quite clear about what this means: "just like 'substance,' 'communion' does not exist by itself: it is the *Father* who is the 'cause' of it" (p. 17).

Here Zizioulas insists that neither "substance" nor some abstract notion of "communion" is ultimate; for him it is of supreme importance that the *person* of the *Father* is first: "the ultimate ontological category which makes something really *be,* is neither an impersonal and incommunicable 'substance,' nor a structure of communion existing by itself or imposed by necessity, but rather the *person*" (p. 18). The radical freedom of God — or, more accurately, the radical freedom of God the Father — is central to Zizioulas's thinking here. As he puts it, "God owes his existence to the Father," and this means that God does not exist necessarily: "God does not exist because he cannot but exist" (p. 18).[9] So it means that the existence of God is a contingent fact; God exists because the Father wills that God exist. But it also means that the essence of God is contingent, and so the fact that the divine essence is one of triune holy love is not necessary. For Zizioulas, the radical priority of the Father entails that this communion itself is contingent, for "that communion is not a constraining structure for his existence (God is not in communion, does not love, because he cannot but be in communion and love)" (p. 18).

We can see some of the importance of this for Zizioulas when we see what he is reacting against and rejecting. It is this: he is concerned with the loss of the sovereign freedom of God. At one level, he is exercised to make sure that the freedom of God *in creation* is not lost. He insists that "biblical theology" shows us that "the world is not ontologically necessary" (p. 39); he wants to protect the absolute freedom of God in creation. In other

---

9. I take Zizioulas to mean "the Trinity" when he refers to "God" here.

words, he is defending a robustly "libertarian" notion of divine freedom.[10] This is what I, following Jay Wesley Richards and Alvin Plantinga, shall call the "Sovereignty-Aseity Conviction."[11] Richards describes the SAC as "the conviction that God is the one reality that exists *a se* (from and of himself) and is dependent on nothing outside of himself for his essence and existence."[12] Only God says "I am" (Exod. 3:14); everything else that exists says "I am *because . . .*" God alone exists *a se;* everything else that exists does so in reliance upon him. As such, the SAC has garnered wide acceptance in the Christian tradition.

But Zizioulas radically extends the SAC. For at another level, Zizioulas is worried that notions of substance and necessity themselves compromise the freedom of God. He is not simply arguing that God has freedom to do A or -A, to create (or "actualize") this possible world rather than another. As Robert D. Turner puts it, for Zizioulas "the doctrine of creation *ex nihilo* alone fails to achieve the goal of maintaining the freedom of God."[13] Zizioulas takes the concept of freedom a step further. And a big step it is, for it leads him to assert the radical freedom of the Father in the face of what he calls the "ultimate challenge to the freedom of the person" — the "'necessity' of existence."[14] Here he shows a close affinity with Heidegger's notion of thrownness.[15] For Heidegger, to be "thrown" is just to find oneself located in a particular setting with a particular set or range of options before you.[16] To be thrown is to "fall prey"; it is to be limited and thus fi-

10. James K. Beilby argues that loss of "libertarian" divine freedom compromises divine aseity. "Divine Aseity, Divine Freedom: A Conceptual Problem for Edwardsian-Calvinism," *Journal of the Evangelical Theological Society* 47 (2004): 647-58.

11. For discussion of this, see Richards, *The Untamed God,* pp. 33-34, and Alvin Plantinga, *Does God?* pp. 34-35. Of course, their contexts are very different: Richards addresses Barth and Hartshorne while Plantinga treats Aquinas's doctrine of divine simplicity.

12. Richards, *The Untamed God,* p. 33.

13. Robert D. Turner, "Foundations for John Zizioulas' Approach to Ecclesial Communion," *Ephemerides Theologicae Lovanienses* 78 (2002): 440.

14. Zizioulas, *Being as Communion,* p. 42.

15. I am not saying that Zizioulas merely baptizes Heidegger (either by sprinkling or immersion), nor do I mean to imply that he adopts Heideggerian thought uncritically. To the contrary, Zizioulas offers several criticisms of the attempt of Christos Yannaras to find "philosophical justification" of Greek patristic theology in the thought of Heidegger. *Being as Communion,* p. 45 n. 40.

16. See Martin Heidegger, *Being and Time: A Translation of "Sein und Zeit,"* trans. Joan Stambaugh (Albany: State University of New York Press, 1996), especially pp. 164-68.

nite. But for Zizioulas, it seems that the radical freedom of the Father — his *ontological* affirmation of the SAC — means that *thrownness* is denied of the Father. The Father — and the Father alone — is radically *unthrown*. *He* is the one whose existence is *a se; he* is the only one whose freedom is so absolute that it chooses both its own existence and its own essence.

A brief comparison with the theology of Karl Barth may be instructive at this point. Zizioulas displays some affinity to Barth's doctrine of God with respect to divine freedom. Like Barth, he wants to insist on the radical freedom of God. Like Barth, he takes this to mean that God wills his own essence.[17] Thus for Zizioulas, as we have seen, the divine essence is contingent. And again like Barth, his affirmation of the BAC places very high priority on the one divine *act* (of communion) that just *is* God.[18] But he criticizes Barth for his lack of success in the utilization of Heidegger due to Barth's "introduction of the concept of time in God."[19] Furthermore, even though Barth insists that God wills his own essence, it is less than obvious that by this affirmation Barth means that God chooses it *from among alternatives.* Thus perhaps God does choose his essence (and so can be said to *freely* be who he is), but it is not as if God could have done otherwise. In other words, it may be that for Barth the freedom of God is some sort of "compatibilism." But for Zizioulas, to say this is to say far too little — if this is true, then God is still "thrown" and thus has "fallen prey" to existence. It seems that even Barth does not go nearly far enough — for Zizioulas, the Father chooses not only his essence but also the very existence of God.

Zizioulas's insistence on the SAC and his view of the radical freedom of the Father are also evidenced in the concerns he raises about the *homoousion.* He applauds Athanasius, whose theology he sees as "a direct consequence of the ontology of communion" that he received from the tradition of Ignatius and Irenaeus (p. 83). He notes appreciatively that, for Athanasius, the Son belongs to the substance rather than the will of God (as for the Arians), and he celebrates the way that Athanasius "trans-

17. See Karl Barth, *Church Dogmatics* II/1 (Edinburgh: T. & T. Clark, 1957).

18. On Barth's "actualism" see George Hunsinger, *How to Read Karl Barth: The Shape of His Theology* (Oxford: Oxford University Press, 1991).

19. Zizioulas, *Being as Communion*, p. 45 n. 40. Here Zizioulas also criticizes Rahner's introduction of the divine economy and revelation into the "ontological structure of the theology of the Holy Trinity." Page numbers in the following text refer to Zizioulas, *Being as Communion.*

formed the idea of substance" by making it relational: "to say that the Son belongs to God's substance *possesses almost by definition* a *relational char-acter*" (p. 83). But Zizioulas also worries that Athanasius does not go far enough, for "the *homoousion* presupposes *ousia* as the ultimate ontological category" (p. 89). So, on his account, it is the Cappadocians who finally bring us to the priority of the Father. Although they extend the relational notion of substance found in Athanasius (rather than correct it outright), it is they — rather than Athanasius — who provide us with an "ontology of personhood" that is adequately grounded in the *person* of the Father.

The theological payoff of this for Zizioulas should not be either over-looked or underestimated. Because of the radical freedom of the Father, the "world is not ontologically necessary" (p. 39).[20] Furthermore, and more importantly for Zizioulas, *personhood* is preeminent. In his words, "the person is no longer an adjunct to a being . . . *it is itself the hypostasis of being.*" Because of the identification of *person* with *hypostasis*, "entities no longer trace their being to being itself — that is, being is not an absolute category itself — but to the person, to precisely that which constitutes be-ing, that is, enables entities to be entities" (p. 39).

In summary, several things should be clear. The freedom of God, or more precisely the freedom of the Father, is metaphysically absolute. The freedom of the person of the Father means that God chooses his own *exis-tence*. As Zizioulas puts it, "when we say that God 'is,' we do not bind the personal freedom of God — the being of God is not an ontological 'neces-sity' or simple 'reality' — but we ascribe the being of God to his personal freedom. In a more analytic way this means that God, as Father and not as substance, perpetually confirms through 'being' his *free* will to exist" (p. 41). The existence of the triune God is contingent — it rests upon the perpetual decision of the Father to exist. But this radical freedom of the person of the Father also means that the *essence* of God is contingent. Zizioulas is clear that the "absolutely crucial point" is that "God as person — the hypostasis of the Father — makes the one divine substance to be that which it is: the one God" (p. 41). So even the communion of holy love shared among the divine persons in perichoresis is contingent; it is only so because the Father freely wills it to be so, and because the Father does so continually.

To this point we have observed what Zizioulas sets out as two founda-

---

20. Cf. his criticisms of Origen's doctrine of eternal creation, p. 75.

tional theses. The first is the BAC thesis, according to which God exists as a relational being. As Zizioulas puts it, "the being of God is a relational being: without the concept of communion it would be impossible to speak of God . . . the Holy Trinity is a *primordial* ontological concept" (p. 17). The results are profound: persons exist only in communion, and the holy love of the Father, Son, and Holy Spirit "ceases to be a qualifying — i.e. secondary — property of being and becomes *the supreme ontological predicate*" (p. 46). The second thesis is the SAC: the Father is prior in an absolute sense and as such is radically free. But these theses do not appear to fit together comfortably, and the conjunction of them raises some difficult questions. How are both of these concepts "ultimate" or "primordial"? How could communion be an ultimate concept if it must be caused by the Father? How can it be so if it is contingent? And how could the Father be a *person* if — given the BAC and its affirmation that personhood exists only in communion — he is prior to the other persons and to the communion itself? It is to a consideration of the difficult issues raised by these theses that I now turn.

II. Problems with the Account

Zizioulas's Trinitarian theology raises worries and concerns on several fronts. For instance, Alan J. Torrance asks if Zizioulas "is really being consistent with himself," and he notes that Zizioulas appears to be committed to "a kind of subordination of the Son to the Father" by his introduction of causal notions into the divine life.[21] As we shall see, Zizioulas's account is not without challenges; these confront both the ascription of the SAC to the Father and the incompatibility of the SAC with the BAC.

A. The SAC of the Father

Several problems confront Zizioulas's predication of the SAC of the Father. One is the issue of arbitrariness. If Zizioulas is right about the radical free-

---

21. Alan J. Torrance, *Persons in Communion: An Essay on Trinitarian Description and Human Participation, with Special Reference to Volume One of Karl Barth's "Church Dogmatics"* (Edinburgh: T. & T. Clark, 1996), pp. 292-93.

dom of the Father — if for the Father to be unthrown he must choose his own existence and essence — then is it not possible for the "Father" to choose to be something other than Father? Could not the Father have chosen to actualize a possible world in which moral atrocities are praiseworthy, one in which holy love is the gravest of all evils? Could he not have actualized a possible world in which Zeus and his brood exist and rule, or one in which the identity of Jesus is that of an Arian (or Aryan) Christ? Could he not first will into existence an evil god and then will himself out of existence? It seems that he could, for on Zizioulas's account anything less would compromise the freedom of the Father. And if so, then we are left to wonder if some abstract principle of freedom as *unthrownness* is finally necessary; it appears as if this understanding of freedom is finally what *is thrown* as a given.[22] In other words, it is simply a brute fact with which the Father must deal. But if not, then Zizioulas's radical version of the SAC is denied.

Even more serious, however, is the issue of subordinationism. Zizioulas himself accepts this: "in making the Father the 'ground' of God's being — or the ultimate reason for existence — theology accepted a kind of subordination of the Son to the Father." For him, this is not to "downgrade the Logos into something created."[23] But it is not clear what is going on here, nor is it obvious how Zizioulas's theology comports with patristic doctrine. Traditional affirmations of subordination have revolved around the "function" of the Son — of course the Son is subordinate to the Father, but for the tradition this is a function of the economy of salvation. Granting that the Son is ontologically subordinate would have meant compromise with Arianism. Functional subordination neither equates nor entails ontological subordination; the temporal and functional subordination of the Son does not reflect an eternal or ontological subordination. Quite the contrary is true for the pro-Nicene tradition; had the church not had recourse to this distinction, they would have been faced with an incredibly daunting challenge from Arian exegesis.

It is hard finally to escape the conclusion that this is ontological subordination on Zizioulas's view. For as Zizioulas thinks of it, the divine com-

---

22. Further concerns regarding omniscience could be raised as well: Would the Father's knowledge of his own actions "throw" him as well? Thanks to Randal Rauser for discussion of this issue.

23. Zizioulas, *Being as Communion*, p. 89.

munion of the triune life is prior to creation and independent of it.[24] So the subordination that Zizioulas refers to is not simply a functional or economic subordination; it is *prior to* and *independent of* the work of the Son in creation and redemption.

This raises the further concern that the Father may have different essential properties than does the Son (and Spirit). I take Zizioulas's BAC thesis to reflect a commitment to some form of essentialism. Beyond this rather basic commitment, it is not clear exactly how to take him, so (in lieu of direct indication on his part) I shall take this in what I take to be a rather standard sense of essence. As I understand it, an "individual-essence" is the "full set of properties, individually necessary and jointly sufficient" to be numerically identical with an individual,[25] while a "kind-essence" is the full set of properties, individually necessary and jointly sufficient for inclusion in a kind.[26] In this light, it is hard to know what to make of Zizioulas's theology.

Zizioulas wants to retain belief in a divine essence; the BAC thesis is that the divine essence is one of this communion of holy love. Beyond this, however, it seems that the Father has different essential properties than do the Son and the Spirit. For on the SAC thesis, the Father has the radical, ontological freedom of being *unthrown*. And the Father *alone* has this property — for the Son and Spirit indeed *are thrown* (by the free choice of the Father). For as Zizioulas has it, it is by the free decision of the Father that God exists, that God exists as triune, and that the triune God exists as

---

24. Recall Zizioulas's criticisms of Rahner on this account; for Zizioulas the ontological Trinity is not to be reduced to the economy of salvation.

25. See Thomas V. Morris, *The Logic of God Incarnate* (Ithaca, N.Y.: Cornell University Press, 1986), pp. 38-41. Graeme Forbes puts this with more precision when he states that "an individual essence of an object x is set of properties I which satisfies the following two conditions: every property P in I is an essential property of x, and it is not possible that some object y distinct from x has every member of I." *The Metaphysics of Modality* (Oxford: Clarendon, 1985), p. 99.

26. On the renaissance of interest in and defense of essentialism in recent analytic philosophy (and the move from modal logic to the metaphysics of modality more generally), cf. Michael J. Loux, "Introduction: Modality and Metaphysics," in *The Possible and the Actual,* ed. Michael J. Loux (Ithaca, N.Y.: Cornell University Press, 1979), pp. 15-64. Major works include Alvin Plantinga, *The Nature of Necessity* (Oxford: Oxford University Press, 1974); David Wiggins, *Sameness and Substance* (Oxford: Blackwell, 1980); and Saul Kripke, *Naming and Necessity* (Cambridge: Harvard University Press, 1972); a well-known recent example of essentialism applied to controversial theological issues is Morris's *The Logic of God Incarnate.*

a communion of holy love. The Father alone has the property of being radically *unthrown* — and he has it by virtue of being *the* primordial person. Consider the proposition *U: the Father chooses his own essence and existence*. To do the ontological and theological work that Zizioulas calls it to do, *U* cannot fail to be true. *U* must be true in all possible worlds.[27] And if *U* is true in all possible worlds, then *U* is *necessarily* true; we are left with the conclusion that the property of being *unthrown* is a necessary property of the Father. Furthermore, since this is, for the Father, a property that he has with *de re* (rather than *de dicto*) necessity, then it appears that it is an essential property of the Father.[28]

But the Son and the Holy Spirit do not have this property. They *are* radically thrown, because the Father decides that they will exist (and indeed that they will exist as they do). The defender of Zizioulas might respond that the SAC of the Father is a *personal* (rather than an *essential*) property; she might take recourse to the venerable distinction offered by the Cappadocians against the assaults of "neo-Arianism." Recall that when pressed by Eunomius that the divine hypostases must be different in either essence or accidents (neither of which was palatable), the Cappadocians responded that the properties that distinguished the divine hypostases were neither essential (which would amount to a denial of the *homoousion*) nor accidental (which would make the divine hypostases contingent), but that the divine hypostases are distinguished by *personal* properties. In other words, the hypostases are distinguished by relational properties — properties had by virtue of the relations to the other divine persons.[29]

But it is hard to see how the property of *being unthrown* could be a *personal* (rather than an *essential*) property. For personal properties (as

27. More precisely, *U* must be true in every possible world in which the Father has existence. But for Zizioulas's theology, the Father must exist in all possible worlds (at least long enough to be able to will himself out of existence), so this detail need not detain us here.

28. On this distinction see Alvin Plantinga, *"De Re* et *De Dicto," Nous* 3 (1969): 235-58.

29. For helpful discussions of neo-Arianism, cf. Hanson, *Christian Doctrine of God,* pp. 598-636; cf. also Richard Paul Vaggione, *Eunomius of Cyzicus and the Nicene Revolution* (Oxford: Oxford University Press, 2000); Michael E. Butler, "Neo-Arianism: Its Antecedents and Tenets," *St. Vladimir's Theological Quarterly* 36 (1992): 355-71; Graham A. Keith, "Our Knowledge of God: The Relevance of the Debate between Eunomius and the Cappadocians," *Tyndale Bulletin* 41 (1990): 60-88; and Thomas A. Kopacek, *A History of Neo-Arianism,* vol. 2 (Cambridge, Mass.: Philadelphia Patristic Foundation, 1979).

traditionally understood) are relational properties; they are the properties that make the persons the distinct entities they are *in relation to the other persons*. But on the SAC of the Father, the property of being radically *unthrown* is a property of the Father only. The Father could have decided to actualize a possible world in which there are no other divine persons, he could have decided to actualize a possible world in which there are only evil divine persons, or he could have decided to actualize a possible world in which he ceases to exist and thus in which there remain *no* divine persons at all (not even himself). So on the SAC of the Father, the property of *being unthrown* is a property possessed by the Father alone. In fact, for the SAC of the Father to work for Zizioulas's theology, it seems that the Father *must* have it alone. And if it is had alone (sans Son and Spirit), then it cannot count as a *personal* property (in the traditional sense). We seem, then, to be faced with this dilemma: the property of *being unthrown* must be for the Father either an essential property or an accidental one. But on Zizioulas's account of the SAC of the Father, it is a property that the Father has necessarily. Even if it could be an accidental property (one that the Father could or could not have), the all-important personhood of the Father would be endangered. So it appears that, on Zizioulas's understanding of the SAC of the Father, the Father has (at least) one essential property that the Son and Spirit do not have. Is he not thus of a different essence?

The defender of Zizioulas might yet have a way out. On the basis of our earlier distinctions between individual-essence and kind-essence, perhaps the Father is of a distinct individual-essence (thus perhaps a Trinitarian *haecceity*)[30] but not of a different kind-essence. This might bring Zizioulas close to the position of Cornelius Plantinga, Jr. Plantinga maintains that the divine persons have distinct personal essences (while sharing the "whole generic divine essence"), but for Plantinga the distinct personal essences just *are* their personal and *relational* properties.[31] Surely this strategy makes the proponents of Latin Trinitarianism nervous, but Plantinga can respond that while the language is unusual, the theology is not heterodox. But it is far from clear what Zizioulas might gain by such a defense, for he cannot access Plantinga's strategy. As Plantinga sees it, the

30. Thomas V. Morris appears to equate individual-essences and haecceities. *Logic of God Incarnate*, p. 38.

31. Cornelius Plantinga, Jr., "Social Trinity and Tritheism," in *Trinity, Incarnation, and Atonement: Philosophical and Theological Essays*, ed. Ronald J. Feenstra and Cornelius Plantinga, Jr. (Notre Dame, Ind.: University of Notre Dame Press, 1989), pp. 21-47.

personal essences are the properties had by the divine persons in relation to one another. But this route is closed to Zizioulas. For, as we have seen, on Zizioulas's account the individual-essence of the Father (which includes *U*) is *not* a property had in relation to other persons (and thus can hardly be said to be a personal property at all). So even if the Father is of a different individual-essence (while sharing the freely chosen kind-essence), on Zizioulas's account this individual-essence of the Father is not a personal essence.

B. Caution at the Crossroads: The BAC and the SAC

As we have seen, Zizioulas's predication of the SAC to the Father raises some serious questions and concerns. Unfortunately, however, yet more problems come at the intersection of the BAC and SAC theses. For at one level, both appear to be ultimate. According to the BAC, the Trinity is a "primordial ontological concept"; there "is no true being without communion . . . communion is an ontological category."[32] The result of the BAC is that (divine) love is "the supreme ontological predicate."[33] But the SAC suggests that the radical freedom of the Father is the ultimate; the Father freely chooses both the love and even the very life of God. But both cannot be ultimate, and we are left to wonder how the two theses might "ultimately" cohere.

Suppose we follow what seems to be the clearest direction from Zizioulas and take the SAC as finally ultimate. Then we are faced with a contradiction, one that goes to the heart of Zizioulas's theology. Consider:

(1) The Father alone is ultimate (SAC);
(2) The Father is a person (SAC);
(3) Persons exists only in communion (BAC).

(1) is clearly a piece of the SAC, for the SAC is predicated of the Father alone. Not even communion is a "constraining structure for his existence"; both the essence and existence of God are contingent upon the will of the Father. Similarly, (2) is central to Zizioulas's thought as well, for it is be-

---

32. Zizioulas, *Being as Communion*, pp. 17, 18.
33. Zizioulas, *Being as Communion*, p. 46.

cause of the free act of the Father *as person* that "entities no longer trace their being to being itself — that is, being is not an absolute category itself — but to the person." And (3) is obviously at the heart of the BAC, for the divine persons are "concrete, unique, and unrepeatable" entities who exist only in communion.

But this is an inconsistent triad. According to (3), without communion there are no persons. Thus, without communion the Father does not exist — at least not as a *person*. But the Father has no communion sans Son and Spirit. The unfortunate consequence is that *both* the BAC and the SAC are compromised by trying to retain both in the manner desired by Zizioulas. The BAC is undermined by the SAC, for the BAC is contingent — and thus hardly the "supreme ontological predicate" — while the SAC is necessary. At the same time, however, the SAC itself is endangered, for on Zizioulas's view it is the Father *as person* who is ultimate — but the Father does not exist (at least not as person) without communion.

I may have misinterpreted Zizioulas; perhaps the BAC is ultimate. But there is still a problem when it is put together with the SAC. Consider further:

(4) Persons exist only in communion (BAC);
(5) The Father is a person (BAC and SAC);
(6) Therefore, the Father exists only in communion.

As we have seen, Zizioulas is firmly committed to (4) and (5). But (6) flatly contradicts Zizioulas's account of the SAC, for he insists that the triune communion of holy love is freely chosen by the person of the Father: "God is not in communion, does not love, because he cannot but be in communion and love."[34]

Perhaps this is too quick. It may be that Zizioulas's view could be rescued by something like an appeal to

(6*) Therefore, the Father exists *as a person* only in communion.

On this account, the "Father" exists alone, but he exists as *Father* — *as a person* — only in communion. In other words, his existence does not depend on the relationality of communion, but his existence *as a person* does.

---

34. Zizioulas, *Being as Communion*, p. 18.

But it is hard to see how this helps much. Zizioulas's motivation, after all, is to protect the primacy of personhood. Going this route would ultimately undercut what Zizioulas wants to affirm by (5) — that the ultimate source of reality is a *person*. Taking (6*) would mean that the ultimate source of reality would be an entity that is merely *potentially* and *contingently* a person, and surely Zizioulas wishes to affirm more. As Zizioulas himself puts it, according to the BAC the divine persons "are so united in an unbreakable communion (koinonia) that none of them can be conceived apart from the rest."[35]

III. Toward Resolution

If I am right, then Zizioulas's ascription of the SAC to the Father is problematic. In addition, it cannot be the case that both the SAC (as understood by Zizioulas) and the BAC are "ultimate." Furthermore, the very convictions that motivate Zizioulas's work are undermined by his effort to hold the two together. To this point I have registered some concerns, but I do not think these concerns should lead to an outright dismissal of Zizioulas. To the contrary, I think there are depth, value, and promise in his theology, for he offers powerful and timely reminders both of the sovereign transcendence and of the holy love of God. But if my criticisms are even close to the mark, surely some adjustments are called for. Hence my modest proposal: we should affirm the BAC and reconfigure the SAC.

A. Persons in Communion: The Priority of the BAC

As we have seen, the BAC works to capture the insight that the "being of God is a relational being: without the concept of communion it would not be possible to speak of the being of God."[36] According to the BAC, the divine persons have their "concrete, unique, and unrepeatable" identities

---

35. John D. Zizioulas, "The Doctrine of the Holy Trinity: The Significance of the Cappadocian Contribution," in *Trinitarian Theology Today: Essays on Divine Act and Being,* ed. Christoph Schwöbel (Edinburgh: T. & T. Clark, 1995), p. 48. Zizioulas's position in this essay seems to be very close to what I am proposing, which raises the question of how well it fits with what he says in *Being as Communion.*

36. Zizioulas, *Being as Communion,* p. 17.

only in the triune communion of holy love.[37] And the holy love of the triune life is no longer conceived of as a "qualifying" or "secondary" property, but is, where God is concerned, the "supreme ontological predicate."[38]

These insights are echoed elsewhere in recent theology. For instance, Thomas F. Torrance thinks of "person" as an "onto-relational" concept: "no divine person is what he is without relation to the other two, and yet each divine person is other than and distinct from the other two,"[39] and he agrees that the doctrine of the Trinity means that God *is* a communion of self-giving love, for "the Father, the Son and the Holy Spirit who indwell one another in the Love that God is constitute the Communion of Love or the movement of reciprocal Loving which is identical with the One Being of God."[40] And these echoes are certainly understandable, for it is arguable that the BAC's account of the divine persons as distinct lovers is both founded on biblical teaching and attested to in the tradition. Although this is not the place for an exhaustive defense of the BAC, a few brief observations serve to remind us that this is central to the teaching of Scripture and the Christian tradition.

After all, 1 John states explicitly that "God is love" (4:8, 16), and the mutual love of the Father for the Son and the Son for the Father is evident in John 17.[41] Here we see what Royce Gordon Gruenler calls "selfless and dynamic love";[42] this is what F. F. Bruce refers to as the "mutuality of love."[43] Jesus prays that the disciples and future believers will be brought to "complete unity" in order to "let the world know" that the Father has sent Jesus and has "loved them even as you have loved me" (17:23). The "glory" that the Father has given to the Son (17:24) is what C. K. Barrett thinks of as "the essential inward love of the Godhead, the love with which the Fa-

---

37. Zizioulas, *Being as Communion*, p. 46.

38. Zizioulas, *Being as Communion*, p. 46.

39. Thomas F. Torrance, *The Christian Doctrine of God: One Being, Three Persons* (Edinburgh: T. & T. Clark, 1996), p. 157. See also William J. Hill, *The Three-Personed God: The Trinity as a Mystery of Salvation* (Washington, D.C.: Catholic University of America Press, 1982), p. 272.

40. Thomas F. Torrance, *Christian Doctrine of God*, p. 165.

41. C. H. Dodd notes how this love permeates the Gospel and holds it together. *The Interpretation of the Fourth Gospel* (Cambridge: Cambridge University Press, 1953), p. 418.

42. Royce Gordon Gruenler, *The Trinity in the Gospel of John: A Thematic Commentary on the Fourth Gospel* (Grand Rapids: Baker, 1986), p. 127.

43. F. F. Bruce, *The Gospel of John: Introduction, Exposition, and Notes* (Grand Rapids: Eerdmans, 1983), p. 329.

ther eternally loves the Son (the love which God *is,* 1 John 4:8, 16)."[44] And the reason for the gift of this glory is clear — it is, Jesus says to the Father, "because you loved me before the creation of the world" (17:24).

The broad Christian tradition also bears witness to the BAC's affirmation that the divine persons are distinct lovers who subsist in relation to one another. A well-known example is Augustine's use of the analogy of the Trinity as lover, beloved, and love itself.[45] Similarly, Richard of St. Victor is famous for his argument (drawn from "Perfect Being Theology") that "perfection of charity *(caritatis consummatio)* requires a Trinity of persons."[46] These brief examples should serve to remind us that what Zizioulas is trying to preserve with his affirmation of the BAC is, at base, a biblical and traditional teaching. Described by Zizioulas in his summary of Basil, "the nature of God is communion . . . the one substance of God coincides with the communion of the three persons."[47] To say that love is of the essence of God; to affirm that God is, sans creation, the triune God of holy love, is mysterious indeed, but to say this is not either to affirm a nonsensical contradiction or to engage in mere fantasy. To the contrary, it seems that the BAC is called for by Scripture and affirmed by the Christian tradition (East and West); it can — and should — be affirmed today as well.[48]

---

44. C. K. Barrett, *The Gospel according to John: An Introduction with Commentary and Notes on the Greek Text* (Philadelphia: Westminster, 1978), p. 515.

45. Augustine, *The Trinity* 8.25. Even if Augustine's critics are right in worrying that this analogy lends itself to a rather binitarian theology, such a theology must be sufficiently *social* to account for a deep and rich relationship of love between (at minimum) two personal agents.

46. Richard of St. Victor, *The Twelve Patriarchs, The Mystical Ark, Book Three of the Trinity,* trans. Grover Zinn (New York: Paulist, 1979), p. 385. For an excellent discussion of Richard, see Nico den Bok, *Communicating the Most High: A Systematic Study of Person and Trinity in the Theology of Richard of St. Victor* (Paris: Brepols, 1996), pp. 259-81.

47. Zizioulas, *Being as Communion,* p. 134.

48. To say that the holy love shared between and among the divine persons is of the essence of God does not — and should not — so far as I can tell, entail that this is *all* that we say of the divine essence. The divine essence, to the extent that we obtain any conceptual grasp at all, is the full set of properties individually necessary and jointly sufficient to be God. Surely this includes omnipotence, omniscience, and other "great-making" properties; what the BAC affirms is that the holy love shared between the Father, Son, and Holy Spirit is at the "core" of what it means to be God.

B. Divine Sovereignty Again: Triune Theism and the SAC

As we have seen, the ascription of the SAC to the Father causes problems for Zizioulas's theology. But the SAC itself is not a problem. To the contrary, it reflects basic biblical and traditionally grounded theological convictions, and it can cohere well with the BAC if the right adjustments are made. But some adjustments must be made: the SAC must be predicated of the Trinity, and the SAC should refer to divine sovereignty and aseity over all that is not God, it should refer to divine sovereignty and aseity in relation to creation (rather than over the divine persons).

The first adjustment is this: the SAC must be seen as a property of the *triune God* rather than as a property of the Father *alone*. As we have seen, to predicate the SAC of the Father alone is to raise several concerns, not least of which is whether this means that the Father is of a different essence than is the Son or Spirit. To assert that the Father alone is *unthrown* and *a se* is to say that the Father has different essential properties than does the Son or Spirit — properties that are not either accidental properties (after all, this seems to be what it means to be the Father) or "onto-relational" properties. But to predicate the SAC of the Trinity alleviates this problem; it makes the SAC an essential property of divinity, one that is had by each and all of the divine persons. Furthermore, the ascription of the SAC to *God* is the way the biblical writers think of it (e.g., Exod. 3:14).[49]

The second adjustment is to predicate the SAC of the triune God *over creation.* This is a robust affirmation that God is sovereign over creation; it is the recognition that the Father, Son, and Holy Spirit are complete and completely fulfilled sans creation. Thus the triune God can be said to be *a se* — God depends on nothing outside of himself to be who he is. Surely this is part of what Zizioulas wants to protect; he argues that "the truth of creation is a *dependent* truth, while the truth of God's being is *communion* in itself."[50]

---

49. For critical arguments that Jesus is worshiped as YHWH in the New Testament, see Richard Bauckham, *God Crucified: Monotheism and Christology in the New Testament* (Grand Rapids: Eerdmans, 1998); Bauckham, *The Climax of Prophecy: Studies on the Book of Revelation* (Edinburgh: T. & T. Clark, 1993); and Larry Hurtado, *Lord Jesus Christ: Devotion to Jesus in Earliest Christianity* (Grand Rapids: Eerdmans, 2003); Hurtado, *One God, One Lord: Early Christian Devotion and Ancient Jewish Monotheism* (Edinburgh: T. & T. Clark, 1998); Hurtado, "Homage to Jesus and Early Christian Devotion," *Journal for the Study of the Historical Jesus* 1 (2003): 131-46.

50. Zizioulas, *Being as Communion*, p. 94.

But as we have seen, Zizioulas wants to affirm much more than this, for he insists that the radical freedom of the Father also includes the Father's choice of the divine essence and indeed of the divine existence.

To predicate the SAC of God in creation says nothing about God's choice of the divine essence and existence. So it does not address Zizioulas's concerns about the radical, ontological freedom of God, and because of this omission, the theologian who finds Zizioulas persuasive here will likely find my proposal unpalatable. But a couple of points are noteworthy. First, it should be clear that what I propose does not necessarily rule out the possibility that God chooses his existence and the divine essence; it just does not address it. So if the defender of Zizioulas wants to insist that God has this radical freedom, she may continue to do so. But if this is going to have any hope of success (without predicating different essential — or at minimum "ungiveup-able" — properties to the divine persons), she will need to attribute this freedom to each of the divine persons, thus perhaps making the Trinity a contingent entity that is dependent on the free choices of *all* the divine persons.

But why should we think that this radical kind of ontological freedom is something we *should* predicate of God? After all, the biblical witness to divine aseity seems to be focused on God's relation to all that is *not God* — it does not seem to address the radical freedom of the Father to choose the divine existence and essence. Surely the biblical witness underdetermines Zizioulas's point. Furthermore, the broad Christian tradition has affirmed that God exists — and exists as triune — necessarily. And it is far from obvious that the property of *being able to choose your own existence and essence* is a great-making property, one that we obviously *should* attribute to God.[51] To the contrary, good arguments to the conclusion that God exists *necessarily* are still available.[52]

These adjustments make it possible to retain belief in both the BAC

---

51. For an account of "Perfect Being Theology" that relies upon "great-making properties," see Thomas V. Morris, *Anselmian Explorations: Essays in Philosophical Theology* (Notre Dame, Ind.: University of Notre Dame Press, 1987).

52. E.g., Alvin Plantinga's Modal Ontological Argument, *The Nature of Necessity*, pp. 196-221. Even though people can block it by denying that there is some possible world where maximal greatness is exemplified, Stephen T. Davis argues that "it still stands as a successful piece of natural theology." "The Ontological Argument," in *The Rationality of Theism*, ed. Paul Copan and Paul Moser (New York: Routledge, 2003), p. 109. I take the Modal Ontological Argument to show (among other things) that if God exists, then God exists necessarily.

and the SAC. Indeed, it is arguable that the BAC enables (or at least supports) belief in the SAC. Some modern theologians take the BAC to entail that the world (at least some world with sentient and volitional creatures) is necessary for God; they reason that since God is love, then this love *must* find suitable expression, and any suitable expression is found in creation.[53] But the BAC, as Zizioulas understands it, actually protects divine aseity. For according to the BAC, God's love is perfect and complete in the triune life of mutual and consummate love. Thus God has no need of the world for God's own fulfillment. As Nico den Bok points out with reference to Richard of St. Victor's argument for the patristic doctrine of divine aseity that he had inherited, "God does not have to create out of other-directed love, because this love is complete as it is in his own Trinitarian being."[54] It is the priority of the BAC that protects the SAC — and with it, the doctrine of creation ex nihilo.

To this point I have suggested that some of the difficulties inherent in the theology of Zizioulas might be alleviated or even overcome by some minor adjustments. To be sure, theologians who are worried that God is somehow *thrown* if the Father does not choose the divine essence and existence will not see these adjustments as minor. But in lieu of reasons to think that Zizioulas's motivating concerns about the SAC *of the Father* are decisive, it seems better to attribute the SAC to the *triune God* over *creation*.

C. Objections Briefly Considered

Some might remonstrate that the SAC is compromised by my proposal. But it is hard to see why this might be so. Yes, we have seen that Zizioulas's predication of the SAC to the Father is not tenable on my proposal. But we have also seen that his view has problems on its own, while the reasons to affirm it are quite obscure. If, at its heart, the SAC means that no divine person is dependent on anything that is not divine, then it is hard to see how the SAC is compromised by my proposal.

Keeping the BAC as ultimate, and relegating the SAC to the complete

---

53. E.g., Jürgen Moltmann, *The Trinity and the Kingdom: The Doctrine of God* (Minneapolis: Fortress, 1993), pp. 106-7.

54. Den Bok, *Communicating the Most High*, p. 294.

freedom of the triune God over creation, indeed does entail that the Father does not have the kind of radical independence that Zizioulas promotes. For according to the BAC, the person of the Father exists only in relation to the Son and the Spirit. But the dependence here does not in any way compromise the SAC. All the divine persons are dependent on one another for their existence as persons. And since all the persons are fully divine (*homoousios*), no divine person depends on anything that is not God. Thus the SAC is not surrendered, nor, by my lights, is it even compromised.[55]

Nor does the ascription of the SAC to the triune God over creation mean that divine action is somehow determined. The BAC reminds us that divine perfection is found in the intra-Trinitarian communion of the divine persons. And this has important implications for the God-world relation; there is no obvious incoherence in maintaining that the triune God who enjoys perfection in the intra-Trinitarian life may desire to share that life while not *needing* to do so to reach fulfillment or perfection. As Colin Gunton puts it, "it is of the essence of God's freedom-in-relatedness that he is not bound to create. He would still be God if he had not created this world or any other."[56] This does not mean that just *any* possible world is feasible for God, for surely some possible worlds would appear to be inconsistent with his nature as holy love (BAC) — it only means that God has robust, "libertarian" freedom in his choice to create this world rather than another or none at all. And if so, then both determinism and panentheism may be avoided. We need not think that the freedom of God is compromised by the ascription of the SAC to the triune God of holy love, at least not in any obviously meaningful way.[57]

---

55. This may be too quick. An objector might worry that if each divine person is dependent on the other two, then it follows that the triune God is dependent on all three and thus the SAC is compromised after all. But such an objection would need to show that the triune God indeed *is* dependent in this way, and it would need to do so without falling prey to the composition fallacy ("if all the players are good, then this is a good team"). But at any rate, according to the suggestion that I offer, the SAC has to do with God's relation to all that is not divine, in which case the SAC of the Trinity would not be compromised even if the Trinity were dependent on the divine persons.

56. Colin E. Gunton, *Christ and Creation* (Grand Rapids: Eerdmans, 1992), p. 121; see also his *The Triune Creator: A Historical and Systematic Study* (Grand Rapids: Eerdmans, 1998), p. 66.

57. There may be any number of galaxies of possible worlds that are feasible for God (where God is understood as perfectly good in accordance with the BAC), and God is perfectly at liberty to choose between and among these. For arguments here see Thomas P. Flint

Some critics may worry that the venerable doctrine of the eternal generation of the Son is endangered or compromised by my proposal. Perhaps they will charge that if Zizioulas's ascription of the SAC to the Father is watered down in any way, then the traditional doctrine of eternal generation is lost. If so, then it seems that they would be arguing as follows. Letting EG stand for the traditional doctrine of eternal generation, and letting SAC* stand for Zizioulas's distinctive version of the Sovereignty-Aseity Conviction, consider

(7) If EG, then SAC*;

(8) EG;

(9) Therefore, SAC*.

But surely this is much too quick. For what we need is an argument that (7) is true.[58] Granting the rather obvious point that the meaning of the doctrine of eternal generation is, well, not exactly pellucid in the tradition,[59] it is far from apparent that the patristic theologians to whom we are indebted for this doctrine intended that it be taken to mean that the Father chooses the divine existence and essence, or, for that matter, that they were concerned about Heideggerian notions of ontological freedom from *thrownness*.

On the other hand, a plausible interpretation of the doctrine of eternal generation is one that coheres well with the BAC — this is the view that eternal generation refers us to (a) the incompleteness of the persons as individuals and (b) their complete and irreducible uniqueness in relation to

---

and Alfred J. Freddoso, "Maximal Power," in *The Concept of God*, ed. Thomas V. Morris (Oxford: Oxford University Press, 1987), pp. 134-67; Thomas P. Flint, "The Problem of Divine Freedom," *American Philosophical Quarterly* 20 (1983): 255-64; Thomas P. Flint, *Divine Providence: The Molinist Account* (Ithaca, N.Y.: Cornell University Press, 1998), pp. 51-59. Edward Wierenga sounds a cautionary note here; he thinks that divine freedom and action are so different from human action as to call into question straightforward ascriptions of various notions of freedom to God. "The Freedom of God," *Faith and Philosophy* 19 (2002): 425-36.

58. Challenges to (8) are also increasing; see, e.g., John S. Feinberg, *No One Like Him: The Doctrine of God* (Wheaton, Ill.: Crossway, 2001), pp. 488-92.

59. E.g., Gregory Nazianzen's famous statement: "Do you tell me what is the unbegottenness of the Father, and I will explain to you the physiology of the generation of the Son and the procession of the Spirit, and we shall both of us be frenzy-stricken for prying into the mystery of God. And who are we to do these things?" "The Fifth Theological Oration: On the Spirit," in *Christology of the Later Fathers*, ed. Edward R. Hardy (Philadelphia: Westminster, 1954), pp. 198-99.

the other persons. Seen this way, the doctrine of eternal generation emphasizes that to be a person — even a divine person — is to be incomplete "alone" or in oneself.[60] Just as the Son is who he is only in relation to the Father, so also the Father is who he is only in relation to the Son. And as the Father is always Father and never Son, so also the Son is always Son and never Father. Indeed, for the tradition the Father is everything that the Son is *except Son,* and the Son is all that the Father is *except Father.* As Zizioulas puts it in his description of Athanasius, "but 'Father' is by definition a relational term (no father is conceivable without a son), and it is precisely this that makes the use of 'substance' in Athanasius un-Greek."[61] Indeed, at some points Zizioulas himself seems to be close to this, for he states that the Father "affirms his existence by a communion-event. He is the Father because he eternally has a Son through whom he affirms himself as Father."[62] At the very least this is an interpretation of the doctrine of eternal generation that is compatible with the BAC and my proposal.

More serious, however, is the worry that what I propose is really a version of *quaternism.* Because at least one property (the SAC) is predicated of the Trinity that is not predicated of the distinct divine persons, we are confronted with a fourth thing in addition to the three divine persons. For if the SAC is predicated of the Trinity *as a whole,* then it seems that the Trinity has a (essential?) divine property that none of the divine persons has alone. That is, if the triune persons together exist *a se,* while the distinct persons "on their own" do not, then the Trinity as a whole has something had by none of the distinct divine persons. Surely such a scenario does not bode well for my proposal. On the other hand, if *each* of the divine persons is, qua person, *a se,* then we are left to think that the Trinity is contingent and simply made up of three individuals who decide to cooperate and get on together. This is surely no better, for it denies the fundamental conviction of the BAC.

But this dilemma may not be as troubling as it appears to be at first glance. With respect to the SAC, within the triune life the divine persons indeed *are a se* over creation, so the SAC is not a property that the Trinity has that is had by none of the divine persons. And even if it were shown that the Trinity has a property had by none of the distinct divine persons,

---

60. I owe this point to conversations with Dennis Kinlaw.
61. Zizioulas, *Being as Communion,* p. 85 n. 60.
62. Zizioulas, *Being as Communion,* p. 121 n. 126.

this would not obviously raise an insurmountable objection. For it simply seems obvious that the Trinity just *does* have some properties that the distinct persons do not have. Such properties as *being triune* or *being three divine persons: the Father and the Son and the Spirit,* etc., are not had by the distinct divine persons. So there are some properties that the Father, Son, and Holy Spirit have together in the triune life that are not the distinct properties of the particular persons, and it is possible that the property of being *a se* is one of those.[63]

Some critics may think that the BAC itself is a problem. After all, it maintains that persons and communion come together; the communion is the communion of *persons* in relation, and the identity of the persons is found only in the communion. Surely, someone might object, one of these *must* come first. But it is less than clear how this objection might proceed, for, as the tradition has held and Zizioulas reminds us, "'Father' is by definition a relational term" — a son is just that only in relation to a father and a father is just that only in relation to a son. So we are not left without any understanding of such a relational account of personhood.

Surely the doctrine of the Trinity is mysterious. Indeed, mystery is what we might expect when encountering what Eleonore Stump calls the "foundations of reality." She insists that "since, on the doctrine of the Trinity, the persons of the Trinity are not reducible to something else in the Godhead, then, *persons* are an irreducible part of the ultimate foundation of reality . . . [thus] the point at which all reduction has to stop will include persons."[64] To admit that it is a mystery is not to say that it is obviously absurd or logically impossible and thus necessarily false. To the contrary, if the BAC is right and the truth of personhood in communion is ultimate, then we are faced with a "brute" — but beautiful — reality.

IV. Conclusion

I am convinced that contemporary theology has much to learn from the theology of John Zizioulas. Although the BAC is part of the tradition of

---

63. It may be objected that these are mere "Cambridge" or "Notre Dame" properties, but this seems unlikely to me, and at any rate is far from obvious.

64. Eleonore Stump, "Francis and Dominic: Persons, Patterns, and Trinity," *American Catholic Philosophical Quarterly* (2000): 1, 25.

Western theology, in the past it has too often been underappreciated and sometimes even marginalized. On the other hand, recent theology has made much of the BAC (or something like it), but with a corresponding and unfortunate loss of emphasis on divine transcendence and freedom. Zizioulas may help us to keep both the love and the holiness of the triune God in perspective.

In this chapter I have tried to shed light on two major themes in the Trinitarian theology of John Zizioulas. One — the SAC — appears to be at base an existentialist thesis: "existence precedes essence." The other — the BAC — is an essentialist thesis: the holy love shared in the perichoretic life of the triune God is "constitutive of his substance." I have argued that Zizioulas's ascription of the SAC to the Father alone is problematic, and I have argued further that these two theses do not work well together. To the contrary, they appear to be incompatible.

Of course, I may be completely wrong in my interpretation of Zizioulas. Maybe Zizioulas means something importantly different by "essence," and maybe his understanding renders my criticisms invalid and lays my worries to rest. If so, then this chapter should be taken as a request for more clarification. Or maybe my concerns are so "Western" that they do not penetrate to the heart of his theology.[65] If so, then this chapter should be seen as a call for those more adept in "Eastern" thought to do some translation work and conceptual bridge building. But if I am right, then these problems remain, and Zizioulas's theology needs adjustment.

My proposal has been that we receive with gratitude Zizioulas's emphasis on the BAC, and that we attribute the SAC to the triune God over creation. Of course, I have not answered all remaining questions, but I hope to have gone at least a short distance toward showing that remaining

65. For a fundamental questioning of the "East v. West" paradigm (a questioning with which I have great sympathy), see Michel René Barnes, "De Régnon Reconsidered," *Augustinian Studies* 26 (1995): 51-79; David Bentley Hart, "The Mirror of the Infinite: Gregory of Nyssa on the *Vestigium Trinitatis*," *Modern Theology* 18 (2002): 541; and Sarah Coakley: "it is ironic to find Lossky at points directly dependent on de Regnon, and Zizioulas on Prestige! To have the 'West' attacked by the 'East' on a reading of the Cappadocians that was ultimately spawned by a French Jesuit is a strange irony." "Re-thinking Gregory of Nyssa — Gender, Trinitarian Analogies, and the Pedagogy of *The Song*," *Modern Theology* 18 (2002): 434; cf. "'Persons' in the 'Social' Doctrine of the Trinity: A Critique of the Current Analytic Discussion," in *The Trinity: An Interdisciplinary Symposium on the Trinity*, ed. Stephen T. Davis, Daniel Kendall, S.J., and Gerald O'Collins, S.J. (Oxford: Oxford University Press, 1999), pp. 131-37.

criticisms may not be fatal. I recognize that my recommendations push Zizioulas's theology in the direction of the "West."[66] This may make it unpalatable to some who are attracted to Zizioulas's theology. If I am right, however, then my proposals might allow us to take the insights and emphases that Zizioulas offers without being forced to accept some of the liabilities and questionable aspects of his thought.

---

66. Ralph Del Colle's generally excellent article brings Zizioulas into more sustained conversation with more traditionally "Western" theology by first focusing on some intersections between the theologies of Thomas (and Alan) Torrance and Zizioulas and then relating these to more traditional Latin Trinitarianism. "'Person' and 'Being' in John Zizioulas' Trinitarian Theology: Conversations with Thomas Torrance and Thomas Aquinas," *Scottish Journal of Theology* 54 (2001): 70-86.

SECTION THREE

The Future of Trinitarian Theology

CHAPTER EIGHT

Moving Forward: Theses on the Future of Trinitarian Theology

To this point I have surveyed some of the main options presented by philosophical theologians who work in the so-called "analytic" tradition. I have offered an overview of some of the most important statements of the major positions, and I have tried to engage these models by raising some distinctly theological issues and evaluating the models accordingly. In this way, I have tried to build a bridge between the Trinitarian theology done by theologians and that done by philosophers of religion. While I am well aware that I have not been exhaustive — indeed, *much* more remains to be said — I hope to have taken some steps toward "bridge building" by bringing some distinctly theological concerns to bear upon the analytic discussion.

I have also tried to open a lane on the bridge for traffic from the other direction: I have worked to provide some analysis of the views of some important and influential dogmatic or systematic theologians. Taking as examples the work of Robert Jenson, Jürgen Moltmann, John Zizioulas, and others, I have attempted to show how the task of contemporary systematic Trinitarian theology might be enhanced and enriched by conversation with the analytic tradition.

But where to now? Whither Trinitarian theology? How might a Trinitarian theologian — one committed and faithful to its sources — make appropriate use of analytic tools? While I do not claim to have the last word on any of these matters, I offer some "theses for scholastic disputation" on the future of a Trinitarian theology that is grounded in the revelation of God in Jesus Christ as presented in the New Testament, consistent with the central creedal affirmations of that revelation, and articulated with the use of the tools of what is sometimes called "analytic theology."[1]

I. Theses on Trinitarian Theological Method

1. Trinitarian theologians should attend to important issues of theological prolegomena.

This first thesis may sound a bit strange. Newcomers to contemporary systematic theology are sometimes taken aback by what must (though probably kindly) be called a preoccupation with issues of theological method. I once heard someone say that beginning with issues of method does for a systematic theologian what clearing her throat before speaking does for a public speaker: clearing one's throat both serves to enhance the speaker's ability to be heard with clarity and gets the attention of the waiting (and perhaps impatient) audience. But if the speaker continues to stand at the podium while doing nothing more than saying "hmm, hmm," she will quickly lose the attention of even the most interested hearers. Indeed, it does not take long before the situation becomes embarrassing for the speaker. Preoccupation with issues of method leaves much contemporary systematic theology in danger of becoming both irrelevant and embarrassing.

On the other hand, however, the situation in contemporary analytic theology is quite different. Here theological prolegomena is often underdeveloped, and indeed many important issues are not sufficiently explored and even appear to be assumed. Consider the issue of theological authority. Dale Tuggy raises some interesting questions along this line. What counts as authoritative in discussions of the doctrine of the Trinity: "Bible only? Bible and all of the 'Church Fathers'? Bible plus the ecumenical councils up through, say, Chalcedon? The whole train of authoritative councils endorsed by the Catholic Church, or those endorsed by Eastern Orthodoxy? The ecumenical councils plus some Reformed creeds? And what about recent statements of faith?"[2] What Tuggy says about

---

1. See Oliver Crisp and Michael C. Rea, eds., *Analytic Theology: New Essays in the Philosophy of Theology* (Oxford: Oxford University Press, 2009).

2. Dale Tuggy, "Tradition and Believability: Edward Wierenga's Social Trinitarianism," *Philosophia Christi* 5 (2003): 452.

Wierenga's essay is largely true of analytic theology more generally: "no stand is taken on this question . . . which documents set the boundaries beyond which we cannot go?"[3]

But without some clarity on this matter, the proponents of various views will likely continue to (at least partially) talk past one another. Those philosophical theologians who are convinced of, say, the Latin theological tradition will continue to think that anything that falls short of the views of divine oneness articulated therein fails as an adequate model of the Trinity, and they will be suspicious of anything that threatens to compromise the doctrine of divine simplicity. Contemporary ST theorists, on the other hand, will likely agree with Cornelius Plantinga that the lease on the doctrine of divine simplicity has expired and should not be extended, for simplicity theories "cannot claim much by way of biblical support . . . [and] are negotiable in ways that Pauline and Johannine statements are not."[4] Many of them will assent to William Lane Craig's contention that "Protestants bring all doctrinal statements, even conciliar creeds, especially creeds of nonecumenical councils, before the bar of Scripture. Nothing in Scripture warrants us in thinking that God is simple and that each person of the Trinity is identical to the whole Trinity. Nothing in Scripture prohibits us from maintaining that the three persons of the Godhead stand in some sort of part-whole relation to the Trinity. Therefore, Trinity monotheism cannot be condemned as unorthodox in a biblical sense. Trinity monotheism seems thus far vindicated."[5] Of course, it would be great if analytic theologians could come to some level of consensus on these issues. But short of that, they need to be self-aware and open to criticism on the issue of authority. At any rate, the extent to which these issues are left untouched will mirror the extent to which we continue to talk past one another. If too much can be made of theological prolegomena (as in much modern and contemporary systematic theology), then just as surely too little attention is not good either.

Or consider the important but vexed issues related to religious language. Many contemporary systematic theologians regard the mere suggestion that

3. Tuggy, "Tradition and Believability," pp. 452-53.

4. Cornelius Plantinga, Jr., "Social Trinity and Tritheism," in *Trinity, Incarnation, and Atonement: Philosophical and Theological Essays,* ed. Ronald J. Feenstra and Cornelius Plantinga, Jr. (Notre Dame, Ind.: University of Notre Dame Press, 1989), p. 39.

5. J. P. Moreland and William Lane Craig, *Philosophical Foundations for a Christian Worldview* (Downers Grove, Ill.: InterVarsity, 2003), pp. 592-93.

our language for God might be (even partially) univocal with nothing short of horror and outrage[6] — but many analytic theologians think this is a perfectly reasonable approach.[7] Again, many contemporary systematic theologians are wary of commitment to robust versions of realism, but this is often *assumed* (in discussions of the doctrine of the Trinity, if not more generally) by the analytic theologians.[8] Continuing to address the more "substantive" theological issues without tackling such issues of theological prolegomena is not likely to move us closer to actual conversation.

2. Trinitarian theologians should work to see the doctrine of the Trinity in the context of the broader biblical narrative.

In saying that Trinitarian theologians should locate the doctrine of the Trinity within the broader Christian story, I am not suggesting that they should merely work harder at "proof texting" their views. Tuggy, for example, advocates what he calls a "radical reformation approach," one that he says will first "see what the scriptures, reasonably interpreted, require, and then accept or reject later formulations insofar as they fit well with scripture and reason."[9] Tuggy apparently takes "reasonably interpreted" to mean in the absence of historical or contemporary biblical scholarship, and he leaves us to conclude that any "reasonable interpretation" is one that provides us with distinct passages that directly prove particular theological propositions. Thus he complains that the "tripersonal God makes no appearance *as such* anywhere in the Bible," and he concludes that since "passages such as the Great Commission, the baptism of Christ, or various Pauline benedictions in which the Father, Son, and Holy Spirit are all de-

6. The movement known as "Radical Orthodoxy" is well known for its insistent polemic against the "idolatry" of univocity; see, e.g., John Milbank, *The Word Made Strange* (Oxford: Blackwell, 1997). See also James K. A. Smith, *Radical Orthodoxy: Mapping a Post-secular Theology* (Grand Rapids: Baker Academic, 2004).

7. For recent defenses of univocity, see, e.g., William P. Alston, *Divine Nature and Human Language: Essays in Philosophical Theology* (Ithaca, N.Y.: Cornell University Press, 1989), pp. 17-117; Richard Cross, "Where Angels Fear to Tread: Duns Scotus and Radical Orthodoxy," *Antonianum* 76 (2001): 1-36; and Thomas Williams, "The Doctrine of Univocity Is True and Salutary," *Modern Theology* 21 (2005): 575-85.

8. For a fascinating discussion of this, see Randal Rauser, "Theology as Bull Session," in *Analytic Theology: New Essays in the Philosophy of Theology*, ed. Oliver Crisp and Michael C. Rea (Oxford: Oxford University Press, 2009), pp. 70-84.

9. Tuggy, "Tradition and Believability," p. 453.

picted or mentioned" do not represent "these three as constituting one God, either in the way that three parts make up a whole, or in the way that individuals compose a community," this is a "big problem" for Trinitarian theology.[10]

This is *not* the approach I am advocating when I call for Trinitarian theology to pay closer heed to the basis of the doctrine as found in the biblical narrative. I *do not* think the way forward is to isolate individual verses of Scripture, press them through some sort of exegetical distillery, and then conclude that only those propositions that can be distilled in this manner are appropriate for theological consumption. And I certainly do not think that ignoring the work of contemporary biblical scholars — or attempting to do an end run around the history of exegesis and doctrine — is the most helpful way to understand the biblical text (indeed, this method smacks of the hubris with which analytic theologians are sometimes charged).

Instead, I am advocating a "thick" reading of Scripture.[11] As David Yeago argues, "the ancient theologians were right to hold that the Nicene *homoousion* is neither imposed *on* the New Testament texts, nor distantly deduced *from* the texts, but rather, describes a pattern of judgments present *in* the texts, in the texture of scriptural discourse concerning Jesus and the God of Israel."[12] Or as C. Kavin Rowe puts it, there is an "exegetical necessity" to the doctrine of the Trinity, because "there is an organic connection between the biblical testimony and the early creeds, and the creeds can serve as hermeneutical guidelines to reading the bible because it is in fact the biblical text itself that necessitated the credal formulations."[13]

It is not simply that the doctrine of the Trinity rises or falls upon distinct verses of Scripture that "prove" (or fail to prove) the doctrine; the doctrine first arises because of the way the first Christians experienced Je-

---

10. Tuggy, "Tradition and Believability," pp. 449-50. Tuggy's target here is Wierenga's ST, but I cannot see why his criticism would fail to apply to Trinitarianism *simpliciter*.

11. On this see Kevin J. Vanhoozer, *Is There a Meaning in This Text? The Bible, the Reader, and the Morality of Literary Knowledge* (Grand Rapids: Zondervan, 1998), pp. 285-335.

12. David Yeago, "The New Testament and the Nicene Dogma: A Contribution to the Recovery of Theological Exegesis," in *The Theological Interpretation of Scripture: Classic and Contemporary Readings* (Oxford: Blackwell, 1997), p. 88.

13. C. Kavin Rowe, "Luke and the Trinity: An Essay in Ecclesial Biblical Theology," *Scottish Journal of Theology* 56 (2003): 4.

sus and the way this is testified to within Scripture. Importantly, the *worship* of Jesus — and the worship of the God who is recognized as Father, Son, and Holy Spirit — is the catalyst for the development of the doctrine in the first place! And this is something that contemporary theologians (and perhaps analytic theologians particularly) would do well indeed to remember. The doctrine of the Trinity is not merely a bad mathematics problem that must somehow be sorted out by very clever logicians, nor is it merely a confusing set of apparently contradictory claims that simply must be sorted out to be believed. No, the doctrine of the Trinity is, in the first instance, an attempt to respond in worship to the only God that exists — the God who exists eternally in the loving communion of the inner-Trinitarian life, the God who as Father sends the Son for the salvation of the world, the God who as Son becomes incarnate for us and our salvation, and the God who as Spirit is present with the church and the world today.

Recognizing the place of the doctrine in the broader biblical story — understanding that the God of Abraham, Isaac, and Jacob, the God who redeems Israel and then who becomes incarnate for the salvation of the world just *is* the triune God — does not for a moment license the theologian to ignore or downplay the important logical and metaphysical issues. Seeing the doctrine of the Trinity in its proper canonical place, at the center of early Christian worship, does not allow the theologian to make all sorts of nonsensical and patently contradictory claims in the name of "being biblical" or "being properly dogmatic." Recognition of the proper place of the doctrine should, however, call us back to the reason that Christians are, and have always been, Trinitarian: worship of the Father who sends the Son, worship of the Son who "humbles himself" for us and our salvation, and worship of the Holy Spirit who continues the work of the triune God in the world today.

3. Trinitarian theology should not conflate Trinitarian doctrine with sociopolitical theological agendas.

To say that Trinitarian theology is in vogue in contemporary theology is to put it mildly. In the past few decades of work in systematic theology, the doctrine of the Trinity has been "recovered," and its importance for all of Christian thought and life has been "reclaimed." Immanuel Kant's now infamous dictum that "the doctrine of the Trinity, taken literally, has *no practical relevance at all,* even if we think we understand it; and it is even more clearly irrelevant if we realize that it transcends all our concepts"[14] has been taken up as a challenge, and theologians of various persuasions have worked to apply the doctrine of the Trinity to all manner of doctrinal and ethical issues.[15] In the words of Catherine Mowry LaCugna,

> The doctrine of the Trinity is ultimately a practical doctrine with radical consequences for Christian life. . . . God is said to be essentially relational, ecstatic, fecund, alive as passionate love. Divine life is also *our* life. The heart of the Christian life is to be united with the God of Jesus Christ by means of communion with one another. The doctrine of the Trinity is ultimately therefore a teaching not about the abstract nature of God, nor about God in isolation from everything other than God, but a teaching about God's life with us and our life with each other. . . . This ongoing revelation and action of God is the proper source for reflection on theological ethics, spirituality, ecclesiology, and the liturgical and communitarian life of the church.[16]

Social Trinitarians have been at the vanguard of this movement. They have worked hard to "apply" the doctrine of the Trinity to various sociopolitical causes. Many of these are commonly associated with the theological and political "left"; for instance, Leonardo Boff is convinced that "social" doctrines of the Trinity support (if not necessitate) a socialist economy, and the ST of Moltmann has been received as an inspiration and support for liberationist theological and sociopolitical agendas of all sorts.[17] But there are ST theorists with other theological and sociopolitical agendas as well; as we have seen, these theologians work to argue "from" the doctrine of the Trinity "to" hard-and-fast conclusions about the permanent subordination of women to men in the church and home (and perhaps elsewhere).

---

14. Immanuel Kant, *The Conflict of the Faculties,* trans. Mary J. Gregor (New York: Abaris Books, 1979), p. 65, emphasis in original. See also Immanuel Kant, *Religion within the Limits of Reason Alone,* trans. Theodore M. Green and Hoyt T. Hudson (New York: Harper and Row, 1960), pp. 132-33, 136-38.

15. Recent examples of such work include Paul Louis Metzger, ed., *Trinitarian Soundings in Systematic Theology* (New York: T. & T. Clark, 2005), and Miroslav Volf and Michael Welker, eds., *God's Life in Trinity* (Minneapolis: Fortress, 2006).

16. Catherine Mowry LaCugna, *God for Us: The Trinity and Christian Life* (New York: HarperSanFrancisco, 1991), p. ix.

17. E.g., Leonardo Boff, *Trinity and Society* (Maryknoll, N.Y.: Orbis, 1988).

I think there is something fundamentally correct about the conviction of contemporary theologians that the doctrine of the Trinity is at the heart of the Christian view of God and the world, and I applaud the concern of these theologians to look for the connections and the "relevance" to contemporary thought and life. After all, if God really is triune, and if human persons are made in the image of God, then surely the doctrine of the Trinity matters for our understanding of individual and corporate human existence.

There is, alas, a real danger here, and we should heed the warnings sounded by critics of this exercise. Karen Kilby raises some concerns about this kind of theologizing. Commenting on the "use" of the doctrine of the Trinity for other agendas, she notes that, especially with regard to ST, something like the following sequence takes place: "First, a concept, perichoresis, is used to name what is not understood, to name whatever it is that makes the three Persons one. Secondly, the concept is filled out rather suggestively with notions borrowed from our own experience of relationships and relatedness. And then, finally, it is presented as an exciting resource Christian theology has to offer the wider world in its reflections upon relationships and relatedness." Kilby says that "Projection, then, is particularly problematic in at least some social theories of the Trinity because what is projected onto God is immediately reflected back onto the world, and this reverse projection is said to be what is important about the doctrine."[18] Her point is well taken; while it need not be true that things *must* go this way (after all, if something like a social analogy is portrayed in Scripture, then surely it is acceptable to make *some* connection with our understanding of human relationships — even if that understanding needs to be corrected), they do so all too easily.

The upshot of all this can be summarized this way: it is wrong to allow other concerns — however legitimate and worthy in their own right — to dominate and dictate our doctrine of the Trinity. To do so is in effect to admit that Feuerbach was right after all, and it is simply going the wrong direction in Trinitarian theology.

Nor should we allow appeals to the doctrine of the Trinity — as in "a 'complementarian doctrine of the Trinity' leads us to a theological anthropology in which women are subordinate to men" or "an 'egalitarian doctrine

18. Karen Kilby, "Perichoresis and Projection: Problems with Social Doctrines of the Trinity," *New Blackfriars* 81 (2000): 442.

of the Trinity' leads us to a theological anthropology in which women are *not* subordinate to men" — to override all other theological sources. It would be one thing if (to stay with the example of the relevance of the doctrine of the Trinity to discussions of gender relations) there were obvious and direct implications from the doctrine to a particular view of gender relations. As I have argued, however, there are no good arguments showing that there in fact *are* such obvious and direct implications. Moreover, the very fact that "complementarians" and "egalitarians" alike can appeal so readily to the doctrine of the Trinity for support should give us pause. If it is so easy for the various sides to make such appeals, do not such appeals run the risk of being vacuous? Is it not obvious that the doctrine of the Trinity can all too easily become a "wax nose"? And should not this prospect be sobering to those Christians who take seriously the biblical warnings against idolatry?

In the case of the relation of the doctrine of the Trinity to gender relations, it seems to me that the efforts of Wayne Grudem and Bruce Ware, on one hand, and those of Kevin Giles on the other hand, would be put to better use helping us understand the biblical texts that speak to those important issues. After all, both parties admit that scriptural teaching is finally authoritative in these matters, and both are (presumably) epistemological and hermeneutical realists who think we actually can make some progress in improving our understanding of what the Bible actually says about such matters. Rather than try to make arguments from the doctrine of the Trinity into "conclusions" that are simply not implied by the orthodox doctrine, the various parties in these disputes would do well to proceed with the remaining hermeneutical and exegetical work.[19]

4. Trinitarian theologians should be clear about the place of "mystery."

Some philosophers of religion seem to think that to admit mystery at all is to throw up one's hands in defeat; they apparently think that any admission of mystery is either the denial that the doctrine might be coherent or the utter and total loss of reason. Tuggy, for instance, complains about "dark assertions about the *perichoresis* or 'coinherence' or 'mutual perme-

---

19. I have argued that the conclusions of Ware and Grudem do not follow from an *orthodox* doctrine of the Trinity — in point of fact, the coherence of their position with orthodoxy is doubtful. Perhaps their anthropological conclusions would follow from heterodox formulations of Trinity doctrine, but that is not my concern here.

ation' of the three divine persons," saying that such claims are "firmly stuck at the metaphorical level."[20] There is "no way," he says, "to 'cash out' this metaphor into literal assertion," and he concludes that "such metaphors simply hide an unintelligible claim."[21] Tuggy asserts that the appeal to mystery is often the effort to "spin a vice as a virtue"; he thinks this is nothing more than a sophisticated way of signaling that the Trinitarian wants the conversation to come to an end.[22] This, he says, is usually a "cop-out," and it is to be rejected forcefully.[23] Even when the appeal to mystery is not a direct "cop-out," he says, it should be resisted nonetheless.

But why should we think that any appeal to mystery is impermissible?[24] I would agree with Tuggy that appeals to "mystery" should not serve as a cloak for what is obviously inconsistent and incoherent. But to admit this is not to deny the place of mystery altogether. Would not theologians accustomed to the mystery of human persons and human relationships (and anyone who is related to family members surely knows something of such mystery) actually *expect* the doctrine that there are three Persons who are one Being to be mysterious in some ways? As Peter van Inwagen puts it, "It is not terribly daring to suppose that reality may contain certain things whose natures we cannot understand."[25]

At any rate, Trinitarian theologians should be clear about the place of mystery in the formulation and defense of the doctrine. They should be clear about *what* it is, and they should be clear about *when* an appeal is legitimate. I suggest that van Inwagen's statement might serve as an example and model: "I do not propose to *penetrate* the mystery of the Trinity. I propose to state the doctrine of the Trinity (or part of it: the part that raises all those pointed logical and metaphysical questions) in such a way that it is demonstrable that no formal contradiction can be derived from the thesis that God is three persons, and, at the same time, one being. . . . I wish only

---

20. Tuggy, "The Unfinished Business of Trinitarian Theorizing," *Religious Studies* 39 (2003): 170.

21. Tuggy, "The Unfinished Business," pp. 170-71.

22. Tuggy, "The Unfinished Business," p. 175.

23. Tuggy, "The Unfinished Business," p. 175.

24. For an epistemologically sophisticated and well-informed response to Tuggy, see James Anderson, "In Defense of Mystery: A Reply to Dale Tuggy," *Religious Studies* 41 (2005): 145-63.

25. Peter van Inwagen, *God, Knowledge, and Mystery: Essays in Philosophical Theology* (Ithaca, N.Y.: Cornell University Press, 1995), p. 225.

to propose a way of stating the doctrine that can be shown to be free from formal inconsistency."[26] This strikes me as a worthy goal indeed, and I suggest that Trinitarian theologians readily and gladly affirm the mystery of the doctrine while denying that outright and obvious contradiction deserves such an honorific title. They should work to show that the Trinitarian claim is not incoherent while not claiming to show — or *know* — just how God is three and one.

5. Trinitarian theology should be clear about its goals; I suggest that attempts to deal with the "threeness-oneness problem" should offer an account that is coherent (or at least not obviously incoherent), is compatible with the biblical portraits of the distinctness of the divine persons, is in accord with the scriptural account of monotheism, and is consistent with the major creeds of Christendom.

The foregoing theses lead us to the conclusion that Trinitarian theology should be clear about its goals. Just what is it that Trinitarian theologians are trying to accomplish? More particularly, what are analytic philosophical theologians attempting to do when they wrestle with the "threeness-oneness problem" of the Trinity? A glance at the various proposals provides no sense of anything approaching unanimity. Indeed, there seem to be competing — though often understated and sometimes unstated — visions of just what the theologian should be trying to do.

Recall, by way of example, Brian Leftow's charges that ST is faced with two hard tasks: "one hard task for ST is to explain why its three Persons are 'not three Gods, but one God,' and do so without transparently misreading the Creed," while the other "hard task for ST is providing an account of what monotheism is which is both intuitively acceptable and lets ST count as monotheist."[27] Several important desiderata are embedded here: adherence to creedal orthodoxy (where the Athanasian Creed is referred to as "*the* Creed" and taken to be the measure of orthodoxy) and an "intuitively acceptable" account of monotheism are valued highly. But one might wonder why it is *this* creed that is privileged? Surely it is a plausible candidate,

---

26. Van Inwagen, *God, Knowledge, and Mystery*, p. 227.

27. Brian Leftow, "Anti Social Trinitarianism," in *The Trinity: An Interdisciplinary Symposium on the Trinity*, ed. Stephen T. Davis, Daniel Kendall, S.J., and Gerald O'Collins, S.J. (Oxford: Oxford University Press, 1999), pp. 206-7.

and I doubt that any theologians who desire to remain faithful to Christian orthodoxy would think it a *bad* thing if their preferred models were found consistent with it, but Leftow never makes a case for why it should be *the* standard of Trinitarian orthodoxy. It was never approved by any ecumenical council — why should it be the touchstone of orthodoxy rather than, say, the Niceno-Constantinopolitan Creed?

One might reasonably wonder as well about Leftow's confident reliance on our intuitions about monotheism. I agree with him that, all else being equal, we really should trust our intuitions on such matters (as elsewhere). But surely he would agree with me that our intuitions on these matters are neither inerrant nor incorrigible. The doctrine of the Trinity (and the doctrine of the incarnation) is in some senses radically *counterintuitive.* To say this is not to admit that it is incoherent (much less that it is necessarily incoherent) or that we cannot make progress toward understanding it, but it is to recognize that the doctrine itself is radically surprising. So we should not be too surprised if it turns out that our initial intuitions about monotheism are in need of correction.

And just *whose* intuitions get to count here anyway? Leftow gives us some indication of what he means by this when he says that "the Christian version of monotheism should complete, fulfill, or perfect its Jewish version. It should be a monotheism that a Jew could accept as monotheistic, and a completion of Jewish monotheism."[28] Similarly, Daniel Howard-Snyder takes Jewish (and Muslim) accounts of monotheism as normative: *they* know what *real* monotheism is.[29] But again, *whose* account of monotheism is to be taken as authoritative? Does the Jewish monotheism that was the inheritance of John, Paul, and the other authors of the New Testament get to count? If not, then we are left to wonder why it would be ruled out of bounds. But if so, on the other hand, then we are left with the possibility that the relevant account of monotheism might differ in some ways — even significantly — from other notions of it.

For the Christian theologian who believes that God has revealed himself personally in Jesus Christ and reliably in the Holy Scripture of the Christian faith, the relevant account of monotheism — and just where and how the Son and Holy Spirit fit into that — is that of the authors of the New Testament. Intuitions about monotheism are surely important, and Trini-

---

28. Leftow, "Anti Social Trinitarianism," pp. 236-37.
29. Daniel Howard-Snyder, "Trinity Monotheism," *Philosophia Christi* 5 (2003): 401-2.

tarian theology would do well to go as far as it can to accommodate them. But for the Christian theologian who believes in revelation, such intuitions should be recognized as defeasible and correctable. So far as I can see, the only reason for Christians to believe in the doctrine of the Trinity at all is on the basis of God's revelation in Jesus Christ as seen in Scripture. Thus all intuitions about monotheism should be accountable to that revelation.

Or consider the criteria put forward by Dale Tuggy. He complains that efforts such as those of Edward Wierenga are "at bottom defensive project(s),"[30] and he insists that any acceptable model of the Trinity will meet three conditions: consistency, intelligibility, and coherence with Christian orthodoxy.[31] What are we to make of Tuggy's claims that any acceptable formulation of the doctrine is to be consistent, intelligible, and orthodox?[32] At first blush, this seems unobjectionable. But as Tuggy seems to understand them, these criteria seem to entail that any acceptable formulation must hold that there is at most only one divine person *and* that there are no fewer than three divine persons. *And* such a formulation — if it is to meet his standards of acceptability — must be easy to understand (= "intelligible"). Small wonder then that Tuggy finds no promise in any of the extant versions of either LT, RT, or ST! But why must the doctrine of the Trinity be easy to understand to be accepted as true? This is the important question, and it is unfortunate that Tuggy merely assumes his answer to it.

Tuggy is clearly unhappy that Wierenga and others are playing defense, but I think it is fair to ask what is wrong with such an approach. If Christians held to Trinitarian doctrine on the basis of elegant or appealing logical or aesthetic arguments, then perhaps we should be unhappy with merely defensive efforts. But Christians have never held to the doctrine for such reasons;[33] they have not been Trinitarians because the doctrine itself is so intuitively acceptable or metaphysically undeniable. Rather, Christians have been Trinitarians because they have been convinced that the revelation of God in Jesus Christ demands it — they have held to the doctrine of the Trinity because of their conviction that this is how God has revealed himself.

30. Tuggy, "Tradition and Believability," p. 455.
31. Tuggy, "Tradition and Believability," p. 447.
32. What Tuggy means by "orthodoxy" is murky at best. He wants to hold ST to the standard of creedal orthodoxy, but elsewhere he suggests a "radical reformation" approach that dispenses with creedal concerns altogether, preferring good "fit with the Bible." See, e.g., "The Unfinished Business," p. 165.
33. Or at least not usually.

If so, then we are left to wonder what is wrong with defensive projects. It is not hard to see why they might be valuable; after all, if the doctrine makes claims that are demonstrably logically incoherent, then it is necessarily false and thus cannot possibly be the deliverance of revelation. A "defensive project" might show that the doctrine is not incoherent, and thus it would perform a real ministry. Such a defensive project might not do much to invite belief, but that is not the intent. As far as I can see, the doctrine is to be believed on the basis of revelation — an incredibly surprising revelation.

I suggest that future work on the threeness-oneness problem not look askance at "defensive projects." Showing that common objections to the doctrine fail, showing that the doctrine is not incoherent, showing that the doctrine is at least possibly coherent — these are worthy and noble tasks (especially when undertaken in contexts where mere mention of the doctrine is enough to elicit smirks and yawns). Theologians should not shirk the challenges; they should realize that Christians can scarcely afford to ignore claims that the doctrine is incoherent and cannot possibly be true, and they should seek to counter such claims. But there is no reason to think they must show that God is triune on the basis of reason alone, and they need not undertake to show *how* God is three and one. Indeed, to attempt to do so reeks of hubris. Theologians can — and should — work to demonstrate that the doctrine is not incoherent, but they need feel no pressure to show *how* God is both three and one.

But they should do so while taking care to be faithful to the biblical portrayal of the distinctness of the divine persons. A temptation for those working to defend the doctrine against charges of incoherence is to shave off any elements of the doctrine that might be clumsy, embarrassing, or potentially problematic. And understanding "person" in Trinitarian theology in a full and robust sense is surely one of those elements. In addition, Trinitarian theologians should promote views that are in accord with the monotheism of the authors of the New Testament. They should not forfeit claims to monotheism; instead they should make the strongest claims for divine unity (or oneness) that are available to them. If they take the monotheism of Paul, John, and the other authors of the New Testament seriously, they will not back down from the position that this is a monotheism that allows for genuine interpersonal relationship within the divine identity.

Furthermore, Trinitarian theology should work to be consistent with major creeds. I confess my conviction that the Holy Spirit has guided the church in its development of these creeds; while they are not infallible, they serve as a generally trustworthy guide. I suspect that I am not alone in this; surely many Trinitarian theologians will be of similar conviction. But even for those who are not so convinced, another point here deserves attention: consistency with the great creeds is arguably important for pragmatic reasons. Models of the Trinity that can claim consistency with the great creeds and confessions are much less likely to be viewed as idiosyncratic (and thus with some degree of suspicion), and they are much more likely to be taken seriously and received positively.

Here I suggest that the great ecumenical creeds receive pride of place. At a minimum, models of the Trinity should be consistent with the statements of the ecumenical councils. Beyond this, they should go as far as possible toward coherence with the Latin creeds and various confessional statements.

In addition, Trinitarian theologians should work to avoid "special pleading" as much as possible, while going as far as possible to accommodate our intuitions and views of monotheism that are acceptable to adherents of non-Christian religious movements. To this point I have insisted that *Christian* theological commitments should receive priority, and I continue to maintain that they should — if our intuitions about "theism" and "monotheism" conflict with the central elements of Trinitarian doctrine, then so much the worse for our intuitions about such things! Nevertheless, we should work to go as far as possible to accommodate our intuitions. We should understand the "as far as possible" to mean *within the constraints of a Trinitarian orthodoxy that is grounded in and faithful to Scripture while consistent with the ecumenical creeds,* and we should realize that violating these boundaries in the defense of the doctrine is to surrender the very thing we intend to defend. But within these boundaries, we should go as far as we can to make claims that are consistent with common intuitions about "three" and "one," "person" and "essence."

II. Theses on the "Threeness-Oneness Problem" of the Trinity

6. Trinitarian theology should be committed to monotheism.

This thesis might seem so obvious as to hardly be worthy of statement. Unfortunately, however, this is no idle condition. Richard Swinburne, for instance, has said that "the first God solemnly vows to the second God. . . ."[34] What is this but a tacit denial of monotheism?[35] Similarly, Jürgen Moltmann has raised "criticism of Christian monotheism."[36] And N. M. L. Nathan has suggested that, when faced with the choice between monotheism and Trinitarianism, Christian theologians would be well advised to give up on monotheism and stick to Trinitarianism.[37] But these moves are as drastic and unfortunate as they are unnecessary. Trinitarian theologians need not — and *should* not — surrender commitment to monotheism.

On the other hand, Trinitarian theologians need to be intentional about the monotheism they claim. They should, I suggest, in the first instance be clear about their commitment to an account of monotheism consistent with the Old and New Testaments of the Christian Scriptures. As for the Old Testament, they will recognize that monotheism is committed to the view that the utter uniqueness of YHWH is testified to in the belief that YHWH is the creator of everything that is not God and in the worship that belongs rightly — and exclusively — to him.[38] With these points in mind, Christian theologians can cheerfully insist that Trinitarian theology is fully consistent with the monotheism of the Old Testament.

With respect to the New Testament witness, they will make a case that the authors of the New Testament are the heirs of Old Testament monotheism as articulated in Second Temple Judaism. They will take seriously the conclusions of such scholars as Richard Bauckham when he says that "Jewish monotheism clearly distinguished the one God and all other reality, but the ways in which it distinguished the one God from all else did not prevent the early Christians including Jesus in this unique divine identity. While this was a radically novel development . . . the character of Jewish monotheism was such that this development did not require repudiation of the ways in which Jewish monotheism understood the uniqueness of

34. Richard Swinburne, "Could There Be More Than One God?" *Faith and Philosophy* 5 (1988): 232.

35. Swinburne does not continue to make such locutions in his later discussions of the doctrine of the Trinity; see, e.g., *The Christian God* (Oxford: Oxford University Press, 1994).

36. Jürgen Moltmann, *The Trinity and the Kingdom: The Doctrine of God* (Minneapolis: Fortress, 1993), pp. 129-50.

37. N. M. L. Nathan, "Jewish Monotheism and the Christian God," *Religious Studies* 42 (2006): 75-85.

38. On these points see Christopher J. H. Wright, *The Mission of God: Unlocking the Bible's Grand Narrative* (Downers Grove, Ill.: InterVarsity Academic, 2007), pp. 75-188.

God."[39] They will point out that the encounter with Jesus Christ forced the earliest Christians to recognize that this Jesus is included in the "divine identity," and they will maintain that this "christological monotheism" is fully consistent with the Jewish monotheism of the period. Though a genuinely new development, it *is* arguably in complete harmony with the monotheism of the Second Temple period.

Commitment to this monotheism should be the hallmark of Trinitarian theology. Of course, it would be a good thing if a Trinitarian account of monotheism would be "strict" enough to be attractive and plausible to Muslims, Jews, and other monotheists. Trinitarian theology should work for the strongest account of divine oneness that is available to it, and it should seek to accommodate our intuitions about such matters as much as possible. But the primary allegiance of the Trinitarian Christian should be to the revelation of the triune God in the incarnation of the Son, and attendant accounts of monotheism should be accountable to that revelation. The primary allegiance of the Christian theologian is *not* to the intuitions of various philosophers of religion or the adherents of other major religions — it is to the way God has revealed himself in Jesus Christ.

The timely "Advice to Christian Philosophers" offered by Alvin Plantinga is appropriate here: the Christian philosopher

> may have to reject widely accepted assumptions as to what are the proper starting points and procedures for philosophical endeavor. And — and this is crucially important — the Christian philosopher has a perfect right to the point of view and pre-philosophical assumptions he brings to philosophical work; the fact that these are not widely shared outside the Christian or theistic community is interesting but fundamentally irrelevant . . . the Christian community has a right to its perspectives; it is under no obligation to first show that this perspective is plausible with respect to what is taken for granted by all philosophers, or most philosophers, or the leading philosophers of our day.[40]

What Plantinga says to philosophers generally should be taken seriously by philosophical and systematic theologians as well. While appealing to com-

---

39. Richard Bauckham, *God Crucified: Monotheism and Christology in the New Testament* (Grand Rapids: Eerdmans, 1998), p. 4.

40. Alvin Plantinga, "Advice to Christian Philosophers," in *The Analytic Theist: An Alvin Plantinga Reader*, ed. James F. Sennett (Grand Rapids: Eerdmans, 1998), pp. 299, 315.

mon intuitions and the adherents of other major religions might not be "fundamentally irrelevant," such concerns should not be the driving force or final judge of what gets to count as "real" monotheism. The Christian theologian who believes that God has revealed that he is the only God who exists, and who believes further that this same God has revealed himself decisively in Jesus Christ (in the relationships of the Son with his Abba and their Spirit), and who thinks further that this revelation coheres well with the monotheism revealed in the Old Testament, can — and *should* — insist that a robustly Trinitarian theology *is* monotheistic.

7. Trinitarian theology should insist on the full divinity of the distinct persons, and it should avoid whatever might compromise the full equality and divinity of the persons.

Again, one might think that something this basic hardly warrants repetition. Unfortunately, however, it is not all that difficult to find endorsement — sometimes *ringing* endorsement — of certain views that undercut belief in the full divinity of the Son and Spirit. As an example of such tendencies I have looked at the doctrine of the "eternal functional (or 'role') subordination of the Son" as promoted by some conservative evangelical theologians. I have argued that the claims of Wayne Grudem, Bruce Ware, and others are ambiguous; they may be understood in such a way that should evoke no controversy whatsoever, but they may also be interpreted in such a way that entails the direct denial of the belief that the Son is *homoousios* with the Father. Such views should be repudiated by Christian theologians who seek to understand and uphold traditional orthodoxy.

8. Trinitarian theology should insist on an understanding of persons that is consistent with the New Testament portrayal of the divine persons, that is, as distinct centers of consciousness and will who exist together in loving relationships of mutual dependence.

Future work on the doctrine of the Trinity should hold to an understanding of "person" according to which to be a person (at least a divine person) is to be a distinct center of consciousness and will who subsists in relation to others. Some critics (especially critics of ST) are convinced that such a view of divine personhood imports into the doctrine of the Trinity a distinctly "modern" or even "Cartesian" notion of person. Such a notion was not even available to the theologians who first framed the Christian understanding of person, and at any rate it was not what they had in mind. Barth states the objection forcefully when he says that "the meaning of the doctrine is not, then, that there are three personalities in God. This would be the worst and most extreme expression of tritheism, against which we must be on guard." Barth rejects the view that there are three divine persons in favor of his proposal that there are three "modes of being" *(Seinsweisen):* "we are not speaking of three divine I's, but thrice of the one divine I."[41]

What are we to make of such criticisms? Is it true that this thesis merely imports a distinctly modern and foreign notion of "person" into the doctrine of the Trinity? And if so, then what should we conclude? Several observations are in order. First, whatever exactly a "modern" notion of personhood *is,* many contemporary Trinitarian theologians are actually working to counter it with a distinctly *theological* understanding of personhood. Interestingly, ST theorists seem to be especially exercised by this; they are concerned to overcome modern ideals of individuality and autonomy. As Plantinga says, "Each member is a person, a distinct person, but scarcely an *individual* or *separate* person."[42] And "if belief in three *autonomous* or *independent* persons amounts to tritheism, the social analogy fails to qualify. For its persons are essentially and reciprocally dependent."[43] Indeed, David Brown makes bold to say that "so far from defenders of the social model being firmly trapped by modern understanding of the person, it is their detractors who are trapped."[44]

The second observation is that the meaning of the objection itself is less than transparent. Sometimes it sounds as though the "modern" view was unavailable to the early Trinitarian theologians, and the implied conclusion is that it should not be available to contemporary Trinitarian theologians either. But at other points it sounds as though this notion was *rejected* by the earlier Trinitarian theologians. Oddly enough, though, the objector cannot have it both ways. If it was not available to the earlier Trinitarian theologians, then they certainly did not reject it! Since the former

41. Karl Barth, *Church Dogmatics* I/1 (Edinburgh: T. & T. Clark, 1936), p. 351.

42. Cornelius Plantinga, Jr., "The Threeness/Oneness Problem of the Trinity," *Calvin Theological Journal* 23 (1988): 50.

43. Cornelius Plantinga, "Social Trinity and Tritheism," p. 37.

44. David Brown, "Trinitarian Personhood and Individuality," in *Trinity, Incarnation, and Atonement,* p. 49.

option is both more common and more plausible, I shall assume that at the heart of the objection is the concern to protect the integrity of traditional understandings by guarding it from any elements that might contaminate it.

But what are we to make of this worry? One response would simply be to shrug off such concerns; after all, is it not possible that we have made some progress in our understanding of personhood, and might this not actually help us in the articulation of the doctrine of the Trinity? A plausible case might be made along these lines, but it is not exactly the route that I shall choose. I think it is important to retain continuity with the Christian tradition, but I am not at all convinced that conceiving of the divine persons in the robust sense of person that I have outlined here loses continuity with the tradition. The contemporary Christian theologian who is interested in contemporary, orthodox articulation and defense of the doctrine of the Trinity should seek to know what the major theologians (and the major creeds) of the Christian tradition have said. But the Christian theologian working in the contemporary context should also want to know if what she says is *consistent with* the same tradition. Consistency with the tradition does not, so far as I can see, demand mere repetition of phrases and formulations from earlier eras, and surely it may build upon what has preceded it.

The extent to which my proposal about divine personhood coheres with the Christian tradition is an open question, and it deserves further consideration (more than I can offer here). I do not for a moment deny that the modern era has seen enormous development in the philosophy of mind, and I am aware of the dangers of reading such notions into the Christian tradition. At the same time, however, I think that a good case can be made for a high level of continuity. I will readily grant that neither Latin nor Greek theologians of the patristic or medieval eras were fond of such expressions as "center of consciousness and will." But it is not at all difficult to find language that coheres well with what I am saying. Gregory of Nyssa, for instance, is claimed by Sarah Coakley as someone who does *not* have such a view of the divine persons.[45] She rightly notes that many of the claims about Gregory made by ST theorists run far past what is warranted,

45. Sarah Coakley, "'Persons' in the 'Social' Doctrine of the Trinity: A Critique of the Current Analytic Discussion," in *The Trinity: An Interdisciplinary Symposium on the Trinity,* pp. 123-44.

but her own claim that Gregory did not hold such a view of the divine persons is itself overstated. Consider the conclusions of Michel R. Barnes on the matter. He recognizes that "a knowledge of Gregory's psychology" makes clear "that personal relationship and consciousness are not important, substantial psychological concepts for Gregory," and he holds that for Gregory a *hypostasis* is "an existent with a real and separate existence" rather than "a center of cognition or volition."[46] But Barnes also recognizes that Gregory "may indeed be said to have a psychology of the Individuals of the Trinity," and he makes this case by pointing to Gregory's discussion of the Holy Spirit: "what is at stake is not simply the 'separate reality' of the Holy Spirit, but the Spirit's status as what we would call a 'person': the Holy Spirit 'acts and says such and such things, and defines and is grieved and is angered.'"[47] Barnes thus concludes that "there is reason to believe that he understood the need for stronger and clearer language on both the distinct and the personal reality of the Holy Spirit — language which made clear that the Spirit *like the Son* was a psychological entity with a distinct existence."[48] Barnes concludes thus for good reason; as Gregory himself says, the Holy Spirit "exists as a person, able to will, self-moved . . . for its every purpose having its power concurrent with its will."[49] Plantinga makes the point in this way: "Gregory does not use the phrase 'center of consciousness,' but he does consistently depict Father, Son and Spirit as distinct actors, knowers, willers, and lovers — what *we* would call centers of consciousness whether Gregory did or not."[50]

The most important question regarding this, however, should be this: Is what I suggest here about divine personhood really consistent with the New Testament portrayal? And the answer to this question, I say, is uncompromisingly affirmative. The Son is portrayed in the New Testament

---

46. Michel R. Barnes, "Divine Unity and the Divided Self: Gregory of Nyssa's Trinitarian Theology in Its Psychological Context," *Modern Theology* 18 (2002): 476, 482. By "separate" I understand him to mean that the divine persons are genuinely distinct.

47. Barnes, "Divine Unity," pp. 485, 487.

48. Barnes, "Divine Unity," p. 485.

49. Gregory of Nyssa, "The Great Catechism."

50. Cornelius Plantinga, Jr., "Gregory of Nyssa and the Social Analogy of the Trinity," *Thomist* 50 (1986): 351-52. See also Lucien Turcescu, "The Concept of Divine Person in Gregory of Nyssa's *To His Brother Peter, On the Difference between Ousia and Hypostasis*," *Greek Orthodox Theological Review* 42 (1997): 63-82; Turcescu, *Gregory of Nyssa and the Concept of Divine Persons* (Oxford: Oxford University Press, 2005).

as someone who is an "I" in relation to a "Thou" — as is the Holy Spirit.[51] Only the Son becomes incarnate, suffers under Pontius Pilate, is crucified, dead, and buried. Only the Son rises again on the third day, ascends into heaven, and is seated at the right hand of his Abba. Only the Son says to the Father, "Not my will but yours," and only the Father says to the Son, "This is my beloved Son, with whom I am well pleased." Peter van Inwagen points this out when he argues that

> Persons are those things to which personal pronouns are applicable: a person can use the word "I" and be addressed as "thou." . . . It is evident that the Persons of the Trinity *are* in this sense "persons," *are* "someones": if the Father loves us, then someone loves us, and if the Son was incarnate by the Holy Ghost of the Virgin Mary, then someone was incarnate by the Holy Ghost of the Virgin Mary. . . . Is it not true that when we count Persons of the Trinity we are counting "someones"? The Father is someone. The Son is also someone. And surely, He, the Son, is someone *else*? If He were not someone else, could He not say truly, using the *personal* pronoun "I," "I am the Father"?[52]

Van Inwagen's position accords well with the New Testament portrayal, and indeed with consensual orthodoxy. As he puts it, "if there is one unde-niable datum in Trinitarian theology it is this: the Son (though he can say 'I and the Father are one') cannot say 'I am the Father.' And, of course, the Father cannot say, 'I am the Spirit,' nor the Spirit, 'I am the Son.' Each of the Father, the Son, and the Spirit is 'thou,' not 'I,' to the other two. That is to say, each of the Father, the Son, and the Spirit bears the following rela-tion to the other two: *being someone else.*"[53] Or as William Lane Craig ex-presses it: "Thus, among the three persons of the Trinity there are three ir-reducible and exclusive first-person perspectives which not even the classic doctrine of *perichoresis* can dissolve. The Father knows, for example, that the Son dies on the cross, but He does not and cannot know that He Him-self dies on the cross — indeed, the view that He so knows even has the sta-tus of heresy: *patripassianism.*"[54] What Trinitarian theologians should

---

51. See Graham A. Cole, *He Who Gives Life: The Doctrine of the Holy Spirit* (Wheaton, Ill.: Crossway, 2007), pp. 66-67.

52. Van Inwagen, *God, Knowledge, and Mystery*, pp. 265-67.

53. Van Inwagen, *God, Knowledge, and Mystery*, p. 266.

54. William Lane Craig, "Does the Problem of Material Constitution Illuminate the Doctrine of the Trinity?" *Faith and Philosophy* 22 (2005): 83.

hold to is this: the divine persons are irreducibly distinct; they are distinct agents who know and love one another. And they are so indivisibly united that their very identity is found in their relationships.

9. Trinitarian theology should reject ST theories that rely upon merely generic or perichoretic unity, RT theories that leave open the door to either modalism or antirealism, and LT.

To this point I have suggested that Trinitarian theologians should be monotheists, and that they should look for the strongest account of divine oneness that is available to them. I have suggested as well that they dare not compromise the full divinity of the persons, and I have proposed further that they embrace a robust account of the distinctness of the divine persons. Putting this together has consequences: any views that remain liable to charges of modalism or antirealism should not be acceptable, and any model that falls short of the strongest available account of divine oneness should not be attractive.

Given this, it seems clear enough to me that at least some versions of ST should not be appealing. For instance, those versions of ST that try to "cling to respectability" with respect to monotheism by claiming that there is only one God because there is only one generic divine essence, because there is only one source of divinity, or because there is only one divine family should be weighed and found wanting.[55] To say that the unity of the Trinity amounts to something much like a family is helpful enough in some ways, but it leaves unanswered the question of what it is that makes the Father, Son, and Spirit *one* God. After all, no one denies that Adam, Eve, and Seth are three humans, and the sense in which they are *one* still seems fairly thin. To locate the unity in one source of divinity (the Father) threatens to make the Father divine in a way that the Son and Spirit are not, and at any rate would tell us only that there is one *source* (one source that is *not* the Son or the Spirit) — it would not go far toward accounting for the fact that there is one God who *is* Father, Son, and Spirit. And to say that God is one in the sense that there is one generic divine essence leaves unanswered Brower's contention that "attributing a sharp distinction between *divinity* and *deity* . . . is no more plausible than attributing a sharp

---

55. Cornelius Plantinga discusses ways that ST's defenders might try to "cling to respectability" as monotheists. "Social Trinity and Tritheism," p. 31.

distinction between *being human* and *being a man* to ordinary speakers of English."[56]

On any of these points the defender of ST might simply dig in her heels and say that her model is consistent with (or at least not obviously *inconsistent* with) the "christological monotheism" of the New Testament while also clearly not liable to charges of Arianism. Fair enough; I have argued that this account of monotheism should be the one that is *most* important for Christians. But I have also made a case that Christians should go beyond this and work for the strongest available account of divine oneness, and I think the Trinitarian should hope that just such a stronger account is available. If this were all that were available to the Trinitarian — if this was the *only* way of clinging to claims to monotheism while also respecting the robust portrayal of the distinctness of the divine persons bequeathed to us by the New Testament — then I would agree that the Trinitarian should dig in here. But I think Trinitarians have reason to be optimistic about other possibilities.

Another option is to conceive of the divine oneness along the lines of "one dance"; that is to say, there is one God in the sense that the divine persons are unified by perichoresis. I think this is a more promising alternative, but, alas, it suffers from ambiguity at several points. It might mean simply that the divine persons are one in the sense that they enjoy a maximal degree of cooperation and fellowship, but this would do little to address the concerns raised by ST's critics. It might be taken to mean that the divine persons are one in the sense that they somehow "interpenetrate" one another, but this leaves us wondering just what this means. On the other hand, the idea of Trinitarian perichoresis might be fleshed out along the lines of Keith Yandell's proposal that the divine persons make up a complex God. This approach engenders much more promise for me; because it comes close to the proposal of Craig and Moreland, I shall discuss it in the next thesis.

If these versions of ST should not be appealing, what should we make of RT? As we have seen, RT has several strengths. Notable among these is its view that the divine persons are not — and cannot be — properly understood as isolated or autonomous individuals. As Brian Hebblethwaite notes, RT forces us to conclude that "we have to think of persons in rela-

---

56. Jeffrey E. Brower, "The Problem with Social Trinitarianism: A Reply to Wierenga," *Faith and Philosophy* 21 (2004): 298. Of course, Brower means "man" in the inclusive sense.

tion, not individuals, as basic."[57] I have noted that many Trinitarian theologians are exercised to overcome modern individualism; it should come as no surprise if they find RT appealing. Moreover, if successful, RT delivers the best of both worlds: it allows for an understanding of divine personhood that is robust enough to suit the proponents of ST, and it offers an account of divine oneness that does not stop short of numerical sameness.

Unfortunately, the puzzles and problems that attend to (most extant versions of) RT seem severe enough to hold it at arm's length. As van Inwagen admits, the purported nontheological examples of relative identity are all open to criticism, so any explanatory power to the analogy is slim indeed.[58] More important, though, are the problems raised by Rea's arguments: the "pure" versions of the doctrine allow for both modalism and antirealism, while the "impure" versions of RT stand in need of further work. So the Trinitarian theologian will want to avoid the "pure" versions! And in lieu of such further work, the Trinitarian theologian should look beyond the "impure" versions.

As I have argued, Leftow's LT is liable to some serious criticisms. Several important issues are ambiguous, and some extremely important questions remain unanswered. The LT proposal could be understood in several different ways, but these interpretations all are weighed in the balances and found wanting: one way leads to positions that are scarcely distinguishable from modalism, while another seems destined for incoherence unless it adopts the logic of relative identity.

10. Trinitarian theology should adopt either the constitution view (CT) or a modified version of ST.

As we have seen, a modified version of ST, such as that put forth by Yandell, and the CT version of RT are very different in many respects.[59] Yet both can claim to satisfy the central theological desiderata. Both modified ST and CT are able to cohere with the New Testament portrayal of the distinct personhood of Father, Son, and Holy Spirit, and both are able to

---

57. Brian Hebblethwaite, *Philosophical Theology and Christian Doctrine* (Oxford: Blackwell, 2005), p. 79.
58. Van Inwagen, *God, Knowledge, and Mystery*, p. 228 n. 7.
59. See also the part-whole proposal of Moreland and Craig.

claim consistency with the monotheism of Paul, John, and the other biblical authors. Moreover, both models have the resources to avoid modalism on one hand and Arianism on the other; both can claim that they do not trespass the boundaries of the ancient ecumenical councils.

This is no small accomplishment! Modified versions of ST still face criticisms about whether a complex God is really one (as in Howard-Snyder's broadside against the model of Moreland and Craig), but its defenders can happily reply that their view accords well with the account of monotheism that should matter most to Christians — that of Paul, John, and the other authors of the New Testament. Similarly, defenders of Yandell's approach will face charges that the defense is unacceptably ad hoc — that it relies upon an idiosyncratic account of parthood and complexity. But the proponent of Yandell's approach can cheerfully admit that such an account is unusual — after all, would we not expect to find some metaphysical surprises if the doctrine of the Trinity is true? — but then go right on and insist that it is possible (on this account) to provide a metaphysical structure showing that the doctrine is neither formally nor informally inconsistent. And the proponents of CT will face worries that their view leaves open the window to modalism (after all, the most obvious and easiest application of the analogy tends in this direction), but the defenders of CT can say that their model does not *necessitate* it.

So far as I can see, the primary *theological* difference comes to this: CT promises greater coherence with the Latin theological tradition. Whereas even the part-whole versions of ST likely run aground of the traditional Latin formulations, CT does not violate the strictures of even such statements as the Athanasian Creed or that of the Fourth Lateran Council. So for theologians committed to the Latin tradition, and even for those who would like to maintain as much continuity as possible, the CT version of RT will likely be more attractive.

Beyond this, most of the debate is over the metaphysics. Critics of CT will again doubt that the Christian doctrine of the Trinity should be tied too closely to something as controversial as the metaphysics of material constitution, and some of these critics will remain skeptical that *any* "supplemental story" can save the theory of relative identity. Similarly, critics of modified ST will raise concerns about how God might be complex without having parts (as in Yandell's model), and they might wonder about the composition of a triune God made up of parts (as in the proposal of Moreland and Craig).

As a theologian, my primary concerns have to do with the major theological desiderata. The theologian, by my lights, is free either to engage the distinctly metaphysical discussion or to leave it in the hands of the metaphysicians.[60] As Craig says in defense of his ST model, "our Trinitarian model . . . is theologically unobjectionable and open to various mereological construals, leaving it up to the metaphysician to choose that construal which best accords with his views."[61] Importantly, both accounts can stake an honest claim to satisfy the major theological desiderata. Both admit mystery — surely there is much about the triune God that we do not know! And both turn back the charges of incoherence while working to remain faithful to the primary theological factors that set the Christian church on the path to Trinitarian theology in the first place.

I suggest that Trinitarian theologians should exercise some restraint and humility in "writing off" one model out of preference for the other. The approach modeled by Brower and Rea is exemplary: "Note, however, that we stop short of actually endorsing the solution that we describe. There are three reasons for this. First, our solution, like most others, attempts to provide a metaphysical account of the ultimate nature of God. But surely here, if anywhere, a great deal of circumspection is warranted. Second, the contemporary Trinitarian debate, as we see it, is still in its infancy; hence a definitive stand on any particular solution, including our own, strikes us as a bit premature."[62] Craig's tone when criticizing their view is similar. He says he does *not* intend his criticisms "as a refutation of the model so much as an invitation to further reflection on it. Rea and Brower have offered us a provocative, new way of understanding the Trinity, but they still have a lot of explaining to do before their interpretation becomes illuminating or plausible. I hope that these brief criticisms will be a spur to further exploration of their model."[63]

Surely further work remains. But as further questions arise on the

---

60. In my view, the theologian both *can* and *should* judge some metaphysical proposals to be inconsistent with the gospel and Christian orthodoxy. But in some cases there may be more than one option that is consistent with the theological desiderata.

61. William Lane Craig, "Trinity Monotheism Once More: A Response to Daniel Howard-Snyder," *Philosophia Christi* 8 (2006): 113.

62. Jeffrey E. Brower and Michael C. Rea, "Material Constitution and the Trinity," *Faith and Philosophy* 22 (2005): 74 n. 3. Their third reason relates to their previous (nontheological) work on material constitution, and need not concern us here.

63. Craig, "Problem of Material Constitution," p. 85.

metaphysical issues at stake, we are left with modified ST (as seen in Yandell's account) and CT (as offered by Rea and Brower). These can claim to satisfy the principal theological concerns while also allowing the Trinitarian to fend off charges that the doctrine is incoherent and thus cannot possibly be true.

III. Theses on the God-World Relation

11. Trinitarian theologians can, and should — although perhaps not always for distinctly Trinitarian reasons — hold that creation is contingent rather than necessary.

Prevalent in contemporary systematic Trinitarian theology is a panentheistic account of the God-world relation.[64] Moltmann, for instance, advocates an explicitly "Christian panentheism."[65] He says that when the Christian doctrine of the Trinity is in view, "it is impossible to conceive of a God who is not a creative God," for "a non-creative God would be imperfect compared to a God who is eternally creative."[66] His theological rationale for this is clear enough: because the triune God is essentially loving, this God must have a proper place to express and exercise that love.

Moltmann and other panentheists seem to think that if creation is contingent, then God's love for creation would also be contingent — and thus God's own love would be contingent! And since Christians understand love to be essential to God, then creation must not be contingent. But this seems confused, for surely a Trinitarian — especially a Social Trinitarian such as Moltmann — need not draw such a conclusion. If the lov-

---

64. For an overview of various versions of panentheism in recent theology, see John W. Cooper, *Panentheism: The Other God of the Philosophers* (Grand Rapids: Baker Academic, 2006), pp. 213-318. In addition to such theologians as Moltmann and Jenson, notable proponents include Philip Clayton, e.g., *The Problem of God in Modern Thought* (Grand Rapids: Eerdmans, 2000), and the essayists featured in *The Work of Love: Creation as Kenosis* (Grand Rapids: Eerdmans, 2001).

65. E.g., Jürgen Moltmann, *The Trinity and the Kingdom: The Doctrine of God* (Minneapolis: Fortress, 1993), p. 106. Process theology, usually shorn of the robust Trinitarianism exemplified by such Social Trinitarians as Moltmann, is if anything even more insistent on the necessity of a physical world for God.

66. Moltmann, *Trinity and the Kingdom*, p. 106.

ing relationships that exist between and among the divine persons are essential to God, then the triune God just is essentially loving. My worry here is not that Moltmann and his fellow panentheists are somehow *too* Trinitarian — it is that they are not Trinitarian *enough* at this crucial point. While I appreciate the theological motivations that drive Moltmann on this issue, his conclusion is simply not warranted by his Trinitarian theology. If God is Trinity, then God's own internal life consists in the loving communion shared between and among the three divine persons, and God is not contingently relational at all but is necessarily so.

William Hasker makes this point with clarity. In dialogue with process theists, he notes that Christian theology "has always rejected" the view that the world is metaphysically necessary for God.[67] He then asks the question that animates many panentheists: "If God could exist apart from any universe, does this mean that the love and the relationality of God, so important to both the open and the process views, are merely contingent attributes of God?"[68] The basis of Hasker's answer rejects the crucial premise of panentheism, and it reflects his Trinitarian commitments: "Not at all. What it does mean is that the love and relationality of God *toward the creation* are merely contingent — though even here, given that there is a creation, it is necessarily the case that God is related to it and loves it. But wholly apart from creation, love and relationship abound within God, in the eternal loving mutuality of the persons of the Trinity, the Father, the Son, and the Holy Spirit."[69]

Trinitarian Christians can affirm (with Zizioulas) that while God's own being is the being of communion, the decision of the triune God to create is completely free and unconstrained.[70] Colin E. Gunton makes two important points. The first is that "God, in creating the world, had no need to rely upon anything outside himself, so that creation is an act of divine sovereignty and freedom, an act of personal willing."[71] The second point is that

---

67. William Hasker, "An Adequate God," in *Searching for an Adequate God: A Dialogue between Process and Free Will Theists*, ed. John B. Cobb, Jr., and Clark H. Pinnock (Grand Rapids: Eerdmans, 2000), p. 227.

68. Hasker, "An Adequate God," pp. 227-28.

69. Hasker, "An Adequate God," p. 228.

70. Recall our discussion of Zizioulas's "Sovereignty-Aseity Conviction."

71. Colin E. Gunton, "The Doctrine of Creation," in *The Cambridge Companion to Christian Doctrine*, ed. Colin E. Gunton (Cambridge: Cambridge University Press, 1997), p. 141.

"it does not follow that creation was an arbitrary act on the part of God. It was, rather, purposive, and in two senses: that it derives from the love of God, not simply his will; and that exists for a purpose — to go somewhere we might say."[72] Gunton makes clear the importance of the doctrine of the Trinity here. Because the doctrine holds that "God is already, 'in advance' of creation, a communion of persons existing in loving relations, it becomes possible to say that he does not need the world, and so is able to will the existence of something else simply for its own sake. Creation is the outcome of God's love indeed, but of his unconstrained love. It is therefore not a necessary outcome of what God is, but is contingent."[73]

Now, whether or not Trinitarian theology *should* affirm divine aseity and deny panentheism is another matter. I think it should, but for reasons that are not strictly Trinitarian in nature and that are thus beyond the scope of this discussion. My point here is that the doctrine of the Trinity enables a theologian to rightly insist that God *is* love — the holy love shared by the Father, Son, and Spirit from all eternity is essential to the identity of God — while also avoiding panentheism.

12. Trinitarian theologians should maintain that creation is the free expression of the holy love that is an essential attribute of the triune God.

Trinitarian theologians can — and should, although not necessarily for Trinitarian reasons — affirm that God creates contingently. But they should also affirm that the radically free creation of the triune God is one that is grounded in, and flows from, the love that God is essentially. Trinitarian theologians as divergent as Moltmann and Zizioulas agree that God's creative action is an expression of his love, and they do so for good reason.[74]

As William Lane Craig points out, the affirmation that the creative action of the triune God is both radically free and grounded in his love is a "remarkable conclusion." "Like the incarnation," says Craig, "the creation of the world is an act of self-condescension on God's part for the sake of

---

72. Gunton, "The Doctrine of Creation," p. 142.

73. Colin E. Gunton, *The Triune Creator: A Historical and Systematic Study* (Grand Rapids: Eerdmans, 1998), p. 9.

74. As I have argued, however, Zizioulas errs in his promotion of an account of SAC that threatens to make the triune loving communion of God himself contingent (upon the decision of the Father).

His creatures. Alone in the self-sufficiency of His own being, enjoying the timeless fullness of the intra-Trinitarian love relationships, God had no need for the creation of finite persons. . . . He did this, not out of any deficit in Himself or His mode of existence, but in order that finite temporal creatures might come to share in the joy and blessedness of the inner life of God."[75] Thomas F. Torrance argues that the doctrine of the Trinity matters immensely both for our understanding of the reason for creation and for our understanding of the divine power that actively creates. With respect to the latter, his comments are worth hearing at length:

> While creation of the universe, in form and matter out of nothing, certainly involved omnipotent power, we must think of that power not in an abstract way as bare unlimited power in itself, not as the power of some "God" complete and enclosed in his loneliness, but as the living power of the eternal Father flowing from his intrinsic nature as Love, as the movement of the Love that God is ever in himself as Father, Son, and Holy Spirit. It is out of that movement of sublime Love within himself, and its free movement outward from himself toward us in his will not to exist for himself or in himself alone but to share the fullness of his Love in fellowship with others, that God the Father became Creator and continues unceasingly to sustain his creation in relation to himself. . . . Far from being some irrational arbitrary power . . . his unbounded almightiness is the sovereignty of his Holy Love revealed to us in the Gospel, the power of the Triune God who is a transcendent Communion of Love in himself and who in the ungrudging and unrestrained overflow of his Love delights to give being and freedom to his creatures.[76]

When addressing the former concern, Torrance is helpful as well: "the relation of God to the world is completely positive for it is never anything else than creative; he loves it, upholds it and blesses it and coordinates its continuing creaturely existence."[77] The central thrust of Torrance's point should be clear indeed, and it is truly powerful. The actions of the triune

---

75. William Lane Craig, *Time and Eternity: Exploring God's Relationship to Time* (Wheaton, Ill.: Crossway, 2001), p. 241.

76. Thomas F. Torrance, *The Christian Doctrine of God: One Being, Three Persons* (Edinburgh: T. & T. Clark, 1996), pp. 209, 211.

77. Torrance, *Christian Doctrine of God*, pp. 211-12.

God in creation are genuinely and supremely free, but they are yet in accord with the holy love that is the essence of the triune God.[78]

13. Trinitarian theologians should affirm Jenson's "Identification Thesis" but deny his "Identity Thesis."

I have argued that Jenson's Identification Thesis is helpful, but that his Identity Thesis is fraught with ambiguity and decidedly unhelpful. I want to briefly reiterate those points now. The first bears repetition because all too often in contemporary analytic discussions of the doctrine of the Trinity the basis for the doctrine itself is overlooked. Theologians such as Jenson are saying something that needs to be heard and heeded in contemporary Trinitarian theology: the triune God of the Christian faith *is* known as he reveals himself in his mighty actions on behalf of his people and in the incarnation — and he is known in the way he reveals himself or not at all! Analytic formulations of the doctrine of the Trinity, with their heavy emphasis on the important metaphysical issues, need to remember the place and prominence of the fundamental Christian story.

On the other hand, however, Jenson's Identity Thesis is a veritable mare's nest of conceptual problems. I have tried to show how these problems are brought to light by analytic reflection on Jenson's work, and I have pointed out that some of these problems may be even more severe than previously thought. If it is understood to entail "The Theory of Worldbound Individuals" (which is an uncomfortably plausible reading of Jenson), then it renders God and creation codependent, makes evil a necessary element both of this world and of God's own life, and produces a Christology that compromises the doctrine of the *homoousios*. We would do well to be skeptical of the Identity Thesis.

14. If properly nuanced, the doctrine of perichoresis can be a helpful category for understanding divine purposes for creation (and the God-world relation more generally).

78. For helpful discussion of how a triune God who is, as the Trinity of three persons who exist in holy love, necessarily good might truly be said to have robust (or even "libertarian") freedom, see Thomas P. Flint, "The Problem of Divine Freedom," *American Philosophical Quarterly* 20 (1983): 255-64; Thomas P. Flint and Alfred Freddoso, "Maximal Power," in *The Concept of God*, ed. Thomas V. Morris (Oxford: Oxford University Press, 1987), pp. 134-67. For a word of caution, see Edward Wierenga, "The Freedom of God," *Faith and Philosophy* 19 (2002): 425-36.

Noting that in many cases the notion of perichoresis is ill defined yet called upon to do a lot of theological work, I have argued that Moltmann's account in particular needs a good dose of careful precision and analysis. I readily admit the truth of the charge that it is often used in an unhelpful manner. Yet I have also argued that it has a proper place in Trinitarian theology (as well as Christology). For it serves to capture — in admittedly halting and less than fully adequate ways — both the concept that the inner divine life is one of mutuality and shared love *and* the concept that creation exists so that the triune God might share that same love with persons made in the "image of God." Creation does not exist to provide God a place to look "big" or "sovereign" — as in some accounts of divine "glory" — as if God needed human creatures and their sin in order to be fully actualized![79] Of course, the notion of perichoresis can turn into a "wax nose" as well as a "black box," but this need not deter the Trinitarian theologian from making use of this venerable concept. It needs nuance and careful qualification, but with such refinement it yet stands to serve a useful and indeed noble purpose. I have suggested that analytic philosophical theology might offer the tools needed for just such a refinement, and contemporary theologians who find helpful the notion of perichoresis would do well to explore such resources.

15. Trinitarian theologians should affirm that the providential and redemptive actions of the triune God should be understood in light of the triune identity and purposes for creation.

It seems obvious enough that if we are to understand the being of God as the communion of love shared between and among the persons of the Trinity, and if we are to understand divine action as consistent with the divine nature, then we should understand divine action in the world as ultimately flowing from that love. As Torrance puts it, "the Love of God revealed to us in the economic Trinity is identical with the Love of God in

---

79. The observations of N. T. Wright about John Piper's theology of divine glory come to mind here. Reflecting on such statements as "it is the glory of God and his essential nature mainly to dispense mercy (but also wrath, Ex 34:7) on whomever he pleases, apart from any constraint originating outside his will," Wright says Piper's theology "cannot escape sounding as though God *needs* sin, in order to display his glorious and to-be-worshiped wrath." Review of *The Justification of God*, by John Piper, *Evangelical Quarterly* 60 (1988): 83, emphasis in original. The statement from Piper is found in his *The Justification of God: An Exegetical and Theological Study of Romans 9:1-23* (Grand Rapids: Baker, 1983), p. 218.

the ontological Trinity; but the Love of God revealed to us in the economic manifestation of the Father, the Son, and the Holy Spirit in the history of salvation, tells us that God loves us with the very same love with which he loves himself, in the reciprocal love of the three divine Persons for Each Other in the eternal Communion of the Holy Trinity."[80]

A danger lurks here; we may all too readily turn to an abstract notion of love — we may assume that we have adequate a priori knowledge of "what love really is," and then simply plug that into the statements that "God is love" and "God loves the world." At this point we especially need to heed the warnings of the theologians who insist that our understanding of divine love should be formed by, and accountable to, the revelation of divine love to be found in the canonical narrative that culminates in the revelation of the incarnate Son of God. Torrance points us back to the incarnation for a proper understanding of love:

> When we turn to the First Epistle of St John we learn that "God is Love," and that this Love is defined by the Love that God bears to us in sending his Son to be the propitiation for our sins, and indeed for the sins of the world. . . . The self-giving of the Son in sacrificial love and the self-giving of the Father in sacrificial love are not separable from one another, for the Father and the Son dwell in one another, together with the Spirit of God, whom we know through his witness to the Son, and through whose dwelling in us God dwells in us. This means that we are to understand the Love that God is in his being-in-act and his act-in-being in a trinitarian way. The Father, the Son and the Holy Spirit who indwell one another in the Love that God is constitute the Communion of Love or the movement of reciprocal Loving which is identical with the One Being of God. It is as God the Father, God the Son, and God the Holy Spirit that God is God and God is Love. As one Being, three Persons, the Being of God is to be understood as an eternal movement of Love, both in himself as the Love of the Father, the Son, and the Holy Spirit for one Another, and in his loving Self-giving to others beyond himself.[81]

Again, the very identity of the distinct divine persons is found in their relations of mutual giving and glorifying love — and this is the same love that the triune God extends toward the world:

80. Torrance, *Christian Doctrine of God*, p. 165.
81. Torrance, *Christian Doctrine of God*, p. 165.